# The State and Private Education:
## An Evaluation of the
## Assisted Places Scheme

2

# The State and Private Education:
# An Evaluation of the
# Assisted Places Scheme

Tony Edwards, John Fitz and Geoff Whitty

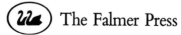 The Falmer Press

(A member of the Taylor & Francis Group)
London • New York • Philadelphia

UK      The Falmer Press, Rankine Road, Basingstoke, Hampshire, RG24 0PR

USA      The Falmer Press, Taylor & Francis Inc., 1900 Frost Road, Suite 101, Bristol, PA 19007

First published in 1989

**British Library Cataloguing in Publication Data**
Edwards, Tony
    The state and private education: an evaluation of the Assisted Places Scheme.
    1. England. Independent secondary schools. Fees. Payment by local education authorities. Great Britain. Department of Education and Science. Assisted Places Scheme
    I. Title   II. Fitz, John   III. Whitty, Geoff
    379.3'22'0942

    ISBN 1-85000-567-2

**Library of Congress Cataloging-in-Publication Data**
Edwards, Tony.
    The state and private education: an evaluation of the Assisted Places Scheme/Tony Edwards, John Fitz, and Geoff Whitty.
    Bibliography: p.
    Includes index.
    ISBN 1-85000-567-2. — ISBN 1-85000-568-0 (pbk.)
    1. Private schools — Great Britain — Case studies.
    2. Education and state — Great Britain — Case studies.
    I. Fitz, John. II. Whitty, Geoff. III. Title.
LC53.G7E34   1989
371'02'0941 — dc20

Jacket design by Caroline Archer

Typeset in 11/13 Bembo by
Chapterhouse, The Cloisters, Formby, L37 3PX

Printed and bound in Great Britain by Taylor & Francis (Printers) Ltd. Basingstoke

# Contents

# List of Tables

# *Preface*

The research reported in this book is a case-study of a particular policy initiative announced by a newly-elected Conservative Government in 1979. It also considers that policy in relation to earlier attempts to define the place of independent schools in the education system and in the light of recent efforts by the Right to alter radically the traditional balance between public and private educational provision. The case-study follows the Assisted Places Scheme from its origins within the private sector, through the mobilization of political support for it while the Conservative Party was in opposition, to its implementation from 1981 onwards and its subsequent expansion. Overall, the books provides a preliminary evaluation of the Scheme in terms of its benefits and costs for individual pupils and for the education system.

In our efforts to understand the origins and implementation of the Scheme, we were greatly helped by Mark Carlisle and Stuart Sexton (political adviser successively to Norman St John Stevas, Mark Carlisle and Sir Keith Joseph); by James Cobban, formerly head of Abingdon School and a major influence on the Scheme's shaping and promotion within the private sector; and by Clive Saville and Roger Morgan, who were successively Registrars for Independent Schools within the Department of Education and Science. Throughout our collection of evidence about the beneficiaries of the Scheme, we received full cooperation from the Assisted Places 'unit' within the DES and we are especially grateful for the help given to us at various stages of the research by Petra Laidlaw, Graham Kirkpatrick, Cathy Christiesan and Colin Seal. We are also grateful to the many individuals who talked or wrote to us at various times about the Scheme's origins and evolution — for example, Gavin Alexander, John Dancy, David Maland and Peter Mason. In our attempts to understand the political opposition to the Scheme, we were particularly helped by Neil Kinnock, Bert Clough, Clement Freud and Elizabeth Maddison. Our greatest debt though is, of course, to the many headteachers, teachers, pupils and parents from both sectors of education whom we interviewed during the course of the research and who made most of the fieldwork so enjoyable. We hope that their voices come through clearly, if anonymously.

The research was supported from 1982 to 1986 by the Social Science Research

Council/Economic and Social Research Council (award number C00230036) and it could not have been carried out without that support or that provided by King's College London, Newcastle University and Bristol Polytechnic. Dr Mary Fulbrook was Research Associate for the first year of the project and made a particular contribution to our attempts to locate the Scheme in its historical context. We are also grateful to Geoffrey Cockerill, who was honorary consultant to the project from 1982 to 1985, took a notably active interest in its development, and gave us the benefit of his long experience as a senior civil servant in the DES which had included being Secretary to the Public Schools Commission. Responsibility for the account and assessment of the Scheme offered in this volume nevertheless rests entirely with its three authors.

Tony Edwards
John Fitz
Geoff Whitty
September, 1989

# List of Abbreviations

| | |
|---|---|
| ACC | Association of County Councils |
| AMA | Association of Metropolitan Authorities |
| AVIS | Association of Voluntary-aided and Independent Grammar Schools |
| CSE | Certificate of Secondary Education |
| DES | Department of Education and Science |
| DGJC | Direct Grant Joint Committee |
| ESRC | Economic and Social Research Council |
| FEVER | Friends of the Education Voucher Experiment in Representative Regions |
| GBA | Association of Governing Bodies of Public Schools |
| GBGSA | Association of Governing Bodies of Girls' Public Schools |
| GCSE | General Certificate of Secondary Education |
| GPDST | Girls' Public Day School Trust |
| GSA | Girls' Schools' Association |
| HMC | Headmasters' Conference |
| HNC | Higher National Certificate |
| HND | Higher National Diploma |
| IAPS | Incorporated Association of Preparatory Schools |
| IEA | Institute of Economic Affairs |
| ILEA | Inner London Education Authority |
| ISIS | Independent Schools' Information Service |
| ISJAC | Independent Schools Joint Advisory Committee |
| ISJC | Independent Schools Joint Committee (later Council) |
| LEA | Local Education Authority |
| NUT | National Union of Teachers |
| OPCS | Office of Population Censuses and Surveys |
| PCS | Public Schools Commission |
| SHA | Secondary Heads Association |
| SPSS | Statistical Package for Social Scientists program |
| SSRC | Social Science Research Council |
| TVEI | Technical and Vocational Education Initiative |

Chapter 1

# The Assisted Places Scheme and its Evaluation

Among the provisions of the 1980 Education Act was a scheme for 'enabling pupils who might not otherwise be able to do so to benefit from education at independent schools'. Between 5000 and 6000 means-tested places were to be made available each year to academically able children whose parents could not afford full fees. Participating schools would 'remit fees that would otherwise be chargeable in respect of pupils selected for assisted places', and the Secretary of State would 'reimburse the schools for the fees that are remitted'.[1]

An explicit pledge to 'restore the direct-grant principle' for the benefit of 'bright children from modest backgrounds' had been part of the 1979 Conservative election manifesto, and the announcement of an Assisted Places Scheme was the first significant policy initiative by the new Government. From the outset, it was defended and attacked with a fervour quite disproportionate to its modest scale. It was justified as an extension of parental choice, a restoration of academic opportunities to many able children whose local comprehensive schools were inadequate, and as essential protection for those individuals and for the nation's resources of talent against the levelling-down effects attributed to the demise of so many maintained grammar schools. It was strongly opposed as an unwarranted Government declaration that the public sector was incapable of providing an appropriate education for very able children, and as likely to produce a Government-sponsored withdrawal of public support from maintained schools which were being so evidently identified as second-best. As portrayed by the head of a prominent independent school whom we interviewed during our research, assisted places made it possible to 'pluck embers from the ashes' of the comprehensive schools. As portrayed critically but in a similar metaphor, they were intended to 'snatch a few brands from the burning fire'.[2] To the Labour Party especially, they were part of a broader policy of 'starving the maintained schools of funds, and then rescuing the brightest children from the surrounding wreckage' (Labour Party, 1980, p. 27).

## An outline of the Assisted Places Scheme

This particular 'rescue operation' was implemented with a speed which reflected the 'secret elite negotiations', as Tapper and Salter (1986a) describe them, which had already taken place within the private sector and between its leading representatives and some Conservative politicians. It was also implemented against strong opposition from the other Parties, and repeated threats that the next Labour Government would end the Scheme in the year in which it returned to office.[3] The coincidence of the Scheme with cuts in public expenditure on education made it politically expedient to reduce its scale considerably. Yet it was a considerable administrative achievement that 4185 of the 5417 places available in September 1981 in 223 English independent schools were actually taken up. Six years later, when the Scheme was almost fully in operation, 26,899 pupils were holding assisted places, at a cost to the Government in 1987–8 of over £48 million.[4] By that time, the average tuition fee in the participating schools had risen to £2346 (compared with £1323 in 1981).

Below a certain income parents pay no fees at all. When the Scheme began that threshold was £4617. It has since been regularly revised in line with inflation, reaching £6972 for 1987–8. Over that six-year period, about 40 per cent of beneficiaries have held free places, while the Government's average payment per place to compensate schools for the fees remitted has risen from £1038 to £1867.[5] Initially, there was to be no Government assistance for anything beyond the costs of tuition. The regulations governing the Scheme also allow schools to reclaim from the DES any additional grants made to low-income families to meet some of the incidental costs (on travel, school uniform and school meals) of taking up places. But there are still no Government contributions to the costs of boarding education, despite the large number of boarding schools which offer assisted places and persistent demands from within the private sector to recognize 'boarding need' as deserving assistance.

The Scheme was introduced quickly to give it time to take root before another election could threaten its continuation, and also to encourage more grammar schools to regard independence as a desirable and practicable alternative to comprehensive reorganization by offering them an entry still partly subsidized from public funds. But while many independent schools (especially those formerly on the direct-grant list) co-operated enthusiastically in this revival of the 'direct-grant principle', the new arrangements were not a replication of the direct-grant system which the Labour Government had dismantled in 1975–6. They could not have been so, if only because many schools on the last direct-grant list had already been absorbed into the public sector or had closed. If the Scheme was to provide anything like the national network of academic opportunities which its architects intended, then it was essential to enlist independent schools which had previously had little contact with the public sector. Of the 223 schools offering places in 1981, 107 had never been on the direct-grant list and twenty-nine were among the 'leading public schools' listed by Honey (1977) in his account of the late-Victorian 'golden age' of elite secondary schooling.

There were also administrative and financial innovations which made the Scheme, as its architects also intended, a 'revised and improved' version of its predecessor rather than a replication. First, all direct assistance to parents is related to an income scale, so avoiding the long-standing criticism that many parents of free-place holders in direct-grant schools had been well able to pay the full fees. Secondly, there are no per capita grants to schools, and so no indirect but equally indiscriminate subsidising of 'full' fee-paying parents. Thirdly, LEAs cannot reserve places for pupils they might wish to sponsor; their involvement was limited to a right (removed in 1983) to veto the allocation of assisted places to 16-year-olds in maintained schools if it could be argued that the transfer would damage their own sixth-form provision. Otherwise, parents apply directly to particular schools. The schools themselves are free to make their academic selection 'in accordance with such methods and procedures as seem to them appropriate', subject only to a general obligation to offer at least 60 per cent of those places to applicants who have attended a maintained school for the previous two years. Fourthly, schools participating in the Scheme remain fully independent. After some initial Conservative uncertainty about whether to restore an intermediate status between 'independent' and 'maintained', it had already been decided by 1979 that each school should make its own contract with the Government, and that its consequent obligations to account to the DES for its assisted-place holders should be extremely light. Schools offering places are under no obligation to appoint LEA or other 'representatives' to their governing bodies as the price of receiving public money.[6] Finally, the embodiment of the Scheme in an Act of Parliament ensured that it could only be dismantled through a prolonged legislative process, and not by any equivalent to the simple withdrawal of regulations after a four-hour debate which had effectively ended the direct-grant system in 1976.

Despite these administrative differences, the Scheme was intended to reflect the 'direct-grant principle' of offering academic opportunities to talented children whatever their social background. In doing so, it diverged sharply from previous attempts to 'integrate' independent schools in its concentration on academic ability and academic opportunity. From the outset, its main justification was that it 'complemented' the public sector by extending access to a high quality academic education which it was claimed many comprehensive schools could not provide. As stated in the letter which the DES sent to independent schools in December 1979 inviting them to indicate at least a provisional interest in offering assisted places, the overriding purpose of the Scheme was to 'help to meet the academic needs of pupils whose talents might not otherwise be catered for'. As Rhodes Boyson claimed a few months before its first beneficiaries were about to enter their schools: 'Able children from our poorest homes will once again have the opportunity of attending academically excellent schools.'[7]

In sharp contrast to earlier proposals to reduce the social exclusiveness of independent schools by meeting a 'need' for boarding education which extended far beyond those families able to pay for it, this new initiative concentrated entirely on modifying the private sector by reviving academic opportunities for the 'poor but able'. As described by one of its principal architects within the private sector, it

> . . . helps society by giving a wider section of the community a share in the opportunities offered by a group of schools of acknowledged excellence. It helps parents by increasing the degree of parental choice. It helps the country by promoting able children. (Cobban, 1980)

Two years into its implementation the junior minister, Bob Dunn, was looking forward to a time when the Scheme was fully grown and its beneficiaries would represent about 15 per cent of all secondary-age pupils in the private sector and about a third of those in the schools offering assisted places. The beneficiaries would be 'pupils from low-income families who are selected on merit alone' and their schools would be 'among the very best in the country'.[8]

## Evaluating the Assisted Places Scheme

From the time of its first announcement, the Assisted Places Scheme was vigorously applauded and as vigorously contested. Alongside the exchange of arguments about the principles on which it was based, confident and contradictory predictions were made about its beneficiaries, benefits and costs. As a research topic, it offered an unusual opportunity to study a specific and controversial policy initiative from its inception to its implementation, and then to assess its early effects against the claims made by its advocates and its critics. It reflected the efforts of a powerful pressure group within the private sector to restore what they saw as the best characteristics of the direct-grant system. It was also an early expression of educational priorities by the incoming Government, to which it offered an inexpensive way of demonstrating simultaneously its commitments to extending parental choice, preserving traditional academic standards, and restoring a traditional 'scholarship ladder' for 'able children from less well-off homes'. From a historical perspective, it could be seen as yet another attempt to define the role of independent schools within the national system. From a sociological perspective, the controversy surrounding it was clearly part of the long debate between those emphasizing the academic costs of egalitarian educational policies, and those emphasizing the socially divisive consequences of academic selection.

It was in these terms that we conceived the research on which this book is based. The grant application which Whitty and Edwards made to the (then) Social Science Research Council in January 1981 placed particular emphasis on testing empirically some of the competing claims being made for and against the Scheme. We also wished to explore the political and ideological contexts in which it had been framed and was being implemented, and to examine its relationship to other components of contemporary educational and social policy.

Any investigation of such a contentious initiative was likely to be contentious itself. Our own application was made at a time when the SSRC was especially short of funds, and when the usefulness of social research was being subjected to close political scrutiny. These circumstances may have contributed to a delay in reaching a decision which prevented us from beginning the fieldwork when the first assisted-place holders were entering the schools. They certainly led to the imposition of conditions which were unusual for a small grant. We were required not to publish any findings until the fieldwork had been completed so as to avoid contributing to premature judgments about the Scheme's effects. But while our research was also supposed to be monitored by a steering group appointed by the Council, the group met only once and made no written enquiries about the progress of the investigation.[9] We discuss later how the 'politics' of researching interacted with the politics of education in the course of the investigation itself. That investigation was intended to explore both the contexts within which the Scheme developed and its consequences for pupils, parents and schools. We now outline the evidence collected at the various levels relevant to understanding the Scheme's implementation and how that evidence is reported in the rest of the book.

In trying to locate the Scheme in its historical, political and educational contexts, our immediate task was to construct a detailed account of how it originated within the private sector in response to the threatened abolition of direct-grant schools, emerged as a Conservative policy commitment in 1976–7, and was formulated into workable arrangements within eighteen months of the 1979 election. The narrative presented in chapters 2 and 3 is based on interviews with the main architects of the Scheme within the private sector, the Conservative Party and the Civil Service, and on documentary research which included analysis of an archive of material made available to us in the course of the project. We were also interested in the Scheme's antecedents — how far it evolved as it did in response to the perceived shortcomings of earlier attempts at 'integrating' independent schools, and how far the terms in which the issues were debated had been altered by the virtual disappearance of grammar schools from the public sector. The work of the Public Schools Commission (1966–70) was critical, partly because of the evidence which it gathered about the social exclusiveness of public schools, but mainly because of the polarization of attitudes towards private education which followed the rejection of its proposals for reducing that exclusiveness. It was in response to an increasingly hostile Labour Party that the private sector began to organize itself more effectively, to present its case for public support more strenuously, and to seek out political allies.

From a wider political perspective, our second line of inquiry was to analyze the

Scheme in the context of other policies being pursued by a Conservative Government explicitly committed to reducing the scale and cost of state intervention, expanding the role of the market in the allocation of national resources, and achieving greater efficiency through wider consumer choice. We were therefore interested in the extent to which the Scheme could be read as manifesting some of the main themes in the educational ideology constructed by the 'New Right' during the 1970s. As part of this search for ideological sources, we re-examined *Black Paper* and associated attacks on the 'progressive consensus'. In chapter 4 we indicate continuities and contrasts between leading *Black Paper* contributors and their much more radical New Right successors. While it was initially tempting to interpret the Assisted Places Scheme as an index of the New Right's ascendant influence in educational policy-making, our research failed to reveal any significant contributions to the Scheme's formation and presentation from those (in and around the Institute of Economic Affairs, or the Centre for Policy Studies) who had engaged so actively in reconstructing the Conservative Party's ideological base.[10] Both the origins of the Scheme and its justification seemed to lie elsewhere, in traditional notions of a ladder of opportunity for the academically able from even the 'humblest' social origins.

That could, of course, be true of the Scheme's primary sources of support, and still leave room for it to be treated as a precursor of (or even a trial-run for) more radical initiatives. Throughout the project, and since its funding ended in 1986, we have been interested in whether the structure of the Scheme has contributed to the changing balance of power between the DES (or other agencies of central government), local education authorities, and educational 'consumers' as these are variously defined. We have therefore had to be aware of other policy initiatives, educational vouchers being the obvious example, with which the Scheme might be seen as practically or ideo-logically aligned. In the final chapter of the book, we look back on the Scheme's objectives and mode of implementation from a position which now has to take account of city technology colleges, grant-maintained schools, and other Government initiatives for which at least some of the advocates of assisted places are unlikely to feel much sympathy.

Before that, in the last section of chapter 4, we illustrate the central claims made for the Scheme by its advocates at the time it was launched, and the counter-claims made with equal confidence in their accuracy by its opponents. From our analysis of these claims we identified predictions about its possible effects and outcomes which could be investigated empirically, and which we put in the form of questions which shaped our decisions about what evidence to collect. In collecting it we worked at three levels — not in a sequence of clearly-marked stages, but as a process of continuous interaction between the general and the particular. The first level is constructed from the national statistics about the allocation and take-up of places which we report and interpret in chapter 5. We then studied the Scheme's implementation in selected geographical areas with high concentrations of assisted places. We describe in chapters 6 and 7 the 'networks' of independent and maintained schools in those areas affected by its operation. Finally, we interviewed over 600 pupils in independent and maintained schools, and over 300 of their parents. Following the example of Connell and his colleagues (1983), we wanted to focus down on individuals affected by the Scheme while keeping in view its broader contexts. Chapters 8 and 9 therefore contain detailed 'cases' drawn from our interviews. While all names of schools and families have been altered to preserve anonymity, we have not imitated the Connell team by constructing 'composite stories' out of real but separate components. Our 'stories' belong to the particular individuals who told them, even when they are used to illustrate common experiences or opinions.

These enquiries at several levels helped us to avoid a top-down approach to policy evaluation, an approach which starts from the perspective of central decision-makers and largely remains there (Sabatier, 1986, p. 30). While we began with national arguments about who would benefit and suffer from the Scheme, and have continued to explore its national origins and implementation, we spent most of our time trying to understand local and individual experience of its effects. Unlike Salter and Tapper (1985), we wanted to interpret and evaluate a policy from positions far removed from its framers and their immediate opponents. In this respect, our methods seemed well suited to studying a Scheme which itself depended for its implementation on devolving responsibility to individual schools and attracting sufficient applications from families persuaded of its benefits.

Those methods were very time-consuming. They also attracted close scrutiny both from potential beneficiaries of the Scheme and from those who felt disadvantaged by it. Our main difficulties in the early stages of the research came not from the formal monitoring instituted by ESRC, but from informal monitoring by heads of schools and LEA officers whose cooperation we were seeking. As we have described elsewhere, a controversial policy innovation of this kind engenders such loyalty and hostility that its gate-keepers are usually inclined to doubt whether any investigation can be impartial, and unusually concerned to discover the views of the researchers themselves (Whitty and Edwards, 1984; Whitty, Fitz and Edwards, 1988). In addition, the Labour Party's declared intention of abolishing assisted places as soon as it returned to power made even the immediate future seem precarious. Before a second Conservative election victory became probable, independent schools were understandably wary of observers who might be looking hard for damning evidence about the Scheme, and negotiating access was initially difficult and time-consuming for that reason alone. Some opponents of the Scheme erected even more formidable barriers to its investigation. The fact that an initiative so objectionable to Labour-controlled authorities was largely protected from LEA intervention led some of them to treat any research as either implying support for it or at best as giving publicity to something they would rather see ignored. For example, one LEA stated openly that its dislike of the policy was a sufficient reason for not cooperating in any investigation of its consequences even though its own chief officer had published explicit predictions about the harm the Scheme would do. We found this position hard to understand.

Even without the background presence of a steering group and the foreground difficulties of negotiating access, we could not have avoided being sensitive to possible charges of bias, or of knowing the answers before asking the questions. Our best defence, then and now, is that we were not judging the Scheme by standards 'imported' from outside, but against criteria identified quite explicitly by its own advocates and critics. For some of its advocates, of course, the *only* relevant criteria were the benefits the Scheme brought to those pupils thereby enabled to attend independent schools, and the freedom to choose those schools which it had given to their parents. Critics, however, concentrated on the damage they foresaw being done to other able children who remained within the public sector. As the mother of one comprehensive school pupil put it during our interview with her — 'Their child's advantage is my child's disadvantage'. It was therefore clear from the outset that it would have been biased to have restricted our inquiry to the immediate beneficiaries of the Scheme when so many commentators viewed its effects more broadly.

We also recognized the impossibility of establishing any 'net balance' of the benefits and costs arising from a policy open to such different forms of evaluation, and seen from such different value positions. We particularly noted the cautionary comment which Chris Patten quotes (from the economist Cedric Sandford) about his own very limited support for educational vouchers. While approving of assisted places, despite their disadvantage of having been introduced 'at a time when spending on the maintained sector was being cut', he could see only 'a thin case' for a few 'careful experiments' to test the feasibility of vouchers. Even then, such cautious testing would settle nothing, because 'while some issues may be resolved by experiment, the extreme individualists and collectivists are unlikely to be brought to a common mind by reference to fact' (Patten, 1983, p. 127). We have no greater expectations of our own facts about the Assisted Places Scheme, but we do hope that our evidence will both interest and inform those policy-makers and commentators who are not committed by political doctrine (of whatever variety) to see only the 'facts' that support their view of the world. What follows is neither an attack on nor a defence of the Assisted Places Scheme, but an attempt to understand its origins and implementation and to explore its initial effects and potential consequences.

### Notes

1  Education Act 1980, Section 17.
2  Editorial in the *Times Educational Supplement*, 30 November 1979.
3  The Party's National Executive motion, moved by Neil Kinnock (then shadow spokesman) on 24 October 1979, gave this rapid extinction as its 'resolute intention'.
4  DES statistical summary, April 1988.

5 Unlike the equivalent scheme in Scotland, there is no ceiling on the total cost for a school year because it is clearly impossible to predict how many places will be offered to parents eligible for full or substantial fee remission. There is a full description of the Scottish scheme in Walford (1988).

6 Schools in the Scheme are however required to publish their examination results in line with the requirement placed on maintained schools by the 1980 Education Act.

7 *Daily Mail*, 25 June 1981.

8 House of Commons Debate, 6 December 1983; Hansard 191–192.

9 Two early publications were 'vetted' by the chairman of the steering group; both described the process of the research rather than reporting outcomes (Edwards *et al.*, 1984; Whitty and Edwards, 1984).

10 Subsequently, however, Stuart Sexton, one of the Scheme's chief political architects, became increasingly associated with some of these New Right groups and he is currently Director of the IEA's Education Unit.

Chapter 2

# Antecedents and Origins of the
# Assisted Places Scheme

When the Labour Government in 1965 appointed a Commission to advise it on 'the best way' of integrating public schools with the state system, those independent schools which were officially 'recognised as efficient' contained 5 per cent of pupils aged 14 and 14 per cent of those aged 17. Although this market-share had fallen quite sharply since the Second World War,[1] hopes that the private sector would 'wither away' into insignificance as public provision improved had to accommodate to the inconvenient facts that it was only minor independent schools which had disappeared, and that the market-leaders still retained a social importance out of all proportion to their pupil numbers.

The coexistence of essentially 'elitist' independent schools[2] with the public sector continued to raise difficult questions. Briefly, did they provide necessary alternatives to public provision, complement it, compete with it, or undermine it? To their defenders, institutional independence was an essential defence against state monopoly, and for that reason alone was not to be tampered with. To some of their critics, abolition was the only effective remedy for the privileges which they perpetuated. The predominant view, however, was that while outright abolition was neither fair nor feasible, the schools were too socially exclusive for their own or the country's good and should broaden their intakes by broadening their purposes.[3]

Arguments for abolishing private education altogether had been put to the Fleming Committee in the 1940s by both the Labour Party and the Trades Union Congress, the main argument being that 'broad democratic principles' required that all children attend 'schools provided by the state' (Banks, 1955, pp. 227–9). But with the practical failure of that Committee's proposals (1944) for extending the private sector's 'association ... with the general educational system', the 'Public Schools Question' dropped temporarily out of sight. Amid all the post-War problems of building or rebuilding schools, training teachers and providing (and defining) 'secondary education for all', there seemed to be far more urgent priorities to attend to. R. A. Butler (1971, p. 120) later claimed that the 'first-class carriage' on the educational train was simply 'shunted on to an immense siding' during the period of reconstruction — a curious metaphor when the public schools offered such an obvious 'main line' to positions of conspicuous power and prestige. His recollection is, however, more accurate as a reference to the successful 'side-tracking' of the policy issues involved. Proposals to enforce the disappearance or even modification of the 'carriage' were rarely on the political agenda during the 1950s. Between 1947 and 1958, for example, no positive decisions about public schools were taken at Labour Party conferences, although in both 1953 and 1958 amendments were put proposing the end of fee-paying and the incorporation of schools into the state system, and that in 1958 was only narrowly defeated on a card vote.[4]

### The Failure of Voluntary Integration 1965–1970

It was the increasingly insistent Labour commitment to comprehensive secondary education which, in the 1960s, focused attention on the possibility of integrating 'both the privileged selective state schools and the private fee-paying schools into the state system'. In the Labour policy statement, *Signposts for the Sixties* (1961), a national enquiry was promised into how the public schools could make 'their best educational contribution' to the national system and so be 'purged of their privileged position'. That promise was then included in the 1964 election manifesto, following which the Independent Schools' Association formally asked the Party's Secretary whether references to 'integration' were to be read as a euphemism for abolition. The Secretary's reply denied any intention of banning private education as such; the public schools were the target for integration because of their special prestige, their privileged position, and their divisive influence (Robinson, 1971, p. 122). The implication was clear that once the 'great' schools had been integrated, a diminished private sector could then be left to decline into irrelevance.

As things stood, however, the public schools were so far from being irrelevant that they had recently been described by the new Education Minister (who was also the Party's leading theorist) as 'the greatest single cause of stratification and class consciousness in Britain' (Crosland, 1962, p. 194). In his earlier book on *The Future of Socialism*, he had described them as 'the strongest remaining bastion of class privilege', and as a far more 'flagrant' source of inequalities of opportunity than the maintained grammar schools with which so many socialists seemed obsessed (Crosland, 1956, pp. 261–5). Yet he continued to dismiss the abolitionist solution as both unacceptable on libertarian principle and unenforceable in practice, and to discount as excessively optimistic any hope that schools which conferred such 'real advantages' on their pupils would conveniently wither away.[5] Their substantial integration 'with' or 'into' the public sector seemed to be the only practicable policy.

The Commission which Crosland (as Secretary of State) appointed in 1965 to enquire into how integration might be achieved was given terms of reference which were, in its own view, 'explosive'. This was because the public schools 'have long been a storm centre of political controversy' and because hard decisions about their future were an unavoidable part of the 'troubled and puzzling journey' being made from a system of secondary and higher education 'designed to educate an elite' to one intended for 'vastly greater numbers'. The Commission had therefore to plunge into 'a whirlpool of arguments about . . . diversity or uniformity, and ask ourselves how far equality of opportunity is compatible with academic excellence' (PSC, 1968, Vol. 1, p. 1).

It was supposed to emerge from the 'whirlpool' with clear proposals for creating 'a socially mixed entry' to public schools which would consequently have to cater for 'a progressively wider range of academic attainment', and for ensuring 'the progressive application of the principle that the Public Schools, like other parts of the educational system, should be open to boys and girls irrespective of the income of their parents' (PSC, 1968, Vol. 1, p. vii). Crosland later explained the Commission's creation partly as an expedient response to strong pressure within the Labour Party for something to be done about the public schools, and partly as a 'once and for all' attempt to establish whether any compromise was possible between the 'nihilist' solution of abolishing them altogether, and the 'fig-leaf' solution of admitting a 'handful of state pupils' to schools which would remain essentially unchanged by their presence (Kogan, 1971, pp. 196–7; S. Crosland, 1983, pp. 149–50).[6] Yet the Commission was widely seen at the time as a stalling device, a way of sending into limbo an issue too controversial for a Government with a majority of three to handle, and as a graveyard of reputations for its unfortunate members. After two years' work, the Commission produced a Report which its second chairman, David Donnison, described as having created 'a record in the history of committees of inquiry', all its recommendations being 'totally rejected by all commentators'.[7]

Essentially, it tried to solve the problem of social exclusiveness by meeting the 'need' for more boarding education. Evidence of the schools' 'remarkable social homogeneity' (Halsey *et al.*, 1980, pp. 52–3) was already available from Graham Kalton's (1966) research, and from the extensive survey of schools and pupils sponsored by the Commission itself. In those boys' schools commonly termed 'public', over 90 per cent of pupils had fathers in professional or managerial occupations and 'would have been away to a good start whatever school they went to'; in contrast, only 1 per cent had fathers in manual occupations (PSC, 1968, Vol. 1, pp. 30, 56, 101). Girls' schools were much less exclusive. As the Girls' Public Day School Trust (GPDST) noted in its evidence to the Commission, many of its pupils and its teachers had some experience of the maintained sector, and girls 'do not gain the same social and professional advantage from the mere fact of having been educated at a public school' (PSC, 1968, Vol. 2, p. 154). Generally, however, there was no doubt that the leading independent schools were highly socially selective in their intakes, nor that their former pupils were conspicuously 'over-represented' in prestigious occupations. In the Commission's view, the schools 'arbitrarily confer advantages and power on an arbitrarily selected membership' (PSC, 1968, Vol. 1, 62.102). The remedy for that arbitrariness lay in transforming their intake by transforming their functions.

Following this diagnosis, seven forms of integration were set out as being appropriate to different kinds of school. But it was hardly surprising that the main proposal, as summarized caustically by one of the Commission's own members (John Vaizey), was to transform the schools by 'changing half the bodies in their beds' (PSC, 1968, pp. 221–4). The Commission's first chairman, Sir John Newsom, had long argued the case for more boarding education for socially disadvantaged children, and most of his fellow members were persuaded by Royston Lambert's (1966) evidence that there was a large gap between supply and demand. They accepted both his estimate that 80,000 boarding places would be needed by 1980 compared with the 35,000 available in 1965, and his recommendation that more than half that larger number should receive assistance from public funds according to national criteria for defining 'need'. Meeting that need would then provide 'a humanely acceptable and administratively feasible' basis for integrating the public schools, because those schools would be seen to be complementing public provision rather than competing with it (PSC, 1968, Vol. 1, pp. 107.210, 110.218; PSC, 1970, Vol. 1, 157.210).[8]

This solution extended a diagnosis and a remedy already familiar to the private sector, and sometimes canvassed within it. Twenty-five years before, the initiative for the Fleming Committee had come ostensibly from a joint suggestion by Headmasters' Conference (HMC) and the Association of Governing Bodies of Public Schools (GBA) that the Government should enquire into how the schools they represented 'could be of service to a wider range of pupils'. The sharp fall in the middle-class birth-rate during the 1930s and the 'democratic spirit' prompted by the War had created enough anxiety about future recruitment to make it seem at least expedient to explore some politically acceptable way of bringing in state-supported pupils.[9] A system of state bursaries to spread the benefits of boarding education more widely seemed an obvious possibility. While the willingness of the schools themselves to serve a 'wider range of pupils' stopped well short of being willing to be socially transformed in the process, the Fleming Committee was surprisingly unanimous in recommending not only that 25 per cent of pupils entering 'associated' independent schools should immediately be recruited from the maintained sector, but that there should be 'a progressive application' of the principle that such schools should eventually become 'accessible to all classes irrespective of wealth and social position' (Fleming, 1944, 55.148). By the time the Report was published, however, most public schools were full again, and queues of fee-paying applicants sharply reduced the attractions of state-bursars. The schools' acceptance 'in principle' of the Fleming proposals reflected a confidence that they were unlikely to be implemented on any significant scale. In practice, few LEAs responded at all to opportunities to take up boarding places, and no minister did much to encourage them — although George Tomlinson hoped that some of the 'great' schools might be opened up through the 'infiltration' of 'deserving pupils irrespective of their parents' income' (cited in Barker, 1972, p. 118; see also Dancy, 1963, pp. 18–29).

When the GBA sought to revive the 'Fleming principle' in 1959 by again proposing 'suitability for boarding' as the basis for a national scheme of assisted places in public schools, it still had in mind small numbers of deserving individuals. The Public Schools Commission, however, proposed a more far-reaching institutional remedy than Fleming had wanted. Given its own diagnosis that the schools' exclusiveness certainly intensified social divisions even if it did not create them, it logically rejected any scheme for scattering assisted places around public schools 'like confetti' because this would preserve unscathed that 'close association' with 'particular classes' which it regarded as socially damaging. The proportion of assisted pupils in every school which opted for integration should be at least 50 per cent of annual intake by the end of a seven-year transitional period to ensure a non-traditional entry too large to be assimilated without radical changes in the schools themselves (PSC, 1968, Vol. 1, 21.43). Most obviously, the schools would have to broaden their range academically, because there was no convenient coincidence between boarding need and high ability. Lambert (1966) had criticized the tendency of LEAs to limit to evidently academic children what little assistance they gave towards the costs of boarding education, and it would have been illogical anyway for a Government now committed to comprehensive secondary schools in the public sector to have 'integrated' public schools on terms which allowed them to remain highly selective academically. For both reasons, integrated schools would have to cater for pupils across the entire CSE-band, and 'preferably beyond' (PSC, 1968, p. 129).

Those were the majority recommendations of the Commission. Three members refused to sign the final Report, being agreed among themselves that the divisive influence attributed to the public schools had been exaggerated, that a 50 per cent minimum of assisted places was too high, that the suitability of many of those schools for educating socially disadvantaged children was doubtful, and that they could only become academically unselective by losing altogether their distinctive qualities.[10] One of that minority elaborated his dissent in a book in which he deplored turning good public schools into secondary moderns 'with poor facilities in inaccessible areas', and advocated the combination of boarding-need and above-average ability as the only appropriate criteria on which to assist pupils and integrate schools (Howarth, 1969, pp. 90–1). A larger minority on the Commission supported the integration of the 'best' public schools solely as centres of academic excellence, on terms which would allow them to recruit the ablest children from all kinds of social background. That proposal more closely resembles the Assisted Places Scheme than anything else in the Commission's *First Report*.

Despite these internal disagreements the Commission's members seem to have been surprised by the pervasively hostile response which their main recommendations received. *The Times Educational Supplement* introduced its catalogue of assorted criticisms by asking if any other educational report had been 'so unanimously damned or derided'.[11] From some directions the proposals were dismissed as mere Fleming-style palliatives which would give the schools increased public subsidies without any guarantee that they would thereby become less objectionable as 'bastions of privilege'. From the private sector they were dismissed as bureaucratic, doctrinaire and unworkable. At the Headmasters' Conference in September 1968, the rejection of the Report was comprehensive and almost unanimous.[12] Particular exception was taken to the intended minimum proportion of assisted places, the Conference chairman arguing that there 'wasn't a hope in hell of a 50 per cent start'; any Government genuinely wishing to encourage integration would avoid 'fixing an exact percentage', but would leave such matters to the good judgment of the schools. It was felt generally that the 'price' demanded for integration had been set absurdly high. At least implicit in Conference discussion was a double fear. If the schools lost their social exclusiveness, they risked losing fee-paying parents for whom it was a salient attraction. If they simultaneously lost their academic exclusiveness, they would lose their strongest appeal to many potential refugees from an increasingly non-selective public sector, and their distinctive function in the training of elites.

As the new chairman of a Commission now reconstituted to consider the future of the direct-grant and other independent grammar schools, David Donnison defended his colleagues against critics who (in his view) themselves had either failed to offer constructive alternatives, or had presented schemes which the Commission itself had turned down as unworkable during its two years of 'serious study'. If its own best efforts had brought 'almost total adverse criticism', it might have to be concluded that there was 'no consensus — no politically viable way forward — in dealing with the public boarding schools'.[13]

Donnison left it unclear whether he expected the consequence of that deadlock to be the schools' eventual abolition, or a continuation of their largely segregated co-existence with the public sector. The direct-grant schools, however, must have seemed an easier case for integration insofar as they already constituted a 'bridge' between the private and public sectors (as their defenders regularly claimed). Crosland had justified their initial exclusion from the Commission's brief by arguing that their future was already provided for in Circular 10/65; either they found ways of cooperating with their local LEAs' plans for comprehensive reorganization, or 'the whole future of the direct grant system will inevitably come into question'.[14] In practice, however, the circular offered no guidance at all about how direct-grant schools might be 'associated' with any of the patterns of comprehensive secondary education outlined within it, or about the institutional status of those willing to be so. It was not surprising, therefore, that very few direct-grant grammar schools had even begun negotiations in that direction by 1968. What was certainly clear to Crosland was the inconsistency of 'requesting' all LEAs to move towards comprehensive secondary education while the same Government continued to subsidize the most academically-selective schools in the country.

The schools' own readiness to change seemed to be limited to recognizing weaknesses in the existing financial arrangements, under which many pupils had 'free places' whose parents could afford to pay while the 'full' fees of others were considerably subsidized by the per capita grants which the schools received from the DES.[15] They were certainly unwilling to be anything other than traditional grammar schools. Recognition of their increasing political vulnerability as the tide moved against academic selection led to the setting up in 1966 of a Direct-Grant Joint Committee (DGJC), partly to monitor the effects of Circular 10/65 on LEAs' take-up of places in non-maintained grammar schools but also to formulate and defend more effectively the principles and purposes which the schools claimed to represent. Although this sudden awareness of the need for collective security is described by Salter and Tapper (1985, pp. 129–31) as representing the private sector's 'first line of defence', it was academic selection rather than independence which appeared at that time to be the critical issue. In the evidence which it submitted to the Public Schools Commission, the DGJC supported a more realistic scale of fee remissions which would widen access to direct-grant schools by replacing free places with means-tested assisted places. But it also offered a strong defence of academic selection, and of the opportunities which the schools it represented made available to able children from all kinds of social background (HMC, 1968).

That was not a defence which the Commission could accept, given that its brief was to advise on 'the most effective method or methods' by which those schools could 'participate in the movement towards comprehensive reorganisation'. At the time of the Fleming Committee, it had been argued that the direct grant should disappear in the post-War reconstruction of secondary education because most of the schools receiving it were insufficiently distinctive in character to justify the special arrangements which covered them. A generation later, the main argument against them was that they had become altogether too distinctive — that it was 'indefensible' to make maintained grammar schools academically comprehensive while 'preserving other grammar schools with similar aims and functions' (PSC, 1970, Vol. 1, 113.204). Against the familiar counter-argument that schools recruiting only 3 per cent of secondary-age pupils could surely be accommodated within an otherwise comprehensive system, the Commission noted that the direct-grant grammar schools in its survey of a sample of LEAs contained almost all pupils with Verbal Reasoning scores above 140 and 62 per cent of those with scores above 130 (PSC, 1970, Vol. 1, 118; Vol. 2, appendix 8). In a detailed case-study prepared for the Commission, Rene Saran showed how one LEA's arrangements for the 2 per cent of pupils it paid for at direct-grant schools shaped its whole policy for secondary education, and how the loss of those pupils depressed the intakes and the status of its maintained schools.[16]

Such evidence of their 'creaming' effects on the public sector convinced the majority of the Commission that 'grammar schools of the traditional kind cannot be combined with a comprehensive system of education; we must choose which we want' (PSC, 1970, Vol. 1, p. 4). They consequently recommended that the schools themselves be forced to choose between 'full independence', and full conformity to public policy on academic selection. While being almost evenly divided about whether those continuing to be publicly funded should receive their money from a national Schools Grants Committee (on the university model) or from local authorities, the majority of the Commission were insistent that the money should be conditional on the abandonment of both academic selection and the charging of fees. Because of the diversity of the schools receiving direct grants, seven different forms of participation in the public sector were suggested. These included becoming a normal 11–18 comprehensive, or specializing in the education of (for example) the musically-gifted. But in sharp contrast both to the later Assisted Places Scheme, and to its own five dissenting members who wanted to retain 'super-selective schools' for the top 2 per cent of the ability range, the majority wanted no publicly-subsidized pupils at any school which was 'only willing to collaborate on academically selective terms'. Schools insistent on remaining selective should be free to choose full independence, since 'the legal right of voluntary bodies to provide efficient private education paid for by parents should not be curtailed' (PSC, 1970, Vol. 1, pp. 7–8, 47–9).

To appreciate how forcefully these proposals were rejected by most direct-grant schools, and also to understand the subsequent reshaping of the 'direct-grant principle', it is necessary to examine the schools' claim to offer exceptional academic opportunities to an exceptional cross-section of children. We do so in some detail because it was almost entirely from this part of the private sector that the Assisted Places Scheme emerged. The direct-grant list originated in 1926, when non-provided secondary schools offering the required minimum of 25 per cent free places had to choose between continuing to receive grants directly from the Board of Education, or being supported by an LEA. Those which retained the direct grant were not necessarily the most academic grammar schools. Most of them either recruited their pupils from several authorities and so were unwilling to be tied to one, or were afraid that LEA control would endanger their denominational character. Having made their decision, they became and remained 'independent schools which have freely entered an agreement to provide services for the state' (PSC, 1970, Vol. 1, pp. 47–9). This intermediate position presented some obvious difficulties during the planning of free 'secondary education for all', and a majority of the Fleming Committee were initially inclined to recommend the abolition of fees in all grant-aided schools. Fears that such a step might drive many direct-grant schools away from the public sector altogether led to a compromise in the final Report, through which the schools were to become 'fully accessible to all classes' either by abolishing fees altogether (as none of them did), or by varying according to parental income the fees charged for the 'residual' places left over when all free places had been filled. Butler's explicit commitment to preserve the 'tradition and variety' represented by the direct-grant system was at least implicitly confirmed by his Labour successors. The re-opening of the direct-grant list in 1945 brought a reduction in the number of schools on it from 232 to 166; some chose to become fully independent, some to become fully maintained, and some were 'dropped' as being academically unsuitable. While there were further changes in membership when the list was again re-opened in 1957, the administrative and financial definitions of direct-grant status remained unaltered.

To its advocates, that status represented an admirable blend of 'freedom and obligation, private enterprise and public accountability', which made possible an equally happy blend of 'academic opportunity and social comprehension' (Cobban, 1969, p. 42). Two closely-related claims were regularly made on the schools' behalf. First, they had better examination results than the maintained grammar schools, their sixth forms were larger, and they had higher rates of entry to the universities — indicators which were confidently treated as evidence of 'good learning and high quality teaching' (HMC, 1968). Secondly, they were said to offer these exceptional opportunities for 'good learning' to pupils from a wider range of social backgrounds than were to be found either in independent schools with intakes limited by parents' capacity to pay the fees or in maintained schools with more geographically limited catchment areas (HMC, 1968; Cobban, 1969). Both claims were disputed as often as they were made. The Commission itself attributed any apparent academic superiority of direct-grant schools to the high levels of social and academic selectiveness which many of them practised. Academically, the majority took their pick of pupils from at least three LEAs, and some took over 60 per cent of their intake from the top 2.5 per cent of the ability range (PSC, 1970, Vol. 1, pp. 51, 155). Socially, they were described as 'predominantly middle class institutions', able to reap the simultaneous benefits of attracting academic high-fliers by their social prestige, and fee-payers by their academic reputation. Insofar as generalizations were possible, they stood socially between the maintained grammar schools and the public schools, but they were considerably nearer the latter. If 'only' 60 per cent of direct-grant pupils came from professional and managerial homes, compared with over 90 per cent in the public schools, it was also true that the proportion whose fathers were in semi-skilled and unskilled manual occupations (8 per cent) was almost as low as in the public schools (PSC, 1968, Vol. 2, table 10; PSC, 1970, Vol. 1, pp. 51–2). Indeed, an earlier analysis sponsored by HMC itself showed the social composition of direct-grant schools to be almost identical with that of fully independent day schools like St Paul's (Kalton, 1966, p. 35).[17]

There was therefore substantial evidence available to those wanting to argue that schools which received 75 per cent of their revenue from public funds were certainly not 'fully accessible to all classes'. In fact, however, most generalizations about direct-grant schools were misleading. The schools often treated as being typical of the category were certainly large, 'regional' and highly selective — like Manchester

Grammar School, King Edward VI, Birmingham, and the North London Collegiate School. But the list also included many much smaller, predominantly boarding schools with relatively high proportions of fee-payers (like Oakham, Kimbolton and Dauntsey's); non-denominational but mainly local grammar schools (like Bromley High School, Kingston Grammar, and the Dame Allen Schools in Newcastle) differentiated by historical accident from their maintained-sector equivalents and Catholic schools recruiting geographically-dispersed intakes but often offering 90 per cent or more free places and being less academically selective than most maintained grammar schools.

It was some of these Catholic schools that were already negotiating moves into the public sector, and most of them were to do so when the choice between full independence and full integration was enforced in 1975–6. In 1970 it was predictably the leading academic schools which promptly rejected the Commission's proposals outright. They could see only the extinction of their special qualities (and quality) in any of the forms of participation they were being offered. They would lose the protection afforded by fee-income against 'dictation' by central or local government. They would also lose the academic selectiveness which was the foundation both of their appeal to parents and their particular contribution to educating the country's future leaders. At their 1968 conference, for example, the Girl's Public Day School Trust headmistresses continued to insist that their schools' main purpose was to prepare able girls for higher education. The Trust's evidence to the PSC repeated that functional definition. Explaining its later rejection of the Commission's Report, it reaffirmed its belief that the freedom to select able pupils and the freedom to charge fees were both essential, and denied that there was any sense at all in trying to transform small, good grammar schools with long-established reputations for academic excellence into poor comprehensives. If faced with a choice between those two essential freedoms as the price of continued public funding, then the Trust would 'reluctantly' choose independence (Kamm, 1971, pp. 194–7).

That was to be the choice of almost all the non-Catholic direct-grant schools after the 1976 Education Act. Their immediate reaction to the PSC proposals would have justified Donnison in repeating his comment on the Commission's *First Report* — that in the context of a public sector being re-organized on comprehensive lines, there seemed to be no possibility of consensus about integration and 'no politically viable way forward'.

### Phasing Out the Direct Grant and Reviving the 'Direct-Grant Principle'

The Public Schools Commission's proposals for integrating the direct-grant grammar schools as (in effect) voluntary-aided comprehensive schools were published in March

1970. Even without the immediately hostile response of the schools themselves, the election of a Conservative Government three months later ensured that 'the dust will appropriately gather on the two reports of the doctrinally directed Public Schools Commission' (Pedley, 1970, p. 61). It brought an abrupt withdrawal of Circular 10/65 by the new Secretary of State, Margaret Thatcher, and its replacement by Circular 10/70 which explicitly rejected any 'imposition' of a uniform pattern of secondary education and any obligation on LEAs to abandon selective schools. This action was welcomed by the *Black Paper* editors as providing the period of 'experiment and comparison' which a properly cautious introduction of comprehensive schooling required. If the next five years brought policies that 'honour and develop talent and ability', and reassert the importance of selection, as Margaret Thatcher's first actions as Secretary of State seemed to promise, then the election result could prove the most fortunate for education for a hundred years (Cox and Dyson, 1970, pp. 3, 11).

Certainly the direct-grant schools were temporarily safe. Indeed, their per capita grants were restored in 1973 to the level from which they had been cut by the Labour Government five years before. The income scale for residuary places was also revised to help lower-income families. The Government was pressed to re-open the direct-grant list so as to allow some independent boarding schools to opt-in to this intermediate status and some aided grammar schools to opt-out of the public sector. Longer-term prospects, however, were uncertain. Anxieties about the future of 'independent' education which had been felt first and most acutely by the direct-grant schools because of their dependence on Local Authority support and central government funds were now pervading the entire private sector. They reflected an increasing polarization between the two main Parties in their attitudes towards the inter-dependent issues of independence and selection.

Until the mid-1960s public debate about private education had focused partly on the inefficiency of some independent schools, but mainly on whether the social exclusiveness of the public schools created or merely reinforced social divisions and on how that exclusiveness might be ameliorated. If the Conservative Party sometimes seemed lukewarm and inconsistent in its support of schools in which about three-quarters of its own MPs (and a higher proportion of its Cabinet Ministers) had been educated, it was because there was no clear threat against which they needed to be defended. The Labour Party's own claim (1980, p. 5) that it had 'consistently objected to their presence' is inaccurate if it refers to anything more than routine expressions of dislike. Until the 1960s their presence was usually treated by the Party either as a background irritation, or as a spectacular form of the class education which was inevitable in a class society and which was only removable through fundamental social change. Certainly, links between the public schools and various occupational elites were regularly displayed and deplored as evidence of how privileges were transmitted unfairly from one generation to the next. But there was no concerted campaign against them, and no mention of them at all except for a threat of HMI inspection in any of the six election manifestos between 1945 and 1964 (Craig, 1982). Abolition was rejected by those (like Hugh Gaitskill) who wanted such evidently good schools to be more widely accessible; by the much larger number who (like Crosland) felt unable to remove parents' freedom to choose private education even when the social costs of its exercise might be high; and by those (like Bevan) who saw the privileges passed on by the public schools as superficial symptoms of much deeper inequalities in the distribution of wealth which it was Labour's primary task to remove.[18]

More generally, Labour arguments against the continued co-existence of public and private sectors were softened by meritocratic confidence in the capacity of the maintained grammar schools to provide opportunities for upward mobility (Parkinson, 1970, pp. 94–118).[19] By the early 1970s, however, the slowly accelerating pace of comprehensive re-organization was sharpening differences which the success of the grammar schools had blurred. It did so more intensely because of those changes within the private sector which have been described as an 'academic revolution', characterized by a heavier and more explicit emphasis on academic results. (PSC, 1968, pp. 79–80; Glennerster and Wilson, 1970, pp. 98–9; Gathorne-Hardy, 1977, pp. 368–92, Rae, 1979, pp. 154–9; Salter and Tapper, 1981, pp. 157–88). This was a response to the 'democratizing' of entry to Oxbridge colleges and to the increasing success of grammar school pupils in general competition for university awards and university places. It now seemed to offer a means of marking out distinctive and defensible functions for the leading independent schools. They would be a continuing source of that 'real' academic education believed to be beyond the scope of many comprehensive schools, and provide a 'measuring-rod' for the academic standards which comprehensive reorganization had supposedly placed in jeopardy (ISIS, 1973; 1974).[20] Presented in this way, they represented so fundamental a challenge to Labour's plans for a 'common' system of secondary education that the continued coexistence of public and private sectors had to be seriously questioned.

There are obvious reasons why the direct-grant schools felt the first force of those questions. In principle their leading exemplars were the most academically-selective schools in the country, and therefore (as the PSC had noted) constituted a notable contradiction of public educational policy in large areas of the country. In practice their intermediate status as 'independent' schools under contract to public authorities to 'receive certain financial benefits in return for services rendered' (Cobban, 1969, p. 39) made them highly vulnerable to a sudden cessation of demand for those services. Some LEAs, like Ealing and Harrow and the ILEA, had already stopped buying places in schools which competed with their own (Saran, 1973; Benn, 1974). And unlike the tortuous legal difficulties in the way of any drastic Government action against the charitable status (let alone the existence) of the public schools, the regulations defining the contractual position of the direct-grant schools could simply be withdrawn.

In general the Labour Party now became unusually consistent and forthright about its opposition in principle to private education, and unusually explicit about how that opposition was to be made effective. Its 1970 manifesto contained nothing more specific than a declaration of support for the 'full integration of secondary education' so as to avoid perpetuating 'educational and social inequalities', while Party conference decisions in each of the years 1969–1972 merely reaffirmed the general intention of 'merging', 'integrating' or 'taking' the public schools 'into the state system' (Craig, 1982, pp. 185–92). But the section on 'education for democratic advance' in the 1972 *Programme for Britain* included a commitment to end the direct-grant regulations as a first step towards the goal of abolishing fee-paying and bringing 'all children of compulsory school age into the national education system'; the schools would have to choose between 'full independence', and 'fully entering the national system' on that system's own terms. In the following year Roy Hattersley (then Shadow spokesman for Education) first told the annual conference of the Incorporated Association of Preparatory Schools (IAPS) that his Party was resolved to 'gradually reduce and eventually abolish' the private sector, and then told them in some detail how it proposed to do so. In his own closing speech the Association's president, Edward Boyle, deplored Hattersley's 'lack of sensitivity to institutions', and affirmed the Conservative Party's commitment to parental choice and its opposition to any form of state monopoly in education. Commenting on the exchange, the *Times Educational Supplement* editorial referred to 'the right to opt out of state education' as being 'about as fundamental a family freedom as can be imagined'.[21] Labour's contrary commitments were then restated by Hattersley at the Party's conference later that month. After summarizing the case against the private sector — that it perpetuated privilege, was deeply divisive, and diverted attention and resources from maintained schools — he repeated that the long-term objective had to be its abolition. He then traced the process of progressive reduction which could be achieved by ending the direct-grant system, ending tax concessions, constraining LEAs from taking up places, and eventually banning the charging of fees altogether. While the procedural details could be left to the Party's Science and Education Sub-Committee, a demonstration of 'political will' was essential (cited in Rae, 1979, pp. 50–7). As an expression of that political will, the Party's manifesto for the 1974 election included a commitment to 'stop the present system of direct-grant schools', and to withdraw 'all forms of tax relief and charitable status' from the private sector. 'Gradual reduction and eventual abolition' has remained Party policy since that time, justified by the damage which the very presence of independent schools is said to inflict on public education and by their importance as 'a huge barrier to equality of educational, social and occupational opportunity' (Labour Party, 1980, pp. 14–15).[22]

As Labour policy towards the private sector became more consistently and specifically hostile, so the sector became more organized and coherent in its own defence. In one recent account a sharp contrast is drawn between its 'dangerously exposed' position in the mid-1960s, and the 'institutional regeneration' through which it rapidly equipped itself for effective 'ideological warfare' (Salter and Tapper,

1985, pp. 127–54). We find this contrast overdrawn and too suggestive of a beleagured 'thin red line'. For example, the falling numbers noted by Salter and Tapper as evidence of institutional decline were mainly a consequence of weaker schools closing. While there was certainly a marked decline in demand for boarding education even among its traditional clients, the very exclusiveness of the 'leading' schools puts them under no pressure to do more than maintain their share of the educational market. And even if public opinion had been swinging against elitist education, as Salter and Tapper argue, some compensating 'flight' might also be expected from a public sector increasingly lacking the attractions of academic selection. Indeed, as we argue later, a major reason for the private sector's regeneration was to be its increasing predomin-ance as the source of 'real' academic education. In short, if the assumed merits of grammar schools largely explain a significant desertion of private education by middle-class parents from 1945 to 1965, then the assumed demerits of comprehensive schools were likely to bring a revival of support.

We therefore doubt whether the direct-grant schools were widely seen in the mid-1960s as the 'independent sector's first line of defence' (Salter and Tapper, 1985, p. 129). Academic selectiveness rather than independence was then the main issue. There was also considerable resentment within the private sector at the extent to which their free and indirectly subsidized places enabled direct-grant schools to escape the full rigours of the educational market and to attract many able pupils who would otherwise have attended fully independent schools. It was the fast-flowing 'compre-hensive tide' rather than a wider threat to 'independence' which led in 1966 to the formation of the Direct-Grant Joint Committee (DGJC). This became a notably effective pressure group in itself and a model of what other more broadly-based com-mittees might do. It provided information and advice to individual schools (for example, about the effects of Circular 10/65 on LEAs' take-up of free places), pressed for the inclusion of direct-grant schools in the PSC's terms of reference, and then presented evidence and arguments to the Commission when it was reconstituted in 1968. It also energetically canvassed political support for the distinctive type of school it claimed to represent (DGJC, 1968; Cobban, 1969), although it had to use some discretion to avoid resentment elsewhere in the private sector that the tail was wagging the dog. Among its activities was the formulation, in broad terms, of pro-posals to improve the direct-grant system by removing its most vulnerable feature — the indiscriminate assistance given to parents who could afford to pay full fees. We return to these proposals for a new form of assisted places in the final section of the chapter.

More general uncertainties about Labour's intentions led to more general forms of concerted defensive action. In February 1973 the GBA set up a sub-committee to examine how 'independent' education was to be defended in principle and in practice. Its report included a lawyer's exposition of the dubious defences available in national or international law against a Government which was really determined to abolish the independent schools and willing to pay the financial (and political) price of doing so. The preface to the report therefore stressed the importance of publicizing the case for independent education, and advised the GBA to decide quickly how far it wished to defend the 'direct-grant principle' since it would be the direct-grant schools which would first bear the brunt of the Government's attack. By this time the traditional ambivalence about the schools within the private sector was being rapidly overcome by the realization that attacks on the direct-grant 'bridge' were unlikely to leave the 'fully' independent 'island' unscathed. In the following year the Independent Schools Joint Committee (ISJC) was established to provide a co-ordinating agency and a common voice for the sector as a whole. Even in the 1960s, the HMC's Publicity Committee had become a public relations committee. In 1972 the evident need both for more information and more professional public relations led to the creation of a national Independent Schools Information Service (ISIS). Its functions were to provide facts and advice to the member schools which funded it (there were 1350 of these by 1983) and to 'inform the public of the true nature of independent schools and their value to the nation'. As a pressure group, it was explicitly intended to mobilize support against a 'growing threat to independence' from all those who believed that 'a state monopoly in education is wrong' (ISIS, 1972). Parents in a free society, it was argued in various pamphlets, had the right to choose efficient schools outside the maintained sector, especially schools which were committed to preserving those high standards of education for which academic selection was necessary (ISIS, 1974; 1976). It was in this new ideological context that the direct-grant schools now began to receive more whole-hearted support as the private sector's first line of defence (ISIS, 1973; 1975).

Although ISIS presented itself as a non-Party organization, it represented pressure groups well aware of where pressure was most effectively applied. The form and force of the attack directed by the Labour Party at both independence and selectiveness aroused strong responses in a Conservative Party which had previously showed little enthusiasm for educational issues.[23] Increasingly close cooperation between some Conservative politicians and some public school and direct-grant school heads is apparent from this time. The Independent Schools Joint Committee (later Council) which was formed in 1974 had a Conservative Minister, Lord Belstead, as its first chairman, and later created its own Parliamentary Committee. But what might otherwise have appeared merely as sectional self-interest was given much broader polemical support in the early *Black Papers*. These were presented by their editors as articulating widespread opposition to 'progressive, non-selective and egalitarian education', and widespread concern at the damage which 'new trends' were doing to educational standards, and especially to the prospects of able working-class children (Cox and Boyson, 1975, p. 3; Cox and Dyson, 1969b, pp. 14–15; Cox 1982). We present in chapter 4 a more general analysis of this 'reappraisal of progressive assumptions', and of the challenge to the 'fashionable left-wing consensus' which arose from it. It included some forceful advocacy of both independent and direct-grant schools.

The extent to which the policies of the two main Parties had polarized since the 'liberal-left' consensus exemplified by Crosland and Boyle was made apparent in the House of Commons debate (November 1973) on the Direct-Grant Regulations, when the Government's proposal to increase per capita payments for pupils in those schools coincided with reductions in expenditure in the public sector. The Labour attack (led by Roy Hattersley) concentrated on the favouring of 'a very selective and very elitist part of the education system', through which schools with 'a woefully inadequate social mix' would be able to undermine further comprehensive secondary education by 'skimming off' able pupils. Conservative speakers made equally familiar references to a 'social mix' better than either the public schools or the 'rigid neighbourhood compre- hensive', and to the necessity of retaining 'absolutely first-class academic education' for the good of the country as a whole and for the particular benefit of 'very bright working-class children'. In his closing speech, Norman St John Stevas emphasized the accessibility of 'good schools' enabled by the direct-grant regulations to charge 'modest fees to those of modest means'. An additional £800,000 for those schools in a total education budget of nearly £300 million was little to pay for avoiding a 'totally state-centred and controlled system', and for preserving — 'the freedom of the parent to choose the education for his child, the freedom of the teacher to follow his profes- sion and to practise it as he likes, and the freedom of the school to maintain standards of excellence'.[24]

In the 1974 Party manifestos, especially those for the second (October) election, the same contrasts appeared in abbreviated form. Labour again presented its proposed sequence of moves against all forms of 'subsidising privilege', starting with the abolition of the direct-grant system. The Conservative prospectus emphasized diversity in educational provision, the right of parents to pay fees, and the importance of preserving all schools 'of proven worth' which helped to meet 'the needs of bright and able children, especially those from disadvantaged areas'. A Conservative Government would therefore re-open the direct-grant list; it would also consider introducing 'a complete system of assisted places so that every parent pays only according to his or her means' (Craig, 1982, pp. 442, 460).

Given a working majority in the second election of 1974, the Labour Government had the opportunity to begin the war of attrition against the private sector which Roy Hattersley had promised, although some doubts among Labour leaders about the political wisdom of that war may be evident in the fact that Hattersley was not appointed to the Education post which he had 'shadowed'. Fred Mulley was certainly unlikely to be in the forefront of that 'demonstration of political will' which Hattersley had demanded. Charitable status, and the tax relief and rate relief which came from it, proved as usual to be an elusive target. The Tenth Report of the House of Commons Expenditure Committee (1975, Vol. 1, p. xv) stated firmly the illogicality of treating as charitable 'activities . . . manifestly devoted to privilege and exclusiveness', but Lord Goodman's Committee on Charity Law and Organisations (1976) preferred to leave the nettle of defining charitable purposes to be grasped (tentatively) by the Charity Commissioners and the courts rather than have it uprooted by legislation.[25]

By comparison with those legal complexities, the ending of the direct-grant system was a relatively simple step to take. The schools were now presented with the clear choice which the Public Schools Commission had recommended. They had to inform the Secretary of State by 31 December 1975 whether they intended to become 'fully independent' or to 'fully enter the national system' as comprehensive schools. There was considerable high-handedness (and ham-handedness) in the Government's approach. Little or no effort was made to persuade schools which might be wavering to move into the public sector, there was considerable confusion over the future status of those which did so, and the absence of any obligation on schools to inform the Government of their decision before the deadline produced complete uncertainty about what proportion of schools were likely to opt for 'full' independence. Shortly after the October 1974 election, St John Stevas had launched a campaign to 'save the direct-grant schools' which was supported by well-organized publicity from the private sector. The schools were presented as victims of the Government's intolerance and dogmatism, their only offence being that they had 'achieved high academic standards and a wider social mix than many neighbouring comprehensive schools' and provided 'centres of academic excellence in the light of which the achievements and short-comings of other schools can be judged'. That was how the Shadow Minister explained 'why they are being done away with', his defence of them being embedded in general arguments about parental choice, opportunities for working-class children, and the 'battle for freedom in education'.[26] There was extensive lobbying of the House of Commons in June 1975 when it debated the Cessation of Grant Regulations, the measure which would enable the Secretary of State to withdraw grants from any school unable or unwilling to meet the requirements for entering the 'national system', and further lobbying at the Party conferences that autumn. Additionally, a petition in support of direct-grant schools attracted half a million signatures, numerous press releases demonstrated how well the schools complemented the public sector, and there was a carefully coordinated campaign of letters to individual ministers and MPs.[27] To contain the damage as far as possible pending a Conservative victory in the next election, schools were encouraged to ask the DES so many reasonable but awkward questions about their future that negotiations would become bogged down and LEAs' reorganization plans would be seriously hampered.

In the end the scale of the exodus into independence was surprising to many both outside and inside the private sector. Fifty-one direct-grant schools decided to become 'fully integrated' — forty-eight of them Catholic schools with relatively unselective intakes (some with heavy capital debts to be paid off) and with a greater commitment to remaining Catholic than to remaining as grammar schools. Four schools closed altogether. The other 119 decided to remain academically selective by accepting the risks of 'going it alone'. Their decisions produced, as Conservative politicians were quick to point out, the largest addition ever made in one 'sweep' to the private sector. The Labour Government's response might well have been phrased as — *sauter pour mieux reculer.*

As the schools were making their decisions, Conservative-controlled LEAs were being encouraged by their Party to give practical support to those contemplating independence (including some voluntary-aided grammar schools) by increasing their take-up of 'free' and 'reserved' places. There was therefore strong Conservative resistance to the Government's next move against the private sector, embodied in the 1976 Education Bill, which sought to restrict the Secretary of State's approval for such purchasing to cases where the places were demonstrably supplementing rather than duplicating (or competing with) provision in that LEA's own schools. Shirley Williams threatened to prevent any places being taken up on the traditional grounds of aptitude and ability, except for special abilities in music. The Conservatives replied that a 'sufficiency' of existing places in the maintained sector had to be defined by quality as well as quantity, and that LEAs were entitled to seek outside provision on those grounds. In practice, however, the power of refusal embodied in Circular 6/77 was much less than the Government had intended — a fact noted with considerable irritation at the 1978 Labour Party conference.

Conservative opposition to the 1976 Bill as a whole was reflected in a series of amendments intended to delay its progress which clearly anticipate policies followed by Conservative Governments since 1979. They included support for parental rights to a 'free' choice of school and to detailed information about examination results on which they could base that choice; support for academically-selective schools within the public sector; encouragement for LEAs to assist able pupils to attend independent schools; and reference to what was described as a 'new direct grant system'. That last amendment reflected an already considerable measure of cooperation between some Conservative politicians and leading figures in the private sector. Indeed, Stuart Sexton, who was already acting as full-time political adviser to St John Stevas, states firmly that he used the amendment to 'float' an Assisted Places Scheme and to establish it as Party policy.[28] What the amendment promised was a 'revised and expanded' version of the previous direct-grant system which would make available to parents, on an entirely income-related basis, places in a 'whole network of independent schools'. These would be schools 'free of political control', and 'free to pursue high educational standards'. It is to the origins and canvassing of that scheme that we now turn.

## The Assisted Places Scheme in the Making

Among the early activities of the Direct-Grant Joint Committee formed in 1966 was discussion of how the existing direct-grant arrangements might be improved. It was widely believed within the schools themselves that the 'direct-grant principle' of offering opportunities for a high-quality academic education to a 'unique social mix' could be more forcefully defended if assistance to parents was more closely matched with financial need. Although there were objections to changing a familiar system, especially from those Catholic schools in which most places were already free, there was also considerable agreement that all fees should be means-tested, and that per capita grants should be ended as a source of indirect subsidy to so-called 'full' fees. There was no intention at this stage, however, of removing the special 'intermediate' status of direct-grant schools, or of denying to LEAs the right to take up places in them.

Some preliminary discussion of these proposals took place with DES officials in July 1970, but seem to have aroused little official interest. Further approaches were made in 1971-2, but Margaret Thatcher's reponse at that time seems to have been that schools which prided themselves on their independence should be willing to face the full rigours of the educational market-place (Rae, 1981, pp. 148–53; Salter and Tapper, 1985, pp. 188–9). As we suggested earlier, that view was also held within the private sector, parts of which were in any case only loosely aligned with the highly academic and meritocratic orientation of many direct-grant schools. But as Labour opposition to academic selectiveness began to be accompanied by increasingly overt threats to private education in general, it became suddenly much easier to elicit support beyond the direct-grant schools themselves for plans not only to make Government assistance with the costs of independent schooling more discriminating but also to extend it to a wider range of schools. To those direct-grant schools in particular which had already resolved to accept the risks of becoming independent rather than cease to be grammar schools, the proposals offered some security in the form of subsidized places and (more importantly) some means of escape from a fate they deplored in principle – that of becoming merely schools for those able to pay. Without some form of assisted places, the social selectiveness of independent schools could be tempered only by whatever scholarships could be provided from past endowments and new philanthropy (GPDST schools, for example, raised some £2 million for scholarships in 1976–8 in an effort to offset some of the effects on their intakes of the ending of direct-grant).

The DGJC's pamphlet, *A Policy for Direct-Grant Schools* (May 1976), was introduced as the outcome of years of discussion which had produced substantial agreement about the proposals it contained. In the previous autumn a 'new and revised direct-grant system' based on those proposals had been circulated for comment within the Conservative Party. Stuart Sexton was active both in canvassing political support and in drafting the relevant amendment we referred to earlier, and which was published on the order paper for the Commons debate of 8 June 1976. In the briefing papers which Sexton prepared at the time for Conservative MPs, there are references to the amendment as having 'received acclaim'; 'it has flown a kite, and the kite has been well received'. The briefing emphasizes that the Scheme would both redeem the Party's pledge to the direct-grant schools, and be the 'salvation' of many voluntary-aided and even some county grammar schools.

Sexton himself saw it as already constituting a Party commitment. But formal approval of the Scheme was still needed from the Shadow Cabinet. Negotiations continued through the following year, with James Cobban (ex-head of Abingdon School) and Peter Mason (High Master of Manchester Grammar School) playing the main coordinating roles for the direct-grant school lobby, and Sexton doing the same for the Conservative Party. Although care was taken to avoid the links between schools and Party becoming too obvious, the proposals made public by St John Stevas on 22 September 1977 closely resembled those 'improvements' in the direct-grant system which the DGJC had been pursuing for nearly ten years.[29] The press releases from DGJC which accompanied St John Stevas' announcement welcomed the emphasis placed on assisting parents genuinely unable to pay fees, and the renewed opportunity for independent schools to 'work in co-operation with the maintained system'. Writing to St John Stevas to thank him 'very, very gratefully' for the Shadow Cabinet's support, Cobban applauded the way the Scheme had been associated so explicitly with the safeguarding both of parental choice and educational standards. He also recognized that however valuable an apolitical basis of support might be, it was also highly unlikely because the Scheme was bound to be fiercely attacked by all opponents of academic selection.[30]

Recognition of the vulnerability of the whole private sector led to the setting-up of a Parliamentary/ISJC liaison committee, which held its first meeting in March 1978.[31] Although the intention was clearly to build up collective defences (for example, some of its members had financial expertise relevant to defending the tax advantages which went with charitable status), there was still some tension between those whose emphasis was on preserving independence *per se*, and those whose main concern was with the continuing availability of a 'grammar school' type of education. It was evident at times in discussions about whether schools offering assisted places should continue to be 'fully independent', or should become 'assisted-place schools' with some form of intermediate status. St John Stevas seems initially to have favoured a new category of 'independent-aided' schools, a compromise which would have contradicted the claims regularly made by the DGJC that it wanted to end all aid to schools and to direct assistance entirely to needy pupils. He also argued at times that some assisted places should be reserved for LEAs to take up, and that there should be some LEA-appointed governors to maintain continuity with the direct-grant system. The direct-grant view, and it was strongly held by Sexton, was that LEAs should be excluded from any involvement in the new arrangements — partly because all the money for assistance would be provided by central government, but mainly because direct contractual arrangements between individual schools and the Government would allow those schools to determine for themselves how many assisted places they wished to offer.

Sexton was determined to establish, by the time the Conservatives returned to office, that there were enough schools willing to enter into a contract of that kind. For more than a year before the 1979 election, he was actively engaged in promoting the Scheme within the private sector, identifying schools likely to offer places, exploring the terms on which they would be willing to do so, and persuading voluntary-aided grammar schools that the scheme would ease their transition to independence if that was the only way they could defeat LEA plans to turn them comprehensive. At times, his openly entrepreneurial negotiating style caused some alarm among fastidious independent school heads. It was clearly important to identify enough schools able and willing to take part. But Sexton had in view a much larger scheme than most of its advocates within the private sector thought realistic, involving as many as 500 schools and 15,000 places a year. His consequently energetic canvassing raised the hopes of some schools which were subsequently judged unsuitable to participate at all, and encouraged others to consider ambitious offers which had later to be scaled down. In pursuit of objectives to which he was personally so committed, he tended to ignore the caution felt in many schools about proposals which, however attractive in principle, were bound to be politically contentious. He certainly met considerable resistance from those unaccustomed to recruiting 'scholarship' pupils in any numbers, or to having any close links at all with the public sector.

Where Sexton and his direct-grant allies were entirely agreed was in seeing independence as the only way of ensuring that traditional academic standards would be maintained. That view was forcefully articulated by the chairman of the 1978 Headmasters' Conference, David Baggley from Bolton School. Arguing for a 'mixed economy' in which 'basic public services at the tax-payer's expense' are combined with 'independent initiative and enterprise in other institutions', he regretted a 'widening of the gap' between public and private sectors which had not been of the independent schools' making. Nevertheless, future cooperation had to be reconciled with the fact that independence is 'a necessary condition of our continuing to be able to do the job which we think it right to do and which a substantial section of the public thinks worthwhile'. Predictably, it was from schools like Bolton that the 'overwhelming support' for assisted places which ISIS frequently announced was strongest. They saw in the scheme a return to familiar ways, bringing an academic education again within reach of all who would benefit from it while avoiding the past error of giving free places to pupils with parents well able to pay. Outside their ranks, there was still some uneasiness that a scheme so emphatically academic in its purposes might devalue other qualities which independent schools claimed to foster. But traditional resentment at the protection which the direct-grant schools had enjoyed had now been overtaken by more widely diffused ambitions to share in the benefits of publicly-subsidized 'independent' schooling.

There was therefore concern to avoid those schools taking too large a share of whatever assisted places were eventually made available. Although it was the DGJC which had so far made the running, it became clear that a more broadly-based body was needed for more formal negotiations with the Conservative Party in the run-up to the election. Its role was therefore taken over by the Independent Schools Joint Advisory Committee (ISJAC), which held its first meeting with the shadow Minister in January 1979.[32] The advanced stage reached in the subsequent negotiations is apparent in a newspaper article by Mark Carlisle three months later, in which he referred not only to the substantial number of assisted places which would be made available in over 200 schools but also to the terms on which those places would be offered and financially supported. Welcoming his plans, an accompanying *Daily Telegraph* Editorial commended this 'restoration of academic opportunities to high fliers from poor homes' both for the benefits it would bring to deserving individuals and because it would help to establish 'a secure basis of academic excellence' against which state schools could be compared.[33] As foreshadowed in the article, the Conservative Party's election manifesto issued later that month included an explicit pledge to 'restore the direct-grant principle' through the means-tested provision of places for 'bright children from modest backgrounds'. And as a result of all the preparatory work we have described, Sexton was satisfied that, as the Party entered the 1979 election campaign, the plans for implementing that pledge were already too far advanced and too well canvassed to be subverted even by the well-practised caution of civil servants.

## Notes

1  The equivalent proportions in 1947 were 8 per cent and 22 per cent.
2  We use 'elitist' here in the 'neutral' sense defined by Mason (1986) as referring to — 'the creation and reproduction of a privileged minority, access to which is limited by inherited rank, wealth or ability'.
3  This view was clearly expressed from inside the private sector by John Dancy (1963), then head of Marlborough and shortly to be a member of the Public Schools Commission.
4  The Labour publication, *Learning to Live* (1958), hoped for integration at some future time when 'maintained schools are improved, when the prestige of the public schools is consequently diminished, and when substantial changes in the distribution of wealth and in public opinion have occurred' (p. 60). In the following year, *70 Questions Asked and Answered on Labour's Education Policy* denied that parents could be prohibited from buying private education 'in a free country'. A much stronger line was taken in a pamphlet written by W. Spikes and P. Ibbotson for the National Association of Labour Teachers and called *A Policy for the Public Schools* (1958); this urged an end to all paying of fees for education as a declaration that 'privilege is not for sale'.
5  There is an obvious inconsistency between Crosland's recognition of these 'real advantages', and his hopes (reported in his wife's biography) that a steady improvement in state provision would make it irrelevant if some parents 'continued to send their children to inferior fee-paying schools for purely snobbish reasons' (S. Crosland, 1983, pp. 149–50).

6  The 'fig-leaf' and 'nihilist' solutions were equally rejected in a speech Crosland made in March 1965 (*Times Educational Supplement*, 12 March, p. 761). For indications of unease that the Government would go too far, or not far enough, see the Commons debate, 1 July 1965 (*Hansard*, Vol. 715).

7  *Times Educational Supplement*, 13 September 1968, p. 453.

8  Later research by Lambert's Unit drew attention to the formidable problems of assimilating such sponsored pupils into schools with very different values to their own, especially where the pupils involved were in their teens, working-class or less able (Lambert *et al.*, 1968). The Commission recognized these problems. Nevertheless, as has been emphasized to us by one of its members (John Dancy) and by its first secretary (Geoffrey Cockerill), meeting 'boarding need' was seen as the only basis for solving the 'Public Schools Question'.

9  Chapter 14 of Peter Gosden's (1976) account of *Education and the Second World War* contains a detailed account of that crisis, and of the close personal links between leading figures in the private sector and at the Board of Education. Among the schools judged by officials to be in danger were Harrow, Malvern, Lancing, Repton and Mill Hill.

10  The three dissenters were Dame Kitty Anderson, head of the North London Collegiate School; Tom Howarth, head of St. Paul's; and John Davies, Director-General of the CBI and a future Conservative cabinet minister.

11  *Times Educational Supplement*, 26 July 1968, p. 169.

12  John Dancy, then head of Marlborough and a member of the PSC, was ill and unable to attend. The hostility of his fellow heads to the Commission's proposals was so strong that he advised those wanting to use him as a referee in applications to public school headships that his support might well prove a handicap.

13  *Times Educational Supplement*, 13 September 1968, p. 453.

14  The threat was made in Crosland's speech at the North of England Conference in January 1966, and was in the context of a forceful defence of comprehensive secondary education (Crosland, 1968).

15  In 1965, for example, per capita payments were £52 for each pupil and an additional £84 for each sixth-former — this at a time when tuition fees in independent schools ranged around the figure of £100. 'Full' fees at direct-grant schools were estimated by Glennerster and Wilson (1970) as being about 58 per cent of economic cost.

16  Her case-study was not published at the time. Evidence from it is referred to in Saran (1973).

17  Their tuition fees, however, were considerably lower because of the indirect subsidy referred to in note 12. For example, among the fees at 'fully' independent schools reported in the PSC's *First Report* were Sedbergh, £234; Repton, £255; Tonbridge, £285; Shrewsbury, £330; and Westminster, £363. By comparison, fees at a similarly random selection of direct-grant schools with boarding places were — Bedford Modern, £95; Loughborough High School, £100; Perse School, £117; and Abingdon, £117. It is easy to see from these figures why the direct-grant schools were seen by many inside the private sector as being excessively protected from the rigours of the market.

18  Gaitskill's strongly meritocratic view is cited in Parkinson (1970, p. 107) who provides a useful account of this tension. Bevan's view is cited in Barker (1972, p. 100). Barker comments that apart from Fleming's intervention, the public schools seemed 'secure in their rural seclusion from the vulgar gaze of socialists and proletarians'.

19  Even a Conservative Minister, David Eccles, argued against a 1961 back-bench request for more publicly-assisted places in public schools on the grounds that it would be a waste of money when so many grammar schools were 'better than the average public school' and no less capable of producing the country's future leaders (cited in Dancy 1963, pp. 30–1).

20  Although written somewhat later when the tide was perhaps turning again, the Methodist Board on Education and Youth issued (April 1977) a statement about the 'theological and ethical implications' of the Church's involvement in private education which reflects a deep ambivalence about a 'great educational tradition' which was restricted to a few. Nevertheless, independent schools are described as a bulwark against state monopoly and state control, a monopoly which might well be used to 'infuse the teaching of a non-Christian ideology', as enabling parents to educate their children 'in conformity with their own convictions', and as providing 'a point of reference' for all parts of the system while being too few to 'significantly damage' the facilities available to the majority.

21 *Times Educational Supplement*, 14 September 1973.

22 See also the *Plan for Private Schools* published the following year by the TUC–Labour Party Liaison Committee.

23 Craig's collection of Party Conference decisions takes only three pages to report Conservative items relating to education 1945–1981, compared with twenty-one pages for Labour (Craig, 1982, pp. 42–5, 184–205).

24 *Hansard*, 15 November 1973, 809–36.

25 The basic objection to the charitable status enjoyed by leading public schools was firmly stated in the PSC's *First Report*; it provided indirect subsidies from public funds to 'people who choose to buy expensive services which they are well able to afford' (1968, Vol. 1, pp. 160–1).

26 Reported in *The Times* and *Daily Telegraph*, 22 November 1974.

27 Replying to a question in the Commons about this canvassing, Joan Lestor reported having received 2500 letters on the matter in the previous three months (*Hansard*, 14 October 1975, 1118).

28 Interviewed by us on 2 February 1984 and 17 December 1984. Sexton was a chemist and former marketing executive for Shell and RTZ. As a Conservative councillor and member of the Croydon Education Committee, he had sent unsolicited advice on educational policy to St John Stevas when he was shadow minister, and had then become his unpaid part-time adviser. It was therefore not surprising that St John Stevas launched his 'Save the direct-grant schools' campaign at a meeting of the Croydon Conservative Association, 22 November 1974. Sexton became a full-time political adviser to the shadow minister in 1975, paid for from the so-called 'Short-money', and continued working in that capacity for Mark Carlisle (in opposition and in government) and later for Keith Joseph.

29 *Times Educational Supplement* editorial (30 September 1977) labelled it immediately 'a direct-grant lifeline'.

30 Letter, 23 September 1977.

31 This committee came into being after a meeting in December 1977 at the Westminster home of Lady Waley-Cohen, who then chaired the ISJC.

32 This was chaired by Frank Fisher, then head of Rugby. Other members included Michael McCrum (head of Eton), Dame Kitty Anderson (retired head of the North London Collegiate School and a member of the Public Schools Commission), Lady Betty Johnston (chair of the GPDST), Tim Devlin (director of ISIS), James Cobban, and Gavin Alexander (head of Hampton School and initiator of the recently-formed Association of Voluntary-aided and Independent Grammar Schools).

33 *Daily Telegraph*, 4 April 1979. The many letters which Carlisle wrote at this time in response to individual enquiries about Conservative intentions refer regularly to 'the direct-grant principle' or the 'direct-grant ideal', and emphasize that a 'network' of schools would be offering opportunities of high quality academic education to 'bright, motivated children'.

# Chapter 3

## *Formulation and Implementation*

In the previous chapter we described how the 'direct-grant principle' was challenged as being incompatible with the principles of comprehensive secondary education. It was therefore discarded (or, from another perspective, betrayed) by the Labour Government. If the matter had then been settled by the withdrawal of the Direct-Grant Regulations in 1976, the last significant group of beneficiaries of free places paid for from public funds would have left their schools in 1983. In this chapter we describe in detail how the revised version of the direct-grant arrangements which had been negotiated between representatives of the independent schools and a few political allies was now translated into a workable scheme which could replace the old one. It was imperative that this was done quickly, while memories of the direct-grant tradition and the manifesto commitment to restore it remained fresh in the public consciousness.

Our account focuses particularly on the negotiations between the independent school lobby and the Department of Education and Science. In doing so, it provides an interesting case-study of the relationship between the activities of an external interest group and the processes of official policy-making within a government department. The account includes evidence of the crucial role in the development of the Scheme of Stuart Sexton as a policy adviser (or 'political civil servant'), both as a 'broker' mediating between the pressure group and the relevant civil servants and as a direct influence on the decisions which were being made by ministers. The energetically partisan role adopted by Sexton throughout the negotiations is in sharp contrast to an earlier description of the dominance of conventional state bureaucrats in the making of educational policy in England (Salter and Tapper, 1981). Yet it will become clear that his was not the only influence on the content of the Scheme which he, together with the representatives of the independent schools and the career civil servants within the department, now had to implement.

As described in the previous chapter, the proposals taken up by the Conservative Party in 1976 had been devised and then actively promoted by heads of direct-grant schools. Prominent members of the DGJC, like James Cobban and Peter Mason, were certainly anxious both to retain the initiative and to avoid appearing too closely linked with the Conservatives. They were also more cautious than Sexton about the scope of the proposed scheme, Sexton being apparently alone in setting targets as high as 15,000 places a year in 500 schools. On the other hand, his insistence that participating schools should remain independent rather than change to some intermediate status was a view to which the private sector did not need to be converted. But while these are reasons for doubting claims that he is the 'acknowledged architect' of the Assisted Places Scheme, his importance as its 'intellectual broker' is certainly evident.[1] Enthusiasm for the Scheme even among Conservative politicians was limited, and there was no discernible contribution to its making from the many other policy advisers (formal and informal) who had been engaged in preparing their Party for office. Even St John Stevas and his shadow successor, Mark Carlisle (for whom Sexton also worked as full-time adviser), showed only intermittent interest in it and Sexton's own consistent enthusiasm was therefore invaluable in enlisting political support for the Scheme. Indeed, far from remaining discreetly in the background, as political advisers were generally expected to do, he appeared increasingly as a public spokesman of the Party's commitment, often deputising for Carlisle at official functions both before and after the Election.[2]

Sexton's long experience as a political adviser, his regular presence in Elizabeth House, his particular commitment to assisted places and relative freedom from other responsibilities, together with his many contacts within the private sector, all enabled him to influence the details of the eventual scheme as no minister would have been able or would have wanted to do. He shared with his future associates in the New Right a suspicion of DES inertia in the face of proposals which he was determined should be brought quickly into effect, and he often showed impatience after the election with official protocol and official caution. After some initial hesitancy about dealing with someone whose style was so overtly entrepeneurial, leading figures in the private sector had come to value his promotional skills and his energy. But they now welcomed the clarity which civil servants brought to early discussions about the terms of the Scheme and their relative wariness about how dependent on assisted places any independent school could afford to become. This interaction between commitment and practicality in the final shaping of the Scheme is a consistent theme in the account that follows.

### Embodying the Scheme in Legislation

During the preparatory negotiations it had already been decided that this 'new and revised' version of the direct-grant system should be established by legislation and not by administrative regulations because legislation would then be required to dismantle it. The old system had been ended in June 1976 by the simple withdrawal of the relevant regulations after a four-hour debate. Its replacement was to be defended against similarly summary execution.

It has been suggested that in the framing of the necessary legislation DES responsibilities were significantly 'eroded' by the preparations described in the previous chapter, and by draft plans which were unusually detailed because of Sexton's determination to avoid the Scheme being either 'emasculated' by official caution or lost sight of by a new Government with other priorities (Salter and Tapper, 1985, pp. 202–3). DES officials certainly showed subsequently a resistance to plans for introducing educational vouchers which their critics attributed to an entrenched partiality towards LEAs and other public sector 'producer interests' (West, 1982; Seldon, 1986; Cox and Marks, 1988). But we found no evidence that the civil servants responsible for constructing a workable Assisted Place Scheme were either dilatory, or obstructive, or uneasy about the close cooperation with the private sector which it involved. Indeed, the main negotiators from that sector regarded them as being notably efficient.[3] The scheme with which they were presented immediately after the election differed in scope from the outline they had prepared themselves as a normal civil service response to a likely new Government's manifesto commitment, and was certainly not ready-made for implementation. The civil servants had to consider (as Sexton did not) the possible impact of the scheme on the public sector, and the consequent need to initiate at least nominal consultation with local authorities and teacher unions. They also had to be much more circumspect than he was about seeming to encourage the participation of grammar schools still undecided about whether or not to 'go independent'. There was a more general contrast too, noted in an internal DES memorandum, between Sexton's dedication to the detailed application of 'his' particular scheme, and the obligation of civil servants to assess the merits of various alternatives.[4] His informal contacts with ISJAC and with individual schools enabled him to exert considerable influence on the details of the emerging arrangements. But it was the civil servants who soon had to respond to many queries from independent schools about (for example) the budgetary controls which might follow an allocation of assisted places, whether all their places would have to be offered on a means-tested basis, and whether safeguards could be offered to entrants against the withdrawal of assistance by a future Labour government.

Within days of the election on 3 May 1979, discussions began between Sexton and such civil servants as Clive Saville (who as Registrar for Independent Schools was the most regularly involved) about how quickly the ISJAC proposals could be translated into a workable scheme. By the end of May an initial draft had already been sent to James Cobban for comment,[5] and Sexton was able to tell heads of HMC direct-grant schools at their June meeting that arrangements were well under way to 'bring the benefits of an academic education within reach of all those who would benefit from it'.[6] Concerted attempts to win support for the objectives of the scheme began early in the autumn. The motion supporting it at the September meeting of HMC defined its prime purpose as that of complementing state education by providing for individual children who needed an academic education which their local maintained schools could not provide. Media interest, however, focused less on the proposals themselves than on what the BBC's *Today* programme described as an unusually 'long and hot' debate about them. This lasted nearly two hours, and ended in the unprecedented taking of a vote. Although the size of the vote in favour (136 to fifteen, with nineteen abstentions) emphasized the scheme's popularity in the most prestigious part of the private sector, the outspoken opposition of John Rae (headmaster of Westminster School) drew more attention to the dissenters. In fact, most of those voting against it or abstaining were heads of boarding schools which could see little place for themselves in a scheme so evidently biased towards highly academic day pupils, or who wanted 'boarding need' included in its provisions. There was no discernible Conference support for Rae's own fundamental objection to assisted places — that they were being 'thrust on the maintained sector by a government telling that sector, "You can't cope".'[7] James Cobban dismissed that objection as the illogical opposition of a maverick who could apparently reconcile himself to selection by money but not to selection by merit.[8]

The publicity arising from the HMC meeting caused problems for Sexton, who had outlined the scheme to Conference members with his usual fervour and was subsequently warned by Saville that he risked intensifying the opposition to it by exaggerating its scope. He himself complained to Mark Carlisle that his words had been 'grossly distorted' in an *Observer* report in which he was made to suggest that the costs of the scheme, then widely put at £50 million, would be deducted from the public sector budget. As Lady Young (a junior Education Minister) commented some time later, this 'rumour' made the scheme vulnerable to what was potentially its 'most damaging criticism' because of its coincidence with considerable cuts in public expenditure. DES briefing papers for Carlisle's meeting with representatives of the ACC and AMA (3 October 1979) emphasized the importance of the question of whether assisted places would be funded from 'new' money.[9] Yet there was still considerable uncertainty about how large a scheme was intended, where the money for it would come from, and whether it should be considered as 'part of the total education budget and not as a separate fund'.[10] At this time Sexton was still assuming that all places in participating schools could be eligible for fee remission, and so was envisaging an annual cost of £12 million to £15 million.

How best to manage public relations was a continuing topic for discussion between Sexton, DES officials and representatives of the independent schools during the autumn of 1979. At a meeting in the ISIS offices on October 5, Sexton warned the schools not to appear too knowledgeable too soon about the details of the forthcoming legislation lest it should appear that the Government was merely acting on behalf of a private sector lobby. But he also urged them to make their case boldly. It was agreed that the 'restoration' of academic opportunities should be emphasized in promoting the scheme, and a list of likely criticisms and plausible responses to them was drawn up for circulation to ISIS members.[11] An Assisted Places Scheme Group began to meet regularly, consisting of equal numbers of DES officials and ISJC representatives, with

ACC and AMA observers. Its first agenda included such obviously sensitive matters as which schools were to be allocated assisted places, and what were to be the 'costs' in lost independence. At its second meeting, the Group turned to the selection of pupils, and the highly complex matter of how fee remissions were to be calculated.

Against this background of rapid consultation, the Education Bill, given its second reading in the Commons on 5 November, included a requirement that the Secretary of State 'establish and operate' arrangements for 'enabling pupils who might not otherwise be able to do so to benefit from education at independent schools'. While the details of how that purpose was to be achieved were left to the subsequent regulations, it was made clear that each participating school was to make its own agreement with the Secretary of State to remit the fees of a specified number of pupils according to a prescribed income scale, and that it would then be reimbursed for doing so from public funds. In an interview immediately following a *News at Ten* report that up to 15,000 'bright but poor' children each year would thereby be enabled to attend independent schools at an annual cost of £55 million, Mark Carlisle had to make it clear once again that such a large figure represented the likely cost when the Scheme was fully in operation. This would not be until 1987–8 (when the actual cost of the Scheme as implemented was £46 million). The immediate objective, which would cost only some £3 million in the first year, was to begin restoring those educational opportunities 'which the direct grant school used to give', and which had become 'limited purely to those whose parents' purse is big enough to pay'.

That objective was so familiar and so laudable to the Scheme's advocates that the hostility with which it was greeted seems to have taken many of them by surprise. Some of the objections came from Conservatives, mainly from areas where assisted places in independent schools seemed to threaten well-established maintained grammar schools, but also from individual critics who argued (for example) that assisted places should be limited to 'a minority of areas of special educational deprivation'.[12] Rapid promises had to be made that LEAs would be consulted about the likely effects of the scheme in their own areas as soon as provisional responses had been received from independent schools. And in an attempt to mollify an obvious source of major opposition, it was announced that LEAs would be able to object to (and so effectively veto) assisted places at 16-plus where the transfer of pupils from maintained schools could be shown as harmful to sixth-form provision in the public sector. When the viability of so many sixth forms was already being threatened by falling rolls in secondary schools, any further threat was bound to be resisted. But LEA opposition to the scheme ranged much more widely than that. There were objections to the 'covert' return of academic selection, the creaming-off of able pupils from comprehensive schools, and most vigorously to the effects on teacher morale and public confidence of so obvious a statement of 'no confidence' in the capacity of comprehensive schools to cater for able pupils.[13]

Almost from the time of its first announcement within weeks of the Conservative election victory, the Scheme restored private education to a position near the top of the Labour Party's agenda. It provoked a fierce debate at the 1979 Party Conference, during which Neil Kinnock (then the Shadow Education spokesman) insisted that it would be impossible for any future Labour Government to tolerate a scheme 'which will expend £70 million from the public purse on the already affluent while pirating scholastic talent from the state sector'.[14] An immediate consequence of the debate was the setting-up of a Working Group on Independent Schools which produced in the following year the most thoroughly documented and thoroughly argued proposals for the 'reduction and abolition' of private education which the Party had ever had as a basis for its policy (Labour Party, 1980). As a direct response to the first DES approach to independent schools (6 December 1979) inviting them to indicate an interest in joining the Scheme, the Party sent its own letter to the same schools informing them that assisted places would disappear by the end of the next Labour Government's first year in office. That letter was attacked by independent school representatives as being certainly improper and probably illegal. Sexton had to convey to them Mark Carlisle's official view that while it was certainly regrettable, it was not unconstitutional.

Even as the canvassing of responses from independent schools was getting under way, however, there was anxiety among some of the Scheme's advocates that it might still not be implemented. The strength of hostility it had aroused brought second thoughts within the private sector itself about the advisability of participating in something so controversial.[15] At this time, Sexton seems to have found it impossible to get backing either from the DES or ISJAC for publishing a promotional pamphlet he had prepared. While reassuring Carlisle that there was little that was new or deserving of attention in the Labour Party's spate of publicity against the Scheme in December, he argued strongly that the Government itself had not done enough to persuade public opinion to support the Scheme. He therefore drafted a statement which the Secretary of State incorporated (almost unchanged) into a speech at Leicester on 7 January 1980, and which Sexton described to Cobban as representing 'the clearest commitment yet' to the Scheme's implementation which would 'scotch suggestions that he [Carlisle] is not really supporting it'. Cobban in turn expressed his pleasure that Carlisle had 'nailed his colours so firmly to the right mast'.[16]

Nevertheless throughout January and February Sexton remained nervous about the future of the Scheme. In a defensive mood he wrote personally to Carlisle expressing alarm at rumours that the Scheme might be dropped altogether, and referring to a manifesto commitment that 'could not have been clearer'.[17] In another note he asked the Secretary of State explicitly whether its abandonment was going to be 'our first U-turn'.[18] Sexton's own attempts to convince Carlisle of the value of the Scheme may not always have been the best means of strengthening his resolve. He was arguing at this time, as Carlisle was not, that competition from assisted places would force all maintained schools to 'pull their socks up' and become 'more selective again, more academic'.[19] However, it was actually the larger controversy about proposed cuts in public expenditure which did most to place the Scheme's future in doubt. Despite Sexton's worst fears, the choice as formulated within the DES was between postponing the Scheme or substantially reducing its scope, rather than abandoning it altogether. Sexton was adamantly opposed to postponement on the grounds that the Scheme had to be confirmed as a success story before the next election so as to make its dismantling difficult even if Labour won, and especially to make the immediate withdrawal of financial support from large numbers of pupils so unpopular as to be politically impractical. Any significant delay also risked reducing the number of voluntary grammar schools which might be persuaded to turn independent under the 'cover' of the Scheme.

The eventual decision to reduce the estimated cost of the Scheme in full operation from £55 million to £25–30 million could be interpreted both as a victory and a defeat. The numbers of assisted places to be made available were certainly far fewer than Sexton had hoped for, and somewhat fewer than many independent school heads had wanted. Yet in view of Carlisle's reputation for weakness in defending educational expenditure, and the undoubted Treasury and other pressures to abandon the Scheme altogether, its retention in reduced form could be regarded as a considerable victory for the political skills of Sexton and the independent school lobby. Carlisle himself claimed that the Cabinet decision was a victory for the education budget in general, since the £6 million 'new' money granted by the Treasury for the Scheme's first year was retained in full, while only £3 million was in fact used to pay for assisted places.[20] In retrospect, however, he admitted that this argument did not satisfy his critics within the public or the private sectors.[21] But provision for an Assisted Places Scheme, albeit on a reduced scale, remained an integral part of the Education Act which received the royal assent on 3 April 1980. We turn now to the complicated negotiations needed to put the Scheme into effect.

### The Details Decided

If momentum was to be maintained so the Scheme began at the intended time, a number of questions had to be answered quickly. How many independent schools were willing and suitable to participate? Could they make all their new places eligible for assistance if they wished? If not, how were their offers to be limited? What proportion of assisted places should be reserved for pupils from maintained schools? How were pupils to be selected, and fee remissions calculated? All these questions had been considered during the preliminary negotiations we have described, so that much of the groundwork had been done before the Bill became law. It was now necessary to make the relevant decisions.

For some time before the first DES letter inviting expressions of interest (6 December 1979), likely independent schools had been canvassed about their participation while others had actively canvassed their own cause. There had also been general discussion about how far participation should extend beyond those schools which had been on the old direct-grant list. It was important to widen the appeal of the Scheme beyond that particular sectional interest. It was even more important that a scheme promoted as restoring academic opportunities endangered by comprehensive reorganization should offer a much more equitable distribution of places around the country than the direct-grant system had provided.

Even before 1979, Sexton had produced detailed maps and plans of what a fully-working scheme might look like, and had argued (as we noted earlier) for the participation of as many as 500 independent schools. That figure has to be compared with the 119 former direct-grant schools which were now 'fully' independent, and which were the Scheme's most obvious recruits. Indeed, the original DES proposals limited participation to these schools. But the notion of schools being 'accepted for Assisted Place status' soon replaced references to 'reviving' the direct-grant list, and implied that schools of very different kinds could merit that status. It was Sexton's view that a larger scheme would be easier to sell politically because it would produce a more significant extension of parental choice and a more equitable restoration of educational opportunities. It was for this reason that he placed such importance on persuading voluntary-aided and special-agreement grammar schools to become independent; they could be expected to make substantial numbers of assisted places available, both to ease their transition to independence and to continue their past traditions of being accessible to scholars from 'poor' homes. Some of these, such as Hampton School and Emmanuel School in London, needed no enticement because they had already chosen independence as the only alternative to becoming non-selective, the latter school being described by its head as an 'independent grammar school in a deprived area' which catered for 'poor boys with rich minds'.[22]

These schools were joined in a new pressure group (the Association of Voluntary-aided and Independent Grammar Schools [AVIS]) by some schools with Section 13 notices already approved, and others (like Wisbech Grammar School and St Marylebone Grammar School) which were still in the maintained sector but actively considering their future status. AVIS, under the leadership of Gavin Alexander, the head of Hampton School, became an important forum for discussions about the feasibility of including such schools in the Scheme, and the original draft was amended to make their inclusion possible.[23] The possibility that they might be given more time to decide was among the matters considered at the first meeting of the Assisted Places Scheme Group in October 1979, which also began approaching the 'minefield' of how 'assisted place schools' were to be selected. It was also well aware of the continuing suspicions that former direct-grant schools would get preference, and the evident need to avoid admitting academically mediocre schools to so academically-oriented a scheme. Against the hopes that enough grammar schools could be persuaded into the private sector as substantial providers of assisted places, there were also some worries that their recruitment might be too successful. Cobban, for example, referred to Sexton's apparent wish to 'rescue' grammar schools whatever the effects on the public sector, and to the alternative view that it would be fairer and more sensible to include schools 'judiciously sited so as not to clobber the comprehensives'.[24]

Sexton's hopes of recruiting grammar schools were accompanied by a determination to cast the net widely towards the 'public schools' and their girls' school equivalents. As he wanted, the DES letter of December 1979 was sent to the governing bodies of all direct-grant grammar schools, and to the proprietors of all independent schools (in England) which provided secondary education even though only those conducted 'exclusively for charitable purposes' were eligible to be considered.[25] At this stage the 1100 schools which received the letter were asked whether they were willing to make all their places 'assisted', and if not what their maximum offer might be. It was emphasized, however, that the Secretary of State would be constrained by his obligation to secure an equitable distribution of places, both geographically and between boys and girls. Indeed, the whole exercise was bound to be a delicate one, since it required enough offers from schools of the right academic 'quality' which were also in the right places. The right quality meant sufficient 'breadth and balance' in the curriculum (particularly in the subjects offered at A-level), and 'good achievements in external examinations'.

Provisional responses were required from schools by 31 January 1980. This was certainly a high-pressure invitation, given the political uncertainty about the Scheme's future, which was highlighted by the Labour Party letter to the same circulation list warning that the next Labour Government would promptly throw the burden of assistance back on the schools. As was intended, that letter induced considerable caution into many schools' deliberations about the risks and the scale of participation. It was suggested by Cobban and others that the DES might counter Labour's ploy by agreeing to pay the relevant fees for a pupil's entire school career at the time of first taking up an assisted place, so removing fears about the demands on schools' own bursaries and scholarships if the Scheme was suddenly abandoned. This suggestion got nowhere.

Despite the obvious reasons for being cautious, 470 schools had made provisional offers of 13,500 places by the revised 'closing date' of early March 1980. DES officials immediately 'graded' these potential volunteers, with HMI advice, largely according to the range and size of their sixth forms. Schools placed in Category A had viable Advanced-level groups in English, mathematics (preferably with further mathematics), three sciences and at least two modern languages. Schools in Category B were judged to have 'otherwise significant sixth forms'. It was thought that schools in Category C should be 'jettisoned immediately' as being irrelevant to the Scheme's objectives. Nine schools still in the maintained sector were among those expressing interest, all of them with large or at least 'significant' sixth forms.[26]

This initial sorting indicated a likely surfeit of places at 16-plus, given especially forceful LEA opposition, and 'almost an embarrassment of offers' at all entry ages from some parts of the country (notably the north-west and south-east).[27] Sexton asked why such an enthusiastic response should be an embarrassment, forgetting that it would be difficult to justify a markedly inequitable distribution of places in a Scheme so explicitly dedicated to creating an equitable 'network' of new educational opportunities. The fact that firm commitments would be needed from schools by the end of the year concentrated attention on some of the critical decisions which had to be made. By the end of March it had been agreed that participating schools should normally offer a minimum of ten assisted places each year, and that 'Category C' schools should promptly be informed of their unsuitability. In a delayed gesture towards consultation, LEAs were circulated by the DES (25 April 1980) with information about independent schools in their area which were intending to join the scheme, asked about the likely effects on their own provision, and reassured that the scheme nationally had been scaled down to a likely maximum of 6000 places a year.

The second, more refined, stage of recruitment was initiated by a DES letter (dated 3 June 1980) to all schools which had already 'expressed an interest and may be suitable'. Firm statements of intent were now called for, although it was stressed that no school would be committed until the Secretary of State had signed a formal participation agreement. Any school offering fewer than ten assisted places at the entry ages 11–13 had to provide good reasons for so limiting their involvement, while no school would be allowed more than five places at 16-plus. Replies were now required by 7 July, such speed being justified with the argument that schools would already have discussed thoroughly the issues and practicalities involved.

By 1 August, after a necessary extension of the original deadline, 290 schools had offered a total of 6705 places at 11–13 (3230 for boys, 2430 for girls, and 1045 at mixed schools), and 2080 places at 16-plus (580 for boys, 860 for girls, and 640 in mixed schools or schools with mixed sixth forms). Some bids were regarded as overambitious because they would make the schools too dependent on the Scheme, and were pruned by fixing an upper limit of 50 per cent to the proportion of any school's intake which could be offered as assisted places.[28] Subject to that limit, the 'acceptability' of the places being offered was now determined by again dividing schools into categories. This time the main criteria were public examination entries and results over the previous two years, the size of sixth forms, and the percentages of pupils going on to higher education. Over half the schools were placed in the 'top' category, which meant that they had more than ten entries a year in A-level mathematics, physics, chemistry and a first foreign language, an overall A-level pass rate of at least 75 per cent, and a record of at least half their sixth formers going on to higher education.

Both Carlisle and his officials regretted that these 'top' schools had not offered enough places for the Scheme to be based almost entirely on them, with 'Category 2' schools only used selectively to fill any gaps. As it was, the DES conclusion was that all the 214 schools placed in the top two categories would be needed to give the Scheme anything like its intended scope, along with a few others whose relative academic weakness had become more apparent since the additional information asked for after the first recruiting drive. Even then, 'accepting just about every acceptable place on offer' would still leave considerable regional and gender differences in the places available. But since those differences could only be avoided either by reducing the total number of places available or by admitting schools known to be unsuitable, the remedies would be worse than the complaints. As was noted in a DES memorandum, opponents of a Scheme presented so explicitly as opening opportunities in academically-excellent schools would be scrutinizing the final list for any signs of academic weakness. Yet some of the schools still applying at this second sifting were 'so weak academically that their inclusion might invite ridicule', while there were others which were also evidently unsuitable.[29] In the light of these judgments within the DES itself, it was at least disingenuous for Sexton to claim that 450 schools had offered over 13,000 places, and to imply that only Treasury limits on the cash available had caused the project to be scaled down.[30]

Throughout the process of recruiting suitable schools, Sexton was more quantitatively ambitious and less discriminating than were the civil servants. He argued that almost all 'Category 3' schools should be accepted, perhaps with small numbers of assisted places allocated to them. He also took a more tolerant view than did his minister (or the officials) of those public schools like Eton, Malvern Girls, Roedean, Radley, Stowe and Sedbergh which persisted in offering no places at all below the sixth-form stage. Sexton emphasized the prestige which even their limited participation would bring to the Scheme; Carlisle expressed his dislike of token 'gestures towards social conscience'.[31] Sexton's advocacy of more liberal entry conditions had only a marginal effect on the final list. As had been predictable from the start, this was dominated by former direct-grant and other independent grammar schools. Carlisle made clear his own special regard for direct-grant schools, and his pleasure that all those which had opted for independence in 1976 were joining the new Scheme. In doing so he was expressing the priority he gave to academic selectivity. Addressing the annual general meeting of ISIS on 2 October 1980, Rhodes Boyson also emphasized that the Government could not admit all the schools which had formally applied for places because it had 'thought it right to apply fairly strict academic criteria for admission to the scheme'.[32]

The names of the 218 schools initially invited to sign participation agreements were made public on 6 October 1980, together with the number of places each was likely to be allocated for the school year beginning in September 1981 within the total of at least 5500 which it was hoped would be available. Between October 1980 and the DES publication of its final list of definite offers in January 1981, there were a number of last-minute exits and entrances. Nine schools had second thoughts, either because the risks eventually seemed too great or because their participation seemed to threaten their relationships (or specific arrangements) with local LEAs. In that second category were Lancing (Sussex), Marlborough (Wiltshire) and Blundell's School (Devon).[33] The places lost by these late withdrawals were more than made up by increased offers from schools already committed, and by seven schools which joined at the last moment. Since these late arrivals were all in areas already well provided with assisted places (for example, Bedales, Sutton Valence, and Aldenham in the south-east), they did nothing to ameliorate the regional inequalities which we examine in chapter 5.[34]

There were other decisions to be made rapidly if the first beneficiaries of the Scheme were to enter their schools in September 1981. First was the contentious question of which pupils were to be eligible for assistance. This was important because of the emphasis in the Scheme's presentation on assisting individuals rather than schools, and because of a less well-publicized intention of creating 'new' clients for the private sector. As we noted earlier, there was support initially for opening up all new places in 'assisted place status' schools, and there was considerable disappointment when the DES insisted on its upper limit.[35] There was also a strong lobby, supported by Sexton, to extend the benefits of the Scheme to pupils already in the participating schools who could meet the relevant financial criteria. This proposal was reluctantly dropped, mainly because it would eat into the money available for the politically more significant entry of new recruits to the distinctive academic opportunities which those schools were claimed to provide.

Much more significant politically was the vexed question of how far pupils already within the private sector should be eligible for assisted places. Independent primary schools contained only some 3 per cent of the age-group, and were even more socially selective than those at the secondary stage. DES officials argued that if the proportion of assisted places available to their pupils was pitched too high, it could enhance unduly the attractions of private primary education. It would certainly make it harder to argue that the Scheme was opening up opportunities in independent schools to large numbers of families who had never considered them before. There were therefore prolonged arguments about the 'right' percentage of places which should be reserved for pupils who had previously attended maintained schools, and how long they should have spent there. The regulations eventually required that 60 per cent of assisted places at each participating school should go to pupils who were attending maintained schools at the time of their selection and who had done so 'for a continuous period including at least the whole of the previous school year'. But the 'right' proportion was strongly contested.

The arguments of Sexton and some independent school representatives in favour of a figure as low as 25 per cent reflected the obvious anxieties of heads of preparatory schools and of independent secondary schools with large junior departments that some of their traditional clientele might be crowded out.[36] The stream of enquiries also included many from heads of former direct-grant schools which had deliberately fostered close links with local private schools which they were unwilling to disrupt for the sake of a scheme which might not last. The preference of civil servants for a high figure received particularly strong ministerial support from Rhodes Boyson, whose belief in the importance of the scheme as a rescue operation for able inner-city children led him to advocate a proportion as high as 75 per cent. Political realism about how the Scheme was to be defended as a source of new opportunities produced a compromise much nearer that figure than Sexton's own preference.[37]

Throughout the early negotiations anxious questions were regularly asked by the schools about the price in lost independence which participation in the Scheme would carry. By the time the relevant regulations were confirmed in October 1980, it was reassuringly clear that the price was going to be low and that 'assisted place schools' would be as independent as any other independent schools. DES supervision and monitoring was to be extremely light, with the main burden for administering the Scheme's financial provisions falling on school bursars and much less financial account-ability to the Government than under the old direct-grant arrangements.[38] The Secretary of State had to be notified of any proposed raising of tuition fees, but this no longer had to wait for formal approval. Logically, though to the surprise of some public school heads, all schools offering assisted places would have to meet the same obligation to publish examination results as had been placed on maintained schools by section 8(5) of the 1980 Education Act.

On the critical matter of selecting academically suitable pupils, schools were left free to use 'such methods and procedures as seem to them appropriate', subject only to the requirement that they recruit a due proportion from maintained schools and to the possibility of an LEA veto on entries at 16 years of age.[39] Apart from those restrictions, each school could therefore decide for itself whether to operate a strict order of academic merit among those financially eligible for places, or to show some positive discrimination in favour of the 'least well-off' or the most culturally disadvantaged.[40] Denominational schools could take religious affiliation into account provided it was not at the expense of academic standards.[41] What they were not allowed to do, however, was to discriminate in favour of those in 'need' of boarding education — the very category which had been so strongly favoured by the Public Schools Commission as the most appropriate criterion for assisting pupils to attend independent schools. There was strong pressure from within the private sector itself to include boarding as well as tuition (and various incidental expenses) among the costs eligible for public assistance, but this potentially very expensive addition got nowhere at a time of budgetary restraint. As a result HMC schools launched, with some DES encourage-ment but no DES money, their own limited scheme funded from schools' own endowments which seemed likely to produce some 400 boarding places a year.[42] Places were eventually allocated to boarding schools on the understanding that such help would be available to deserving applicants. But complaints continued to surface at meetings of the Assisted Places Scheme Group (especially from the GBA) that the DES attitude to boarders was 'grudging', and that there was an excessive bias in the Scheme towards day schools in urban areas.

The single most important determinant of whether the Scheme would reach its intended target groups was obviously going to be the income scale on which fees would be remitted. Defining that scale was both a politically controversial and a technically difficult exercise. Evidence was soon being gathered from and volunteered by schools long practised in means-tested bursary schemes (for example, the GPDST, the Bristol charity schools, and the King Edward foundation schools in Birmingham). A meeting of HMC's Direct-Grant Committee in June 1979 derived from the experience of its members what turned out to be an over-cautious estimate of how fee remissions should be calculated — for example, the suggestion that families with a gross income of not more than £5800 or a net income of not more than £3800 should pay no more than half the fees normally charged. Sexton himself had serious reservations about the gross income scales initially produced by DES officials, and sought unsuccessfully to base those scales on parental income after tax — partly on the grounds that take-home pay was more readily understood by the manual worker. Like many independent school heads, he was especially anxious to avoid cut-off points which would produce a 'poverty trap' for 'middle-income' families earning £8500–£11,000 a year. Expressing this widespread concern, the head of a northern direct-grant school wrote to Carlisle in February 1980 applauding the Scheme for enabling schools like his to return to their 'true tradition of service as independent schools which yet keep their doors open to all classes of society', but urging the importance of so defining fee remission that middle-class families would not have to decline places.[43]

It had been agreed at the meeting of the Assisted Places Scheme Group in January 1980 that the income scales had to be comprehensible, easy to administer, dependent only on evidence which could be readily provided, and compatible with other schemes of family assistance. In the draft figures then produced for further discussion in February, a family with a 'relevant income' of not more than £4100 would pay nothing towards the tuition fees of an only child holding an assisted place (fees then averaging about £1000 a year), and that this threshold would potentially benefit a third of the population.[44] At an income level of £6000, the parental contribution would be £354; at £7800, it would be £894. 'Relevant income' for this purpose was defined as the combined incomes of parents (before tax) for the previous year, excluding child benefits but including any unearned income of dependent children apart from academic scholarships. An 'allowance' of £300 was being suggested at this stage in the negotiations for each child other than the place-holder, and for any other dependent relative. Independent school heads argued strongly that the real benefit to families with several children would be no more than £100, and that an allowance of at least £750 would be necessary to avoid obstructing their participation in the Scheme.

Throughout the consultation period ISJC and AVIS and the independent school members of the Assisted Places Scheme Group pressed hard for more generous income scales. The revisions announced on 3 June 1980 doubled the dependent allowance, reduced the parental contribution for a second assisted-place holder from the same family, and were intended to soften the sharp cut-off points at the upper end of the scale. Table 3.1 shows the scale on which parental contributions for the first intake of assisted-place pupils were calculated. Family expenditure data indicated that about a third of all family incomes were then near or below the lowest point.

**Table 3.1 Parental contribution to school fees, 1981–2 based on relevant income 1980–1**

| Relevant Income | | One place-holder | | Each of two place-holders | |
|---|---|---|---|---|---|
| £4767 | (6973) | £15 | (15) | £9 | (9) |
| 5000 | (8000) | 36 | (123) | 27 | (93) |
| 5500 | (9000) | 99 | (273) | 72 | (204) |
| 6500 | (10000) | 267 | (471) | 198 | (354) |
| 7500 | (11000) | 480 | (681) | 360 | (510) |
| 9000 | (12000) | 840 | (921) | 630 | (690) |
| 10000 | (13000) | 1170 | (1161) | 876 | (870) |
| 11000 | (14000) | 1500 | (1449) | 1125 | (1086) |
| — | (15000) | — | (1779) | — | (1335) |
| — | (16000) | — | (2109) | — | (1581) |

*Note*: The equivalent figures for the school year 1986–7 are given in brackets.
*Source*: ISJC: *Assisted Places Scheme: a guide for parents.*

The maximum relevant income at which pupils were eligible for assistance varied according to the fees which their schools charged, and there were many schools in 1981 at which fees were lower than the maximum parental contribution of £1500 (as there were in 1986 for the equivalent figure of £2109). This illustrates why it was impossible to estimate precisely what the Scheme would cost. Unlike the equivalent scheme in Scotland (Walford, 1988), schools were free to select pupils all or most of whom were eligible for the highest levels of fee remission. Commenting on the financial uncertainties which this produced, Lady Young suggested that while the Government doubted whether the Scheme would attract (at least initially) many parents from the lowest income bracket, and so was more likely to undershoot than overshoot the Treasury's expenditure target, any overspending could be justified politically as evidence that the Scheme was successful in attracting the least well-off.[45] It had also been apparent to DES officials much earlier than to Sexton that assistance had to cover far more than fees if the Scheme was to reach the target groups most in need of the opportunities it claimed to offer. After detailed discussions within the DES, but with apparently little regard for any equivalent benefits available to pupils in maintained schools, Mark Carlisle announced in October 1980 that schools could offer assisted-place pupils from the lowest-income families financial help towards the incidental costs of school meals, school uniforms and travel which the schools could then reclaim from the DES.

With the regulations now completed and due to come into operation from 17 November 1980, formal agreements to participate in the Scheme were signed by schools in October. Each school entered into an independent contract with the Government which could only be varied by agreement on both sides, and which could only be ended by due judicial process. The Scheme's purpose had been defined by Mark Carlisle when he opened the Commons debate on the draft regulations on 21 July. It was not there for the benefit of the independent schools or teachers or even parents, but to extend opportunities for able children from 'ordinary hard-working homes' who could benefit from the 'highly disciplined academic atmosphere' to be found in selected independent schools and 'most especially the independent day grammar schools'. At the September meeting of HMC, less than a year before the first assisted-place pupils would enter their schools, he repeated the claim made so often in defence of the Scheme — that it would complement rather than compete with the public sector. The 5000–6000 places being offered for the next school year were an insignificant number compared with the 700,000 pupils who transferred each year from primary to secondary schools. But those places were being made available for pupils 'whose academic needs might not be best catered for in the school they would otherwise attend'. When he spoke at an 'informatory conference' organized by ISJC a few weeks later, he thanked his audience for joining the Government in an 'exciting venture' which was the culmination of years of effort which the DGJC had initiated. Opportunities which Labour had removed in 1976 were now being restored in a much wider cross-section of schools and without the disadvantages of the previous system. The great objective of that venture was to help 'bright children' by 'making the private sector more widely available'.[46]

### Notes

1 Sexton presented himself as the Scheme's effective creator at both our interviews with him. His 'broker's role' in selling it to the Conservative Party is emphasized in an *Education* article, 21 September 1979, which also describes him as its 'acknowledged architect'.

2 For example, at the meeting of HMC direct-grant school headmasters in Birmingham, June 1979.

3 We found no evidence either of that zealous personal commitment to controversial Government policies displayed subsequently by some DES officials.

4 DES internal memorandum, 8 June 1979.

5 Cobban immediately drew attention to the understandable alarm in the public sector at the 'creaming-off' of able pupils.

6 ISIS press release, 16 June 1979. A survey carried out by the DGJC had elicited replies from fifty-nine schools indicating 'a strong sense of moral obligation' to participate in the proposed scheme which

reflected their traditional claims to combine high academic standards with socially mixed intakes. Almost all those schools had responded to the ending of direct-grant by instituting their own bursary schemes, funded from endowments, appeals, or surcharges on normal fees.

7  John Rae, interviewed on the *Today* programme, 27 September 1979.

8  In a letter to the national press following the HMC debate.

9  Ministerial briefing paper, 2 October 1979.

10  Sexton was already using this argument in a letter to the new Secretary of State as early as 16 May 1979.

11  Insistence that the Scheme 'complemented' the state sector is a main theme in ISIS publicity at this time, as it is in the *Guide for Parents* published by ISJC as soon as the final list of schools offering places was published early in 1981.

12  Letter from Matthew Parris, MP, to Carlisle, 29 October 1979.

13  For an early attack on Government-sponsored withdrawals of public support from maintained schools, see Dudley Fiske (1980) 'Responsibilities, power and the LEA', *Local Government Studies*. 6, 6, pp. 39-46.

14  Labour Party Conference Report, 1979, p. 357.

15  Salter and Tapper (1985, p. 194) describe the strength of hostility to the Scheme as having 'taken the independent schools unawares'. We doubt this. Strong objections to 'creaming-off' able pupils, and to the more general demonstration of 'no confidence' in public education, were entirely predictable; they were certainly expected by (e.g.) James Cobban and other leading representatives of the independent schools.

16  Exchange of letters between Sexton and Cobban, January 1980.

17  Note, Sexton to Carlisle, February 1980.

18  Note, Sexton to Carlisle, February 1980. A memorandum of 29 January making a similar point is quoted by Salter and Tapper (1985).

19  Note from Sexton to Carlisle, February 1980. Throughout their respective presentations of the Scheme, Carlisle was consistently more discriminating in his doubts about the capacity of comprehensive schools to cope with able children; for him, it was some schools, in some areas.

20  A DES memorandum dated 11 February 1980 estimated the initial cost at £3 million, rising to £12 million by 1983–4 and to £25–30 million by 1987–8. The initial estimate was accurate, but the 1983–4 cost was almost £15 million while that for 1987–8 was £48 million. Sexton saw an annual cost of £50 million as an entirely reasonable reflection of inflation, since the last full year of the old direct-grant arrangements had cost the Government £39 million. He also wanted to argue that the Scheme was a bargain anyway; because the average cost of an assisted place was approximately that of a maintained place, many more academic opportunities were being provided with almost no extra expenditure. He had to be dissuaded by civil servants from 'being sidetracked into necessarily inconclusive arguments about relative cost' (DES note, 7 May 1980)

21  Interview, 16 November 1982.

22  Letter to Carlisle, autumn 1979.

23  A change in regulations at this time allowed the Secretary of State to treat 'a proposal to establish assisted places as one of the circumstances to which he is to have regard' in deciding whether a school could be given more time before making a final decision about continuing to receive grants from public funds for pupils entering in September 1980, or becoming 'fully' independent.

24  Letter to DGJC, 30 May 1979.

25  But the letter still made particular reference to former direct-grant schools intending to become independent, or which had 'applied to enter the maintained sector but have not yet completed the process'.

26  A first sorting was done as early as 4 March 1980. On 25 March it was made more formal at a meeting attended by Carlisle, two of his ministers (Young and Boyson), Sexton and four DES officials. It was then discussed the following day at a meeting between a DES team, and Frank Fisher, James Cobban and Lady Johnston.

27  DES note, 4 March 1980.

28  Among the schools whose enthusiasm for the Scheme had to be dampened were Latymer Upper School and Haberdasher's Girls School in London, Bristol Grammar School, Wolverhampton Grammar School, and a cluster of former direct-grant schools in and around Manchester and Liverpool.

29  DES memorandum, August 1980. Among the schools deemed unsuitable for the Scheme were several HMC schools.

30  He made this claim, for example, in a briefing paper for Conservative MPs prepared for the Commons debate in July 1980.

31  Reported in an internal DES note, 15 September 1980.

32  R. Boyson, Speech to ISIS AGM, 2 October 1980.

33  The other disappearances were Kimbolton School, Queen Anne's in Caversham, St. Leonard's Mayfield (Sussex), and Tormead (Surrey).

34  The other late arrivals were Gresham's School (Norfolk), Bradfield, St Swithun's (Winchester), St Catherine's (Bramley, Surrey) and Charterhouse.

35  Cobban, for example, objected strenuously.

36  There were formal submissions to this effect from the Incorporated Association of Preparatory Schools, and the Association of Headmistresses of Preparatory Schools.

37  He conceded 50 per cent 'for political reasons', had to accept 60 per cent reluctantly, and then fought a rearguard action to make the rule apply to the take-up of places rather than the quota.

38  For example, Saville reassured the chairman of AVIS that the DES 'hoped to get as little involved as possible in the financial affairs of participating schools' (3 July 1980).

39  The LEA veto on sixth-form transfers was a sore point with Sexton, who saw it as a 'sop to the NUT'. He encouraged Conservative MPs to query it in the House, supplying them with the argument that if the Scheme was intended to help individuals, and if compulsory schooling ended at 16 years of age, then LEAs had no right to interfere.

40  Note from Frank Fisher to Saville, 15 January 1980.

41  Briefing paper prepared for Carlisle before the ISJC Conference 1980.

42  The initiative for this internal support for boarding education came from Ian Beer, the head of Harrow School, who was chairman of the Headmasters' Conference in 1980.

43  Letter dated 11 February 1980.

44  DES memorandum, 7 February 1980.

45  Report of meeting, 13 August 1980.

46  ISIS press release.

Chapter 4

## *Arguments and Predictions*

Expressing what he claimed to be the collective astonishment of independent school heads at 'the manner in which politicians obfuscate a very simple issue', the High Master of Manchester Grammar School described the emergence of the Assisted Places Scheme as a straightforward revival of opportunites for 'poor scholars'. Insisting that 'schools independent of political control' were among the necessary conditions for a free society, he went on to argue the undesirability of making them available only to the rich.

> For centuries, the provision for 'poor scholars' has been a characteristic of most of the distinguished independent schools in this country. Until 1976, the direct-grant regulations allowed this school and many other schools to admit pupils regardless of their parents' means and in accordance with their parents' wishes. The Assisted Places Scheme was designed to replace the lost direct-grant system, to improve it, and to extend provision to a wider range of schools — all of which it has done. That is how we simple professionals see it, and we would be glad if politicians would try to see it in the same uncomplicated way.[1]

That brief account encapsulates many of the justifications for assisted places which we review in this chapter. It also exaggerates the simplicity of the issues. Having described the Scheme's initiation, we now identify main themes in the controversy which attended its appearance and place them in their ideological contexts. In doing so, we hope to show how a Scheme deliberately limited in scope nevertheless highlights fundamental disagreements about the functions of private education, and provides something of a bridge between two significant traditions within Conservative education policy.

It is always difficult in policy analysis to show ideological commitments being directly expressed in Government action (Norton and Aughey, 1981; Gamble, 1983). In the case of the first Thatcher Administration, it took office in 1979 largely unencumbered by detailed manifesto promises but unusually well-equipped with ideological reference points from which specific policies could be constructed. The Assisted Places Scheme was among its few formal commitments, its announcement in June 1979 being the first significant initiative taken by the new Secretary of State (Mark Carlisle), and one of the first policy initiatives of any kind by the incoming Government. Such speed was the product of effective groundwork, and we described earlier the negotiations which had preceded the 1979 general election and provided the government with a well-worked-out proposal. The Scheme also had obvious ideological attractions. At relatively little cost in public expenditure, the Government could express simultaneously its commitment to *quality* by supporting traditional academic education in 'excellent schools'; to *opportunity* by sponsoring able children from all kinds of social backgrounds; and to *parental choice* by bringing within range of 'less well-off families' schools usually restricted to those able to pay high fees.

At the same time virtually all varieties of Conservative opinion were readily mobilized to support the 'cause' of private education as Labour's commitment to abolish it became an apparent threat to personal freedom. Amid the 'progressive collapse' identified in the *Black Papers* and other publications, independent schools also came to represent an oasis of traditional academic values and standards. A rejection of the 'cult of egalitarianism' is evident in a wide spectrum of Conservative writing. It was argued that 'Conservatives should never feel it necessary to be apologetic about inequality' (Clarke, 1978, p. 13) so long as the talented were encouraged as they deserved. The onrush of comprehensive secondary education was rejected as social engineering incompatible with high standards, reasonable parental choice, and the opportunities for personal advancement which should properly be available to able children. In any society which claimed to be 'open', 'equality of opportunity' had therefore to take precedence over 'millenarian' notions of 'equality' (Blake and Patten, 1976, p. viii; Bogdanor, 1976, p. 126; Joseph, 1976, pp. 75–80; Patten, 1983, pp. 85–9). In addition, the 'natural' right of parents to purchase education for their children if they wished was defended as a necessary part of a democracy, any inequalities arising from the exercise of that right being preferable to 'the danger to the quality of society from a State monopoly' (Peele, 1976, p. 25).

Presented in this way, the defence of private education could be represented as a 'cause' rather than as the protection of a vested interest. In contrast to the increasing hostility from other political directions, it could now reasonably be argued that 'only the Conservative Party continues fully to support the independent sector of education as an equal and valuable partner with the state sector in overall educational provision, and only under a future Conservative Government will the independent sector continue to be safe'.[2] Opinions were divided, however, about how 'equal' that partnership should be. The traditional view was that independent schools generally constituted the 'top end' of the educational market, making a distinctive contribution to the training of the country's future leaders and setting standards for maintained schools to strive for if not to attain. As we shall see, it was that view, bolstered by the demise of most maintained grammar schools, that was originally at the heart of the Assisted Places Scheme rather than any deep-seated preference for a significant extension of the role of the private sector in the provision of education.

### The Restoration of Opportunities for 'Real' Academic Education.

Once again the boy or girl from an inner-city area, where the aspirations and achievements of his local comprehensive aren't such that he will be stretched the way he should be, can now once again join the ladders of social and economic mobility, and to me that's part of an open society. And I'm astonished anybody opposes it. (Rhodes Boyson)[3]

It was definitely promoted . . . as an opportunity through a scholarship scheme. Particularly in my mind always was that in inner-city areas for the children to benefit from the education that was available at King Edward's [Birmingham], Bradford Grammar School and Manchester Grammar School. (Mark Carlisle)[4]

These quotations illustrate the predominant view of what the Assisted Places Scheme was for. It was often welcomed as a meritocratic 'ladder' for the 'poor but able', made necessary by the academic 'failure' of the comprehensive schools.[5] That welcome reflected a broader commitment to restoring access to the distinctive academic and occupational opportunities which grammar schools were believed to offer, a view embodied most clearly in and around the *Black Papers* on education which had appeared in the late 1960s and during the 1970s (for example, Cox and Dyson, 1969, 1970, 1971; Cox and Boyson, 1975, 1977). In our view an understanding of *Black Paper* opinion provides important insights into the origins and the rhetorical appeal of the Assisted Places Scheme as a scholarship 'ladder'.

Leading *Black Paper* contributors regularly drew attention to their own boldness in challenging 'progressive' assumptions, and to the predictable outrage which their 'heresies' provoked. Although they also insisted on their political independence, addressing their strictures on the state of education to MPs of all parties, there were obvious connections with the attempts then beginning in the Conservative Party to challenge its post-War drift into the policies of the 'social democratic consensus' (Baron *et al.*, 1981). Angus Maude, for example, published a broad statement of his unease in the same year (1969) that he contributed to the initial *Black Papers*. The first editors also insisted that their contributors represented a wide range of educational views, and that it was wrong to treat them as a tightly-knit group of like-minded ideologists. There were, nevertheless, certain strong main themes in their 're-appraisal' of 'progressivism'.

They intended first to 'break the fashionable left-wing consensus on education', and then to replace it with a frame of reference in which standards, discipline and opportunity were the key terms (Cox and Dyson, 1971, p. 11; Cox, 1982). Musgrove (1987) locates the prominent contributors in a 'literary-moral tradition' preoccupied with preserving a minority culture against various forms of barbarism and utilitarianism, and with rationing opportunities of acquiring it. These were the preoccupations later exemplified in Bantock's (1980) account of the curriculum 'dilemmas' of mass secondary education. Certainly a clear strand of cultural elitism is evident in *Black Paper* doubts about how far higher education could be 'safely' expanded. More generally, it is reflected in the distrust of 'discovery methods' as being too deferential to the ignorance of learners, and in equally strong belief in the discipline of subjects and the authority of teachers. More particularly, it shaped the ways in which grammar schools were defended. Exempted from criticism of the deteriorating levels of attainment attributed to comprehensivization, they were seen as complementing the public schools as a source of the country's future leaders — its 'surgeons, scholars and engineers' (Cox and Dyson, 1969, p. 14; Cobban, 1969; Pedley, 1969). By continuing to 'uphold the finest academic and cultural values', they stood in relation to the 'newer' secondary schools as did Oxford and Cambridge to the newer universities — 'as a continual reminder of what excellence is' which helped to prevent standards elsewhere from sliding even further downwards (Boyson, 1975, p. 14). In a postlude to Black Paper writing, they were described as an oasis of 'order and harmony' amid the comprehensive chaos (Cottrell, 1982).

These overtly elitist views were accompanied, however, by meritocratic objectives which Musgrove neglects — a strange omission given his own denunciation of Labour for 'betraying' the working class by destroying the grammar schools and with them the best hope of 'circumscribing class power' (Musgrove, 1979, pp. 107–14). For if 'equality' and 'quality' were seen from *Black Paper* perspectives as being entirely incompatible, so were 'equality' and 'equality of opportunity'. The impossibility of having both was firmly asserted among the '*Black Paper* basics' proclaimed at the beginning of the fourth collection (Cox and Boyson, 1975); equality meant 'the holding back [or the 'new deprivation'] of the brighter children', since 'without selection the clever working-class child in a deprived area stands little chance of a real academic education'.

Meritocratic arguments were therefore prominent, even predominant, in the defence of the grammar schools. If it was necessary to defend 'a fine and well-tried system of education against the envy of inverted snobbery and vague class hatred' (Cox and Dyson, 1969a, p. 3), it was also necessary to preserve the 'openness' of society by sponsoring talent from every kind of social background. 'Selection by neighbourhood' was especially disliked. It risked reinforcing local influences unhelpful to high educational achievement, and it risked again reinforcing those 'class barriers' which the 'wide social mix' attributed to grammar schools was believed to have countered (Szamuely, 1969; Pedley, 1969; Boyson, 1975, p. 78; Bogdanor, 1976, pp. 126–8; ISIS,

1976). Able children were now being denied the opportunities which their ability merited by a futile pursuit of 'fairness' and 'social justice', and a consequent levelling-down of standards.

As these comments imply, there was a particular preoccupation with the harm already being done to the prospects of able working-class children by the rapid disappearance of grammar schools from the public sector, and with the further harm threatened by political moves against the direct-grant system. As long as grammar schools were available, it was argued, able working-class children had the chance to 'break down the class barriers and achieve unrestricted scope for their talents'; if such schools disappeared, or were forced to become academically comprehensive, then selection would again be based on income, and 'the cash nexus will reign undisturbed . . . ' (Szamuely, 1969, pp. 50–1). The first *Black Paper* editors felt 'bitter and angry that the fine opportunities given to them in the 1940s are from now on to be denied to children from similar backgrounds' (Cox and Dyson, 1969a, p. 6; see also their successive editorials, 1969b, pp. 5-6; 1970, p. 5; 1971, p. 11). C. S. Hilditch (1970), writing as retiring chairman of the Assistant Masters Association (then very much a 'grammar school union') but also as a Labour Party member since 1932, portrayed the 'capacity-catching' function of grammar schools in a way long practised in his Party (Barker, 1972; Dean, 1986); they were essential to giving working-class children 'a chance to compete with the product of the public school', and to attack them was 'not only misguided but evil'. Also writing as a professed socialist, Iris Murdoch (1975) argued that while able middle-class children would succeed in any system, 'poor clever children with an illiterate background' would be denied their *right* to 'rigorous education' if 'good grammar schools' became available only by accident of birth. In the same *Black Paper* collection, Rhodes Boyson (1975, pp. 76-9) restated the now familiar assumption that most low-achieving comprehensive schools were in 'poor working-class areas', and saw a 'terrible irony' in the fact that Labour's 'reform' of secondary education would damage most 'the intelligent working-class child' who needed to be 'placed in an academic atmosphere at an early age'.

There was considerable diversity of view amongst *Black Paper* contributors, however, about the timing and scope of academic selection. Lynn (1969) wanted to undo the 'dreadful mistake' of 1944 by restoring grammar schools as 'independent fee-paying institutions' offering scholarships to 'intelligent children from poor families'. In contrast, Cox and Dyson (1970) accepted comprehensive schools as the 'normal mode of education', provided that the ablest 5–8 per cent could still attend grammar schools; such a strictly limited entry would avoid the stigma of 11-plus 'failures' and be too small to create 'an exclusive elite of self-sustaining meritocracy'. At that time a still 'moderate' Boyson included an academically-balanced intake among the necessary conditions for a successful comprehensive school, co-existence with grammar schools creating only 'misnamed secondary moderns' (Boyson, 1969, p. 60).[6] Yet even though the capacity of a 'truly' comprehensive school to cope with able pupils is vigorously asserted in his account of how Highbury Grove flourished under his own leadership (Boyson, 1974), he was soon arguing that working-class pupils would 'only become scholars' if selected early. And in the last *Black Papers*, a case is made for restoring academic selection for as high a proportion as 20 – 40 per cent of children so as to safeguard both academic standards and the country's economic future (Cox and Boyson, 1977, p. 61).

By this time Boyson was already associating himself with some of the free-market ideas of the New Right and he did much to generate a sense of continuity between the agenda of the earlier *Black Papers* and that which was increasingly to become the educational agenda of the Conservative Party under Margaret Thatcher. His move into an editorial role in the *Black Papers* brought with it a more radical approach to educational policy which included some approval of vouchers, and specifically of vouchers which could be 'cashed' in maintained or independent schools (Cox and Boyson, 1975, pp. 4, 27–9; Cox and Boyson, 1977, pp. 8–9, 87–9). Even so, these more radical departures had little backing from the private sector itself, though there was growing and insistent support within that sector for the idea that it could play a major role in reversing that 'betrayal of working-class education' for which the 'cult of egalitarianism' was held responsible (Cox and Boyson, 1977, p. 60). On that aim at least, leading figures in the private sector and some New Right publicists were entirely agreed. Stuart Sexton, for example, in a contribution to the last *Black Papers* written while he was actively engaged in preparing the way for assisted places, includes in his vision of an educational market freed from political constraints 'a network of highly academic schools throughout the country to which any child regardless of parental income would be free to apply' (Sexton, 1977, p. 87).

It was essentially on the basis of agreement with that specific element of Sexton's vision, rather than with his broader espousal of market forces, that the Assisted Places Scheme was initiated, and later justified. Simply, egalitarian educational policies carried high costs in diminished equality of opportunity, and the Scheme would help to alleviate them. In the words of that leading independent school head whom we mentioned earlier, it would make it possible to 'pluck embers from the ashes' of comprehensive reorganization. More traditionally expressed, it was the belief in the 'capacity-catching' function of 'great schools' which Harold Lever (a prominent member of the 1974–9 Labour Government) used at the Manchester Grammar School prize-giving in 1981 to justify the spending of public money so as to create 'ever-widening opportunities' of entering them (cited in Sampson, 1983, p. 136), and which Mark Carlisle emphasized to us as his priority in supporting the Scheme. Even so, Carlisle also candidly admitted to us that the Scheme itself would have been less of a priority for the incoming government had it not been for the disappearance of maintained grammar schools in most areas.[7]

Framed as it was in this way, reactions to the Scheme highlighted some starkly opposed views in the long debate about the consequences of comprehensive reorganization for educational standards and for the life-chances of able children. Boyson, well practised in deploring a 'levelling down' towards mediocrity, presented it at its inception largely as 'an opportunity for able children from our poorest homes to again attend . . . superb ex-direct grant schools'.[8] Mark Carlisle was always more inclined to emphasize its importance for those pupils who might not be catered for academically in some comprehensive schools, avoiding the blanket condemnations for which his junior colleague was noted.[9] But the overarching assumption within the private sector was that the inability of many comprehensive schools to cope with the ablest children gave the best independent schools an indispensable 'complementary' function provided that access to them could be more widely based on academic merit. Given that broadening of access, they could make 'a real contribution to social mobility' (ISIS, 1981, p. 9).

## The Emergence of the New Right

The 'quiet revolution' which Edward Heath promised when he took office in 1970 was explicitly intended to reduce the scale and scope of government provision, so creating conditions in which enterprise and competition could flourish. These objectives, though similar in some ways to those of his successor as Conservative leader, were presented more managerially than ideologically — as efficient responses to the problems created by what had come to seem an 'excess of welfare'. When the problems of government turned out to be much more intractable than the solutions devised in opposition, there was a considerable retreat by the Heath Government to 'collectivist' orthodoxies — a retreat which some commentators treated as evidence that the 'intellectual revolution' needed to challenge them had not yet occured (Blake, 1976; 1985, p. 310; Lindsay and Harrington, 1979, pp. 267–9). While most of those who voted for Margaret Thatcher in the first Party ballot of February 1975 did so more from an unfocused wish for change in the style of leadership rather than in deliberate pursuit of an 'intellectual revolution' within their Party, conditions were more propitious than they had been ten years earlier for a more principled, less pragmatic, redirection of policy. It certainly brought to the leadership someone whose instincts 'corresponded to the intellectual structures of the New Right' (Cosgrove, 1985, p. 20).

Nine years later, Thatcher told a meeting of Parliamentary lobby correspondents that she wished her Administration to be remembered as the one which 'decisively broke with a debilitating consensus of a paternalistic Government and a dependent people, which rejected the notion that the State is all-powerful and the citizens merely its beneficiaries, which shattered the illusion that the Government could somehow substitute for individual performance' (cited in Kavanagh, 1987, pp. 251–2). 'Winning the battle of ideas', a phrase she often used, meant redefining completely the limits and possibilities of social policy. For, as Keith Joseph had argued at the time of his own conversion to 'true' Conservatism, policies may be constrained in the short run by what is considered politically feasible, but the possibilities themselves can be redefined by changing the whole frame of reference. The so-called 'middle-ground' of consensus politics had proved to be 'a slippery slope to socialism and state control' down which the 'moral and material benefits of the market order' had been allowed to sink from view while the public sector 'spread like bindweed' (Joseph, 1976, pp. 19-35; see also Cowling, 1980). For the architects of the 'new Conservative' challenge to the orthodoxies of 'welfarism', breaking the consensus meant questioning all assumptions about the scope and scale of state provision and being willing to advance 'extreme' arguments previously excluded from 'serious' debate. It required a deliberate lack of respect for policies 'which ever since 1945 Labour has promoted and Conservatives had accepted', because the effect of that acquiescence had been to leave less and less room for individual freedom, opportunity and enterprise (Blake, 1976). And it created an intellectual momentum through which it was the 'stupid party', traditionally distrustful of theory, which 'made the intellectual running' (Sherman, 1986; Scruton, 1984, p. 11).

There were common themes in this reappraisal of 'welfarism', notably a strong wish to halt the excessive growth of public expenditure and see 'leviathan chained' (Waldegrave, 1978). But much more radical variations were propounded alongside them, to be sponsored or translated into populist form by the new leadership. One major source was the Centre for Policy Studies, founded in 1974 by Thatcher and Joseph to counter the still predominantly consensual (and collectivist) approach of the Party's existing Research Department.[10] Another was the Institute of Economic Affairs (IEA), which at last found the time to be ripe for monetarist ideas it had been propagating for twenty years. It had been founded in 1957 to promote study of the market as 'a device for registering individual preferences and allocating resources to satisfy them', and to demonstrate the 'true democracy of the market-place' in which consumers cast their 'votes' every day and providers of goods and services were 'disciplined' into efficiency by having to cater for consumer preferences (Harris and Seldon, 1979, p. 5; see also Harris, 1980; Seldon, 1981). Particularly important were its various surveys of public attitudes to welfare provision and the taxation which paid for it — surveys intended to demonstrate how far 'progressive' politicians of all Parties were out of touch with popular opinion, which was 'shown' to favour greater freedom for individuals to make their own choices with their own money (e.g., Harris and Seldon, 1970). Such demonstrations of what might be done by 'freeing' market forces were intended to redefine possibilities by offering fundamental opposition to 'collectivism'.

The foundation of this opposition was a faith in the market as 'the subtlest and most efficient system mankind has yet devised for setting effort and resources to their best economic use' (Enoch Powell, cited in Kavanagh, 1987, p. 78; see the very similar statements of belief in Joseph, 1976, p. 57; Howell, 1981, pp. 3–4). More simply stated, 'private means better means more'; state provision in education and other social services should therefore be reduced to 'a reasonable minimum above which individuals are left free to rise rather than an imposed maximum which stifles initiative' (Seldon, 1981, pp. 18, 24). By 'registering individual preferences and allocating resources to satisfy them', market forces brought producers under the inescapable discipline of having to satisfy consumers; either they satisfied public demand and prospered, or they failed to do so and declined. That 'iron law' should apply to the so-called 'public' services as it applied to private enterprise (Harris and Seldon, 1979, p. 5). Economically, the market was simply more efficient. Politically, it not only offered the rational alternative to welfarism by revealing the true cost of services; it also offered a democratic alternative because it gave individuals more control over how their money was spent and because the 'incorrigible differences in cultural power' which brought very unequal access to the 'free' services of the welfare state were replaced by the 'corrigible differences in purchasing power which determined access in the market' (Seldon, 1981b, p. xxi). Morally, and this strand of New Right thinking is especially strong in 'Thatcherism', 'choice is the essence of ethics'. An excess of welfare had weakened the country's economic performance, but it had also denied the just rewards of 'originality and skill and energy and thrift' and the opportunity to take action for oneself rather than rely on the intervention of others (Thatcher, quoted in Cosgrove, 1978, pp. 191, 218–19). These arguments were given further expression in the field of education and social work by the establishment in 1980 of the Social Affairs Unit, which shared premises with the Institute of Economic Affairs in Lord North Street.[11]

There is no doubt that these ideas have influenced the policies of the Thatcher Government and that they have been successfully accommodated within the Conservative ideological repertoire alongside more traditional Tory themes. Gamble (1983), amongst others, argues that what is distinctive about Thatcherism as a force within British Conservatism is its capacity to link the neo-conservative emphasis on tradition, authority and national identity with an espousal of neo-liberal free-market economics and the extension of its principles into whole new areas of social activity including the provision of welfare. What we term New Right ideology is based on a blend of moral and economic academic and philosophical doctrines, and it holds out the possibility of reconciling the ideas of the traditionalists that figured so heavily in the *Black Papers* with those of the advocates of the free market that have recently gained ascendancy on the political agenda.

However, the political predominance as well as the homogeneity of such intellectual structures of the New Right (Cosgrove, 1985, p. 20) can easily be exaggerated, particularly in the period during which the Assisted Places Scheme was being developed. Quite apart from the internal tensions between the New Right's free-market, libertarian strand and its moral authoritarianism, for example, some

Conservative intellectuals continued to assert traditional notions of welfare and community and to defend the traditional Tory distaste for dogmatically-derived panaceas for economic and social problems. Indeed, particularly strong scepticism was expressed towards those who seemed to exalt the sanctity and power of market forces beyond all common sense (Gilmour, 1977; Peele, 1976; Waldegrave, 1978, pp. 43–5; Patten, 1983, pp. 101–114). There was a considerable contrast, too, at least until the budget of 1981 and the Cabinet reconstruction which followed it in September, between the rhetorical stridency of 'Thatcherism' and its frequent caution in action. The 1980 Education Act, which contained the Assisted Places Scheme, certainly reflected this caution.

## The Assisted Places Scheme and the New Right

I didn't look upon it as a privatisation of the state system . . . I didn't look upon it as a privatisation measure at all . . . I did promote it on two points — one the basis of the scholarship idea and secondly as a general widening of choice for parents. Obviously, a widening of choice that was only available to the parents of children who had the ability to pass an entrance exam, but to them it was a widening of choice. (Mark Carlisle)[12]

If choice is a good thing and variety a good thing, which I obviously believe it is, then it should be open not only to academically able children but to all children . . . That is why I moved towards the voucher system or contracting out . . . in the long term, without denying the virtues of the assisted places scheme. (Rhodes Boyson, cited in Albert, 1982)

As we have seen, the Assisted Places Scheme was centrally a demonstration of confidence in the special qualities of grammar schools, and was most often presented as a restoration of opportunities to benefit from the kind of education they offered. This was the central justification usually offered by Carlisle, but linked in the quotation cited here to a limited extension of parental choice that was consistent with the other limited moves in this direction embodied in the 1980 Education Act. As Carlisle acknowledged, the Scheme's deliberate concentration on the academically meritorious necessarily limited its scope, and by doing so made it largely irrelevant to those who wished to subject all schools (by some mechanism like educational vouchers) to the 'discipline' of consumer choice. For that reason it was not initially a scheme that was actively promoted by the more enthusiastic free marketeers on the New Right, there being no significant contributions to its formulation from those groups cited earlier who were then actively engaged in reconstructing the Conservative Party's ideological base.

However, it is also the case that the Scheme soon came to be seen by a few supporters (including Boyson as quoted here) as a forerunner of, or as a trial for, much more radical mechanisms for extending parental choice or even privatizing large elements of the education system. We have seen that even by the time he became an editor of the *Black Papers*, Boyson had begun actively to promote the free-market ideas of the neo-liberal strand of New Right thinking. Certainly the last two collections, especially in his own contributions, show a marked shift towards making popularity with parents the 'real' test of a school's efficiency and subjecting all schools to the discipline of consumer preference through the mechanism of vouchers (Cox and Boyson, 1975, pp. 27-9; 1977, pp. 8-9, 87-9). Even in the second collection, the director of the monetarist Institute of Economic Affairs had drawn from his involvement in a parents' campaign against the closing of Enfield Grammar School the 'larger lesson' that state schools would only become fully responsive to their clients when those clients could take their business elsewhere because 'consumer sovereignty rests securely on the power to choose between competing suppliers' (Harris, 1969, p. 71). By 1975 that view was becoming more prominent.

Nevertheless, as we have seen, the predominant themes of the *Black Papers* resonated most strongly with traditional Tory preoccupations, even if their neo-conservatism also contributed to that new blend of ideas that constituted the emergent ideology of the New Right. It was certainly in their more traditional form that they influenced the planning and initial implementation of the Assisted Places Scheme. Yet, although in his early ministerial advocacy of the Scheme even Boyson usually restricted himself to the traditional themes, it is scarcely surprising that a Scheme launched by a Government increasingly influenced by the New Right should be seen by some commentators to reflect a new agenda rather than a continuation of a long-standing one. We explore in our final chapter the extent to which the Scheme can reasonably be seen in this light. Meanwhile, at the same time as emphasizing the more traditionally meritocratic objectives which assisted places were originally intended to serve, it is important to recognize the wider ideological changes from which the private sector as a whole benefited politically just as the Scheme was getting under way.

When the Scheme was introduced, the political climate was far more favourable to the private sector than when that sector had to mobilize for a 'war of attrition' in the early 1970s. Commenting on this transformation, John Rae (1982) noted the contrast with his first attendance at a Headmasters' Conference in 1966, when members of the newly appointed Public Schools Commission mingled with the delegates and were canvassed by heads anxious to save their own schools from the awful fate of being 'integrated'. Sixteen years later, he saw 'a tantalising vision of a Britain in which privatization has become philosophically respectable, school fees tax-deductible, and ritual noises about wanting to broaden the intake can be quietly forgotten'. If that was visible on the horizon, it was already apparent that both the general case for private education and the distinctive virtues claimed by independent schools had obvious attractions for the 'new' Conservative Party. Independent schools exemplified parents' 'right to choose'. Their dependence on fees made them directly accountable to parents, and necessarily responsive to market demands. 'If they were not so good', it was argued, 'no-one would pay to go to them'.[13]

The relevance of such claims to some New Right priorities seemed at times to be carrying private education from its 'first-class siding' (to adapt Butler's comment) towards the main-lines of policy debate. Partly for this reason, it has sometimes been tempting to 'read' a Scheme which emphasized parental choice and seems to benefit the private sector as a logical expression of the ideological commitment of the New Right towards privatization — and thus as an unusually clear example of a Government acting on a 'policy preference' rather than reacting to the pressure of events (Dale, 1983). Certainly, as we have seen, at the very time the Scheme was introduced, some Conservatives were beginning to argue for a huge increase in private provision as part of their vision of a new social order in which public and private services would compete freely for the allegiance of consumers. It was from this more 'sectarian' perspective that Rae (1982) derived his 'tantalising vision' of privatization made respectable. From New Right perspectives, private education was favoured in principle in so far as it was 'freely' chosen by families willing to compare the costs and quality of competing schools and to take direct responsibility for their eventual choice. The schools themselves were thereby constrained to be responsive to market forces, and the quality of what they offered could be taken as evidence of the 'disciplining' effects of that accountability (Boyson, 1975, pp.144-9).

However, it did not appear in 1979 that the new Thatcher Government would espouse such policies in the field of education with any great vigour. Thatcher's three years as Secretary of State for Education preceded the 'intellectual revolution' in her Party, and were not notably radical. There was some increase in per capita grants to direct-grant schools, some support in principle for greater parental involvement in the running of schools, and a failure to check the 'destruction' of maintained grammar schools which she later attributed to her 'helplessness' against the 'equalisation rage' still fierce at that time (Wapshott and Brock, 1983, p.96). But even when she became Party Leader, neither of her shadow ministers of Education was a 'new' Conservative. St John Stevas' defence of quality against equality was eloquent, but in the traditional mould. Mark Carlisle's confirmation as Secretary of State in 1979 was a disappointment to the Right, especially as Boyson's inclusion in the ministerial team was offset by his exclusion from responsibility for schools. And despite its concern to extend parental choice and increase the accountability of state schools, the 1980 Education Act was very much a measure designed to elicit support from all strands of Conservative opinion rather than a narrowly sectarian one.

It is therefore perhaps not surprising that to those thoroughly committed to releasing the 'energizing' effects of parental choice and market forces, the Assisted Places Scheme was altogether too limited in scope and elitist in purpose. Commentators from the New Right remained sceptical and anxious for further progress (West, 1982). It is significant that Boyson, despite remaining fully supportive of the Scheme's meritocratic objectives, quickly found in vouchers the 'political and philosophical' direction in which he felt he had to move. It was a market mechanism which Carlisle's replacement as Secretary of State, Sir Keith Joseph, found 'intellectually attractive' even while he remained unconvinced of its practicality (Argyropulo, 1986b; Seldon, 1986, pp. 36–8). Yet, even with the benefit of hindsight, it would be misleading to suggest that the Assisted Places Scheme was originally conceived, either by its ex-direct-grant school sponsors or by the Government of the day, as a significant step towards an espousal of market forces in education that would make drastic inroads into public sector provision.

The Assisted Places Scheme cannot then be 'read' straightforwardly as an expression of New Right policy preferences, its contribution to enhancing parental choice being altogether too limited and academically-orientated. Its justification through the arguments of the *Black Papers* certainly give it a consistency with the neo-conservative elements of the thinking of particular New Right groupings such as the Hillgate Group (1986; 1987) which focus on academic selection as the means of raising standards of achievement, on the preservation of traditional values and on the traditional academic curriculum as a bulwark against any dilution of national culture and identity. However, its ideological roots lie most firmly in traditionally meritocratic arguments for a 'ladder of opportunity' that go back to the turn of the century, and the ideological climate shaped by the privatizing priorities of the neo-liberal strand of New Right thinking was, at most, only marginally influential in the genesis of the Scheme. However, as we shall see more clearly in chapter 10, the Scheme was increasingly reinterpreted in that light, and right from the start some commentators certainly attributed motives to the Scheme that related to that way of thinking. For example, critics held the view that, even on its limited scale, the Scheme constituted an expression of no-confidence in public sector education which was intended to promote a more general exodus of parents into the private sector. It was also seen by some of its advocates as having a potentially galvanizing effect on state schools, which would 'have to' improve academically if they wished to keep some of their ablest pupils. But such conflicting claims only reflected a broader tendency to attribute profound advantages and disadvantages to the Scheme despite its apparently modest scope. In the final section of this chapter we identify in more detail those predictions about its likely consequences which provided the starting points for our own empirical exploration of the Scheme in practice.

### Beneficiaries, Benefits and Costs

In a presentation of the 'Tory Case' which is often sceptical about 'the politics of the simple answer' and specifically sceptical about the efficacy of market forces, Chris Patten (1983) defends 'quality' against the 'egalitarian onslaught' in terms similar to those outlined earlier in this chapter. Educational opportunity had been sacrificed to the vain pursuit of equality, and should now be given its proper priority. Labour had abolished the direct-grant 'bridge' which many (like himself) had crossed to their own advantage and 'no-one else's disadvantage'. He therefore welcomed the introduction of assisted places as a revival of educational opportunity, while admitting that the Scheme 'would be easier to defend if its criteria were wider drawn . . . and if it had not been introduced at a time when spending on the maintained sector was being cut'.

### Table 4.1 Examples of conflicting claims and predictions about the Assisted Places Scheme taken from the public debate surrounding its inception and implemention

Mr Carlisle said that the Labour Party had chosen to attack the scheme on a party political basis, regardless of the fact that it was underprivileged children who would gain most from the Scheme. (*The Times*, 8 January 1980)

Able children from our poorest homes will once again have the opportunity of attending academically excellent schools (Boyson, *Daily Mail*, 25 June 1981)

The government's intention (is) to give priority first to inner city areas without grammar schools. (*Times Educational Supplement*, 30 November 1979)

It is not instantly obvious that the maintained system would be shattered if say, 5000 (of the 86,000) two A-level candidates had been syphoned off to the independent sector. (*Times Educational Supplement*, 30 November 1979)

On the income scale published, the help through the Assisted Places Scheme would go to people who otherwise would be educated in the state system (Carlisle, *Times Educational Supplement*, 15 February 1980)

It helps parents by increasing the degree of parental choice. It helps the country by promoting able children. (Cobban, *Sunday Times*, 8 June 1980)

For the sake of the system (critics of the scheme) would sacrifice not only the needs of these children but of a country which is desperately short of graduates in mathematics and modern languages (Maland, *The Times*, 21 March 1980)

The future of hundreds, even thousands of children is at stake. The NEC document speaks much of the viability of schools and the morale of teachers and the size of sixth forms, but says nothing of the needs of individual children. And the prime point we must make in our defence of the scheme is that it is meant to help children, not schools (*Conference*, February 1980)

It is complementary to the provision made by the maintained schools, indeed it can be fairly looked upon as an extension of the maintained sector (Carlisle, Speech at Harrogate, 24 February 1980)

I don't believe that a provision which will be no higher than the old Direct Grant intake used to be even when fully operational will harm anyone. (Carlisle, *Times Educational Supplement*, 15 February 1980)

It was meant to give certain children a greater opportunity to pursue a particular form of academic education that was regrettably not otherwise, particularly in the cities, available to them (Carlisle, *Education*, 11 March 1983)

Expressing his scepticism about vouchers as a means of enhancing opportunity more widely, he made the comment which we quoted at the end of our opening chapter — that fundamental value differences between their proponents and opponents made both sides immune to any evidence which even the most careful investigation of their feasibility might provide (Patten, 1983, pp. 93–4). Table 4.1 illustrates how aptly that comment applies to competing claims about the consequences of the Assisted Places Scheme. Having identified the wider contexts of the debate surrounding its inception, we now turn to some of the main predictions about the effects of the Scheme made by advocates and opponents. Although these predictions were a main starting-point for our research, we had (and have) no expectation that empirical investigation would produce a 'common mind' about the value of the Scheme.

---

The Scheme is designed for pupils from middle class families who are intent on giving their children educational advantages and privileges over the majority of children in comprehensives (*Labour Councillor*, April 1981)

Only a very small proportion are likely to go to the sons and daughters of Andy Capp. All previous experiences suggest that the places will be monopolised by the middle classes (*Guardian*, 2 February 1980)

The Scheme would not only undermine the comprehensive schools but also the grammar schools in the catchment area (Labour Party Information Paper, December 1979)

Comprehensive schools will lose numbers and in turn some will lose sixth forms or at least courses particularly in certain minority subjects (*PRISE News*, December 1979)

It is sensible to anticipate that parents who seek to use APS would have been likely to send their children to private schools in any case (Kinnock, Press Conference, 11 December 1979)

Some schools [would] coach their most able pupils for the exams and more teaching resources would be transferred from helping the low and average ability pupils (Labour Party Information Paper, December 1979)

The Scheme has been endowed with all the condescending virtues of philanthropy, 'pursuit of excellence' and 'moderation', when in reality it means robbing the public purse to support the already affluent whilst pirating scholastic talent from state schools (*Guardian*, 29 September 1979)

The Assisted Places Scheme would also prop up private education by increasing the number of places in independent schools and bailing out those independent schools whose recruitment has been flagging (*Labour Weekly*, February 1980)

The Assisted Places Scheme tells them [state school teachers] in effect that they are not good enough to teach clever children (Tim Heald, *Daily Telegraph* 10 August 1985)

The trouble is that a scheme designed to attract working class children who would otherwise go to a poor neighbourhood school, may simply attract middle class children who would otherwise go to a good comprehensive (*Conference*, February 1980)

To claim the scheme will provide a link between the sectors is a nonsense. You don't provide a link with a school by stealing its best pupils against its will (John Rae, *Times Educational Supplement*, 13 January 1984)

---

Despite the Scheme's limited scope, Table 4.1 makes it apparent how widely the competing claims ranged over the expected benefits and costs to individuals, schools, systems of schools, and to society at large. Some of those claims reflect value positions which can be debated but not 'tested'. Others make confident predictions which clearly call for evidence. The most obvious of these are about the likely beneficiaries of the Scheme. The regulations which established assisted places defined the target group only as 'pupils who might not otherwise . . . be able to benefit from the education at independent schools'. Some critics of the Scheme predicted immediately that many places would be acquired by families able to mislead school bursars about their income. Others pointed out that in any sort of welfare the middle-class can always milk the benefits much better than anyone else.[14] The real financial need of pupils receiving assistance was therefore a critical matter for the Scheme's advocates, especially since the direct-grant schools themselves had recognized how indiscriminate the previous system had been. On the evidence of two years' intake, the junior Minister (Bob Dunn) felt entitled to claim that a third of all places in participating schools were being progressively opened up to 'pupils from low-income families who are selected on merit alone'. By concentrating assistance on 'those who most need it', the Scheme had been successfully 'widening the educational opportunities open to children from less well-off families' by enabling them to 'enjoy the best of the secondary education that is provided in good independent schools'.[15]

We have deliberately chosen a statement here which reports 'facts' rather than makes predictions so as to indicate something of the difficulty of ever assessing whether the Scheme has really met its target. To give his facts a human face, the Minister held a well-publicized meeting with five assisted-place pupils evidently selected to illustrate the wide social range covered by the Scheme. The parents included a Merseyside bus-driver, an unemployed electrician, an unemployed accountant, a Nigerian-born teacher, a single parent training to be a teacher and a single parent currently studying full-time.[16] As we note in chapter 8, there was no evidence at that time that such occupations were anything but untypical of the Scheme's beneficiaries. More substantial evidence that the Scheme was reaching 'those who most need it' was found in the high proportion of families with incomes low enough to qualify for free places. This meant incomes significantly below the national average. Where the direct-grant system had certainly been vulnerable to the charge of subsidizing many who could well have afforded to pay 'economic' fees, the new Scheme was defended as casting its net more discriminatingly and so more widely. From this perspective, the only relevant test of the Scheme's success was whether places in independent schools were going to those who could not have afforded them otherwise. The target group was therefore not defined in terms of occupation or social class, but simply as 'low-income families'. It did not matter to the Minister whether 'the parent is an MP, a farmer, a dustman or a road sweeper', and to inquire about occupations was a typical socialist obsession.[17] We return to this issue in chapter 8.

From other perspectives, however, the situation appeared more complicated, as is clear from some of the quotations in table 4.1. Within the private sector, if not apparently by the Government, the Scheme was welcomed as achieving on a sensibly limited scale an objective which the Public Schools Commission had pursued so energetically and which had long been canvassed by independent schools themselves — that of extending the social range of recruits to private education. Pupils from 'less well-off homes' (the preferred euphemism in official statements) would surely alter the overwhelmingly middle-class intakes which successive surveys had revealed (Kalton, 1966; Public Schools Commission, 1968, Vol. 2; 1970, Vol. 2; Halsey *et al.*, 1980). Such pupils might come from 'the lowest economic groups', as Conservatives usually claimed when identifying those who would suffer most if a future Labour Government abolished assisted places. But they might also come from families of the kind described by Douse (1985) as having been made 'artificially poor' by death or unemployment or separation. Would the reasons for poverty be relevant to the purposes of the Scheme? Assistance would still be going to those who needed it financially. But it might not be attracting pupils with no previous 'family tradition' of using independent schools, which was certainly a subsidiary objective of assisted places, nor compensating for the cultural disadvantages of pupils drawn from 'illiterate backgrounds' and dependent on the Scheme 'to give them any sort of chance'. An HMC Minute of 1981 admitted that the purposes of the Scheme would be frustrated if the beneficiaries turned out to be confined to 'distressed gentlefolk and the children of staff' (cited in Tapper and Salter, 1986a, p. 325).

In the chapter which follows, we discuss the limited national evidence about the social distribution of assisted places, and note here only that the annual press releases issued by the ISJC Assisted Places Committee emphasize both income-related and occupation-related illustrations of the Scheme's success. In 1985, for example, 42 per cent of places were awarded to children from families with incomes low enough (i.e., below £6376) to qualify for full remission of fees, 57 per cent were taken up by children from families with incomes below £8000, and 'the unemployed and one-parent families were again 'the largest categories of need'. The 'wide variety of occupations' represented included 'bus and lorry drivers, miners, butchers, bricklayers, and semi-skilled and clerical workers'. Insofar as that chosen sample of occupations is weighted towards the manual working class, it may reflect awareness of how the scope of the Scheme was initially presented. For as we argued earlier, the defence of direct-grant schools rested heavily on their claim to be fully accessible to able working-class children, and *Black Paper* concern at the opportunities for economic and social mobility being lost through the disappearance of academic selection was directed especially at the consequences for 'deprived working class children from poor neighbourhoods'. The target group for any revival of those opportunities was therefore defined predominantly in class terms. While this was not true explicitly of most early official justifications for the Scheme, ministerial references in the period

1979–81 were nevertheless mainly to 'children from inner urban areas' or from 'deprived backgrounds', or to 'academically-minded children of poor parents'. There can be little doubt that these phrases conjured up images of able working class children for whom opportunities for upward mobility through educational success were being restored. More recently, there has been a significant change from earlier images in how the typical assisted-place pupil is represented within the rhetoric of legitimation. Again, we return to this issue in later chapters.

Alongside these uncertainties about who would and should be receiving assisted places, there were basic disagreements about how far the Scheme could be judged solely by the benefits it brought to individuals. It would be misleading to suggest a simple polarization between individual benefits and social costs. Arguments in support of the Scheme often refer to the necessity of developing the nation's resources of ability to the full, to recruiting as widely as possible those 'occupational cadres' on which its future depends, and to the valuable discipline imposed on maintained schools by having to compete for able pupils with high quality alternatives (see, for example, ISIS, 1981). Nevertheless, as we noted in our opening chapter, some of its advocates sought not only to emphasize the benefits to individuals, but to deny that any other criteria for judging it could be proper or valid. In part that view reflects a persistent theme in the 'reappraisal' of egalitarian educational policies which developed during the 1970s — namely, that the rights of individuals were being sacrificed to millenarian (and mistaken) notions of social justice. Ideologically, individual freedom was defined as a superior (and more attainable) 'good', and it was a freedom which included the right of parents to have their children educated at schools of their own choice, and of children from whatever social background to enjoy equal chances of educational and occupational success. The best education in the best schools should therefore be available to those who deserve it, not restricted to those who can afford it.

On the other hand, the most obvious social and educational costs attributed to the Scheme by its critics arose from the consequences of 'returning selection through the back door'.[18] Directly, competition for assisted places would greatly increase the number of children taking what was in effect an 11-plus (or a 13-plus), re-erecting what Neil Kinnock called the 'greasy poles scaled most easily by the crammed and pampered offspring of the middle-class'.[19] Indirectly, it enhanced the status of highly selective schools. It would also enhance the academic quality of their intakes, taking bright children out of the maintained schools 'and into the private sector's roll call of success'.[20] Apart from the more general and pervasive effects of identifying public secondary education as something from which the brightest had to be 'rescued', there were the more immediate consequences of depriving comprehensive schools of 'a core of high ability pupils whose presence contributes to the stimulus and motivation of their peers'.[21] This was the central objection in LEA responses to the Scheme. Especially serious were the projected effects on sixth-form provision. The beginning of the 30 per cent decline in the 16–19 age group by the early 1990s was already compounding the formidable difficulties facing most comprehensive schools in creating and sustaining viable sixth forms, difficulties which dominated the entire planning of secondary education in many authorities (Ruffett and Chreseson, 1982, chapter 5; Edwards, 1983). The specific provision in the Scheme for pupils to transfer from maintained schools at 16-plus therefore caused particular alarm, the critics noting that the private sector already contained almost a quarter of all sixth-formers and produced 27 per cent of those leaving the sixth form with the three passes at A-level which were the critical credential for entry to higher education and the careers to which it led (Benn, 1980; Labour Party, 1980).[22]

As we saw in our earlier discussion of its links with the arguments at the centre of the *Black Papers*, critics of the Scheme were quite correct in seeing it as an attempt to turn the clock 'back' towards academic selection — as 'a toehold in advance of a foothold'.[23] Indeed, this was one of the central justifications for the Scheme. It therefore had to be placed in the context of the new Government's encouragement of those local authorities wishing to retain grammar schools, or even (like Solihull) to revive them. Even amongst the Scheme's most ardent supporters within the private sector, however, there were doubts about what James Cobban (1980) called the 'lifelines for meritocrats' justification of assisted places. In his view, it risked marking out a 'charmed circle of schools', with the obvious implication that high academic opportunities were not available outside them. This was clearly a slight on the public sector. But the wholehearted emphasis on academic ability did not appeal to the heads of less obviously academic independent schools either. Nor did it please those who wanted to extend eligibility for 'assistance' to those 'needing' boarding education. There are long-standing tensions within the private sector between its elite academic day schools (mostly direct-grant), and those mainly boarding schools which define their purposes and announce their qualities more broadly. Given the nature of the Scheme, its natural constituency of support within the private sector was clearly displayed by the independent grammar schools which offered most of the places.

The most strenuous, certainly the best publicized, opposition from within the private sector came from the head of Westminster School, an elite boarding school which itself had an impeccable academic record. John Rae's main objection was that public money was to be used to subsidize the transfer of pupils from the public sector without there being any clear evidence (or any intention of collecting it) to show that their move was strictly necessary to their academic development. It therefore risked wasting that money, while Rae too felt that it would cast an unjustifiable slur on the public sector and so damage relationships between local authorities and independent schools (Rae, 1981, pp. 178–83; 1982).[24] These were clearly also the kinds of arguments employed against the Scheme from within the public sector. Mark Carlisle was firmly told by the Association of Chief Education Officers that there was no evidence that independent schools offered distinctive benefits not available in maintained schools. Pretending that they did so therefore constituted an offensive public declaration by the Government 'that the national system of education is incapable of providing education for our most able children'.[25]

The extent to which maintained schools would be harmed by the loss of able pupils was the object of frequent speculation. Supporters of the Scheme tended to refer back to the direct-grant system in support of their argument that assisted-place holders would be so geographically dispersed that no maintained schools would thereby lose more than a handful of able pupils; schools participating in the Scheme were not 'local' enough in their intakes, and in any case were taking too small a proportion of the age-group, to justify accusations of 'creaming' and of doing 'serious harm' (Lord, 1984, p. 68). As an additional safeguard care was to have been taken during the allocation of places to those schools to avoid unneccessary competition with (or duplication of) public sector provision, though the eventual allocation of places showed little sign of any such systematic fine-tuning. As we noted in the previous chapter, there was certainly anxiety among some Conservative MPs about the effects of the Scheme in those (mainly Conservative) LEAs which retained grammar schools (for example, in Kent, Bexley, Buckinghamshire and Trafford). But the main defence in principle against the accusation of 'creaming' was one in which the private sector was now well practised; selection by ability for assisted places was less invidious, and certainly less socially selective, than was entry to neighbourhood comprehensive schools.

Critics of the Scheme rejected what they saw as deliberate understating of its direct effects on the intakes of many comprehensive schools, and of the consequent injury to their more 'academic' courses. They also referred more broadly to the damage inflicted on morale in those schools by being so explicitly identified as incapable of catering for able children, to the danger of an accelerated flight of ambitious parents from schools undermined in this way, and to the accompanying risks of revived parental pressure on many primary schoools to coach children for the special opportunities which the Scheme was supposed to offer. The more the Scheme drew attention to the distinctive, even unique, opportunities available in independent schools, the more it was likely to be seen as 'an insult to and a sabotage of the state sector'.[26] As the Chief Officer of the ILEA argued, it was likely to promote a significant withdrawal of middle-class support from schools so identified as being second-best, thereby risking the creation of 'a fee-paying grammar school system and a maintained secondary modern sector'.[27] And it was this sort of prediction that led some commentators to suggest that the Scheme itself was actually conceived as part of a broader ideological commitment to the privatization of state services.

From our analysis of such claims and counter-claims we identified a set of predictions about the effects and outcomes of the Scheme which, despite the difficulties of doing so, we felt could be investigated. We put these predictions in the forms of questions which guided our collection of evidence, although some of them emerged or were modified as the research proceeded. The chapters which follow report our attempts to answer those questions.

To what extent, for example, has the allocation and take up of places achieved the objective of creating a national scholarship system — a ladder of opportunity accessible to able and financially eligible children wherever they lived? Relevant evidence is available in the statistical surveys carried out annually by the DES and for the ISJC by ISIS, and more usefully from the information collected by the DES from each school offering assisted places. This evidence is analyzed in the next chapter.

Were assisted places reaching the intended target groups? Did the recipients meet the formal eligibility criteria? Were they mainly underprivileged children who would otherwise be educated in poor schools within the state system, which was the critical question for the Scheme's most ardent supporters within the private sector? These are questions which cannot be answered adequately from the evidence which the Government itself collects, and which guided the extensive programme of interviews with pupils and parents which we report in chapters 8 and 9.

What were schools' reasons for participating in the Scheme and what were its immediate effects on those schools? How did the Scheme affect the state primary and secondary schools around them? Was there evidence that the availability of assisted places was having a detrimental effect on competing state schools? Or was it having a beneficially stimulating effect on comprehensive schools faced with increased competition? Was the Scheme particularly significant in inner city areas without grammar schools? Each of these questions indicates the inappropriateness of limiting the monitoring of the Scheme to its immediate beneficiaries. To answer them, we not only interviewed many pupils and parents in state schools but also tried to keep in view the local 'systems' of schools, maintained and independent, in those parts of the country in which our main fieldwork was done. In chapters 6 and 7, we therefore try to describe particular schools and the connections between them.

In what respects did assisted-place pupils and their parents differ from pupils and parents paying 'full' fees in the same schools, and from academically able pupils and their parents in state schools? At the time of their children's impending transition to secondary school, how were parents' perceptions of the opportunities open to them affected by the existence of assisted places and by the prevailing pattern of state provision in their area? What relative advantages did pupils and parents see themselves as gaining from being sponsored by the state to attend independent schools? How far these questions were answered in our interviews with pupils and parents is considered mainly in chapter 9.

Finally, what evidence was there that the Scheme was bringing about a systemic change in the relationships between the public and private sectors? That question pervades chapters 6–9, and is inseparable from larger questions about the 'right' balance between public and private educational provision and about the complementary and competitive relationship of the two sectors. The concluding chapter is therefore an attempt to locate the Scheme in the context of subsequent and much more radical measures to promote the privatization of schooling.

## Notes

1  Geoffrey Parker, in a letter to *The Times*, 8 October 1985.
2  Speakers Notes, prepared by the Conservative Central Office for the 1983 election, and evidently drawn mainly from ISIS material.
3  Taken from the transcript of the London Weekend Television programme *Starting Out*, 11 September 1981 — in the week that the first assisted-place pupils entered their schools.
4  Taken from our interview with Mark Carlisle, 16 November 1982.
5  Even at a time when Conservative opposition to comprehensive re-organization was muted, Edward Boyle argued at the 1965 Party Conference that some grammar schools should be retained because neighbourhood comprehensives in inner cities could not cater for the ablest working-class children. A similar view persisted in some sections of the Labour Party, and in some Labour-controlled LEAs like Durham.
6  This was the orthodox view from the Left (for example, Benn, 1974; Benn and Simon, 1972).
7  See note 4 above.
8  *Daily Mail*, 25 June 1981.
9  For example, in his opening speech in the Commons debate on the Scheme, 29 October 1980.
10  Its first director was Alfred Sherman, whose comments on the 'stupid party's' discovery of an interest in theory we cited and whose contribution to that 'discovery' was energetic.
11  Its first fruits are published in Anderson (1980). Among the Unit's early publications about education is the attack in Flew *et al.* (1981) on the 'progressives' still leading education astray. Some of those associated with the Unit became members of the influential New Right Hillgate Group later in the decade; see, for example, Hillgate Group, 1987.
12  See note 4 above. However, even Carlisle himself did appear to endorse some of the arguments for privatization when he was quoted in October 1982 as saying that 'not only is it one's responsibility rather than that of the state to provide for one's own family . . . if one is fortunate enough to be able to afford to do so, it is one's right and duty' (quoted in Pring, 1987, p. 295).
13  See note 2 above.
14  The Scheme was thus potentially susceptible to New Right criticisms of free welfare in general (eg. Seldon, 1981b, cited earlier this chapter).
15  Commons debate, 6 December 1983; *Hansard* 191–2.
16  See Hodges (1984).
17  Bob Dunn, Commons Standing Committee on Statutory Instruments, 24 April 1985.
18  For example, the Labour Party's National Executive statement October 1979; see also Caroline Benn (1980).
19  In the Commons debate reported in *Education*, 8 February 1980.
20  *Guardian*, 5 September 1980.
21  The Labour National Executive press release, 11 December 1979, circulated to all independent school heads and characterizing them as a 'gang of poachers', was commented on with predictable indignation in the HMC journal (*Conference*, 6 January 1980).
22  In 1961, 40 per cent of those leaving independent schools had A-levels and just under 20 per cent had three passes; in 1981 the equivalent figures were 63 per cent and 45 per cent. This evidence of the 'academic revolution' might also be taken as evidence of the schools' responsiveness to their market.
23  Martin Flannery's phrase in the House of Commons debate, 6 December 1983.
24  Rae's view that many assisted places would be offered in circumstances which made them a waste of public money and an 'insult to the public sector' was unchanged when we interviewed him in 1984, the year in which Westminster School first offered such places. By that time he had announced his resignation of the headship.
25  LEA opposition is described in *Education*, 5 December 1980, pp. 516–17.
26  Quoted in *Education*, 8 February 1980.
27  Peter Newsam, then Chief Officer of the ILEA, appearing on the same London Weekend programme as Rhodes Boyson (see note 3).

Chapter 5

# The Allocation and Take-up of Assisted Places

As an embodiment of the 'direct-grant principle', the Assisted Places Scheme was intended to improve on the previous version by avoiding the indiscriminate awarding of 'free' places without reference to parental income. But as a national scholarship 'ladder', it inherited a significant weakness from the arrangements it replaced. The uneven distribution of direct-grant schools across the country had always been a problem for defenders of the special academic opportunities they were believed to provide. It became even more of a problem, as the maintained grammar schools began rapidly to disappear, for those convinced that academic selection was a necessary condition for 'real' academic education — especially for 'bright children from modest backgrounds'. It was therefore important in justifying the new Scheme that any interested and eligible family should have a suitable independent school within reach, Section 17(2) of the 1980 Education Act referring to the 'desirability of securing an equitable distribution of assisted places throughout the country and between boys and girls'.

An analysis of the allocation and take-up of those places is therefore an obvious check on whether the Scheme, judged on its own terms, has met the requirements of 'equity'. Our main source of relevant data has come from the monitoring 'unit' at the DES — a group small enough, and sufficiently involved in other duties, to reassure any independent schools worried that the price of participating in the Scheme might be an unacceptably close bureaucratic supervision. Each school has to provide little more information annually than is needed for it to reclaim from the DES the fees it remits to parents, and any incidental grants made to low-income families. It reports how many of its quota of places were taken that year; how many assisted pupils it has altogether; how many of them hold free places; what proportion were recruited from maintained schools; what grants it made towards the incidental costs of uniform, travel, and free or half-price meals; and what the average 'relevant income' was of parents benefiting from the Scheme. There is no reporting of parental occupations. Nor is information gathered about where (or even within which LEAs) assisted-place holders live, despite its obvious relevance to claims that some comprehensive schools are suffering considerably from a sponsored loss of able pupils. The academic performance of pupils is not asked for either in this annual enquiry. However, their results in public examinations have been collected separately — an obvious form of evaluation for such an explicitly academic scheme.[1]

From all these returns the DES produces each year a statistical summary showing (for example) regional differences in the take-up of assisted places, the proportion of pupils paying no fees at all, the relevant parental incomes of other beneficiaries, and the rising costs of the Scheme as it moved towards its full year of operation in 1988. We have also been given access each year to the school-by-school information on which these summaries are based. We are most grateful to staff at the DES for making the material available to us, and for their readiness over the years to answer our many questions about how the scheme was being administered and monitored. It is on our own analysis of this more detailed evidence that the present chapter is largely based.

The Independent Schools Information Service also publishes a brief report each December, based on a questionnaire survey of schools offering assisted places. There is considerable overlap with the DES statistical summaries, although there are also additional questions about (for example) whether there has been a good choice of candidates, whether heads of maintained schools have been helpful or unhelpful, and what proportion of assisted-place leavers has gone on to higher education. As we note in more detail in chapter 8, the lack of systematic evidence about parental occupations does not seem to inhibit the highlighting of individual children from manual working-class backgrounds. They are used to displaying the wide range of social backgrounds from which assisted-place holders come, without any indication being possible about how typical or untypical these cases might be.

Such limitations in the evidence being collected by the Scheme's most obvious monitors were among the main starting-points for our own investigation, as we reported in the opening chapter. In this present chapter, however, we limit ourselves to what can be reported and inferred from 'official' statistics, and to a broad survey of the Scheme's scope.

## A Network of Schools

If the schools offering assisted places were indeed raising 'embers from the ashes', then it was desirable that there should be a fairly even distribution of opportunities to benefit. Yet the construction of an equitable 'ladder of opportunity' was considerably impeded by history — by the philanthropic activities of wealthy individuals and merchant companies who had founded those 'town' grammar schools which later outgrew their local status; by the creation of new 'country' schools to meet the rising Victorian demand for boarding education; by the decisions of some grammar schools in 1926 (or on some later occasions) to receive grants directly from central government; and by the choice of 'full' independence by only two-thirds of the schools which were still on the direct-grant list in 1975. The outcome of these various historical decisions was a very uneven distribution of 'academically excellent' independent schools which also felt able to offer substantial numbers of assisted places.

The most obvious sources of such offers were the former direct-grant schools. Almost all of them volunteered immediately for the new Scheme. Most offered at least twenty places a year. They saw themselves as returning to long-established notions of 'partnership' with the public sector, and to the direct-grant 'ideal' of academic opportunities dependent only on academic merit. In doing so, they also avoided the unattractive consequence of the Labour Government's action — that by 1982 their intakes would be determined almost entirely by parents' capacity to pay 'full' fees. For while many of these schools had responded to the withdrawal of direct grant by launching appeals for money to support their own bursaries and scholarships, their efforts could not begin to match the 'free places' available under the old system.[2] Public money was now to be made available again to support 'able children from less well-off homes', and the schools welcomed it.

Some of the Scheme's supporters (including Norman St John Stevas) had regarded it initially as a simple matter of re-opening and extending the recently abandoned direct-grant list. But however generous the independent schools formerly on that list might be with their offers of places, there would certainly not be enough places from that source alone to meet the Scheme's objectives. Of the 174 direct-grant schools which the Public Schools Commission had considered, fifty-five had subsequently either closed or moved fully into the public sector;[3] those which remained were erratically distributed by any criteria of 'rational planning', as table 5.1 shows. It was therefore essential to the appearance of the Scheme as a fair and efficient scholarship ladder that other independent schools should be persuaded to participate, especially in parts of the country which the direct-grant system had hardly reached.

The most obvious complementary source of places was the independent day (or 'mainly day') schools like St Paul's, Dulwich, and St Paul's Girls', which the Public Schools Commission had grouped with the direct-grant schools for the second stage of its inquiry. Unfortunately for the Scheme's purposes it was also something of a geographical grouping because, of the thirty-four such schools which eventually offered assisted places, fifteen were in and around London and another three were in the northwest of England — areas relatively well-provided with former direct-grant schools. The two other potential sources of supply were certainly better dispersed geographically. The first we mentioned in chapter 2, where we related how governing bodies of voluntary-aided or special-agreement grammar schools facing comprehensive reorganization were encouraged to consider whether joining the Scheme might not ease their transition to independence by creating a safety-net of publicly subsidized places underneath the risks of going into the educational market-place. We also noted the active involvement of AVIS (the Association of Voluntary-aided and Independent

**Table 5.1 Distribution of direct-grant schools 1970, and those remaining independent in 1979[4]**

|  | Location of English direct-grant schools in 1970 | Former direct-grant schools still independent in 1979 |
|---|---|---|
| North-east | 10 | 4 |
| North-west | 15 | 4 |
| Merseyside | 15 | 8 |
| Greater Manchester and Cheshire | 25 | 16 |
| Yorkshire and Humberside | 19 | 11 |
| East Midlands | 9 | 9 |
| West Midlands | 9 | 7 |
| East Anglia | 10 | 8 |
| South-west | 22 | 19 |
| South-east | 20 | 14 |
| London | 20 | 19 |
|  | 174 | 119 |

*Source*: PSC Second Report 1970 and *Education Year Book 1979*.

Grammar Schools) in negotiations preceding the Scheme's implementation, and Stuart Sexton's hope that as many as forty grammar schools might be tempted out of the maintained sector to participate in it. In the end, only ten former maintained grammar schools which had chosen independence offered places from September 1981, and most of these were well-established as independent schools long before the Assisted Places Scheme came into existence. However, they were later joined by Kirkham (1982), Wisbech (1983) and Worcester Royal Grammar School (1984), and in these cases the Scheme certainly eased the transition to independent status. Six of the total of thirteen such schools were in or around London.[5]

The second main source was the traditional public school sector. Its participation, of course, was sought for other reasons than to even-out the distribution of places. The presence of public boarding schools in considerable numbers would enhance the prestige of the Scheme. It would also emphasize that the new arrangements were not merely a restoration of the direct-grant system in revised form, and so would offset any continuing resentment in other parts of the private sector at the relatively protected position which those schools had enjoyed. Despite the Government's refusal to include 'boarding need' among the criteria for assistance, seventy-six boarding or 'mainly boarding' schools joined the Scheme in 1981. They included twenty-nine of the 'leading public schools' listed by Honey (1977, pp. 263–75) for the late-Victorian period, and fifteen of the twenty-nine included by Walford (1986) in his 'Eton' and 'Rugby' groups of present-day elite schools. Most schools of this kind which now offered assisted places had not previously sought any substantial links with the public sector. They did so now from a mixture of motives — a sense of *noblesse oblige*, a real commitment to the new opportunities which the Scheme was claimed to provide, a wish to attract some non-traditional clients, or a hope of raising the academic quality of their intakes. It is unclear what those schools hoped to gain from participation which limited their offers to a few sixth-form places. We commented earlier on Mark Carlisle's resistance to 'token gestures'. As we show shortly, some gestures have remained so 'token' that it is hard to see why the schools concerned have been allowed to retain even a nominal presence in the Scheme.

Although efforts were certainly made to persuade the most cautious schools to raise their offers, and to encourage others which were wavering about whether to offer places at all, the main difficulties in negotiating the final list came from the large number of academically unsuitable schools which applied for 'assisted place status', especially in response to the first DES letter of invitation in December 1979. We noted earlier the striking success of the private sector in associating academic excellence with selectiveness, which has increasingly meant associating it with independence. Some advocates of the new Scheme, like Stuart Sexton, assumed that while the maintained grammar schools had been able to match their independent equivalents as providers of 'real' academic education, comprehensive schools almost by definition were unable to do so. Carlisle, in his ministerial capacity, was usually more discriminating, highlighting the 'failure' of many inner-city neighbourhood comprehensives but recognizing that there were many other comprehensive schools which did not evidently need the 'good example' of private education to do their job properly. Certainly, generalizations about independent schools being obviously good because otherwise 'no one would pay to go to them' are not borne out by the process of selecting 'assisted place schools'.[6] Of the 470 schools whose provisional offers of 13,000 places were considered in the initial sifting process, over 200 were discarded as being unsuitable for the Scheme's explicitly academic purposes. As we noted in chapter 3, it was at best disingenuous of ministers therefore to claim that only Treasury constraints had prevented the launching of a very much larger Scheme in 1981 than the 5446 places which were eventually on offer. The criteria used by civil servants and HMI to sift the applicants gave priority to substantial sixth forms with a wide range of subjects, A-level pass-rates of at least 70 per cent, and a 'proven record of achievement' in sending pupils forward to higher education. Assessed against these criteria, some schools were discarded because they were too small. Others were judged to be academically too poor or mediocre to stand the scrutiny which would inevitably be given to schools which were supposed to be demonstrably better than the maintained schools from which they would draw pupils. A few which barely met DES criteria had to be admitted to fill gaps in some regions, or to reduce the bias against girls. Several schools which had passed the admission test withdrew at the last moment, as governing bodies weighed up again the advantages of recruiting some able pupils against the disadvantages of antagonizing nearby LEAs or the risks of having to support needy pupils from school resources if the Scheme was suddenly ended. These were all boarding or mainly-boarding schools. During the period between the provisional 'final' list of October 1980 and the final list published in January 1981, they were replaced by a similar number of schools of similar character in similar parts of the country.[7]

Altogether, the final list of schools offering assisted places in September 1981 shows much more diversity than a mere revival of the direct-grant system could have achieved. And it included most of the academic (and social) market-leaders within the private sector.

**Table 5.2 English schools offering assisted places, 1981**

|  | Boys | | Girls | Mixed | All | |
|---|---|---|---|---|---|---|
| HMC boarding schools | 35 | (37) | — | 13 | 48 | (50) |
| Other independent boarding schools | — | | 11 | 2 | 13 | |
| HMC day schools (excluding ex-direct grant) | 14 | | — | — | 14 | |
| Other independent day schools | 3 | | 17 | | 20 | |
| Former direct-grant schools [8] | 47 | (48) | 53 | 14 | (15) 114 | (116) |
| Former LEA grammar schools | 8 | (9) | 1 | 1 | (3) 10 | (13) |
| Totals | 107 | (111) | 82 | 30 | (33) 219 | (226) |

*Note*: 1988 figures in brackets where these have changed
*Source*: Aggregated School-by-School Statistics.

Between 1981 and 1988, seven other schools joined the Scheme. Two were public schools — Bishop Stortford College, and Westminster School which joined in 1984 despite the opposition of its head (John Rae) who resigned shortly afterwards. Two former direct-grant schools also joined late — West Buckland in Devon (a boarding school), and Nottingham High School after its governors had second thoughts about whether they could afford to stay out. The other new recruits were the former aided grammar schools at Kirkham (Lancashire), Wisbech and Worcester.

These late additions were obviously too few to affect significantly the overall distribution of assisted places. In the 1987 election, however, the Conservatives promised as part of their plans for extending educational choice and competition to expand the Scheme to 35,000 places compared with the 33,228 reached in its first full year in operation 1987–8. In July 1987 many other independent schools were invited by the DES to consider (or in some cases reconsider) joining the Scheme. Of the 132 which replied, fifty-two have been accepted; subject to completing formal participation agreements, they will offer assisted places for the first time in September 1989. The criteria used to judge their suitability have apparently been the same as in 1981, although the energetic canvassing of the 'best' schools which preceded the

Scheme's introduction make it likely that many of the newcomers met them with greater difficulty than their predecessors. The list includes, however, several schools which had been accepted in 1981 and then changed their minds (for example, Kimbolton and Tormead), and a number of others which would have been warmly welcomed earlier if they had applied (for example, Cheltenham Ladies College, Christ's Hospital School, Sevenoaks, Haileybury and Oakham). These schools are untypical of the list as a whole, which contains a surprising number of small schools which might be thought unlikely to have the range of A-level subjects and size of sixth form teaching group which participation in the Scheme supposedly requires. More than half the fifty-two have fewer than 400 pupils, and four have fewer than 300. There is also a preponderance of boarding or partly-boarding schools among them which is quite unlike the proportions shown in table 5.2 for the Scheme as it began. Given its initial orientation towards academically successful day schools, it is unlikely that there are many suitable schools of this kind still left outside the Scheme. That its current extension is based primarily on boarding schools is reflected in the uniformly low allocation of only five places at the ages of 11-13 to each of the fifty-two newcomers, a quota which represents no risk for the school and is likely to be filled. The resulting addition of (at most) 260 new places a year will do little to reduce the regional and other inequalities which we identify in this chapter. For the appearance of scope and diversity which is given by counting schools is considerably undermined by counting places. Predictably, assisted places are concentrated most heavily in those parts of the country which for historical reasons are relatively rich in independent day schools and especially rich in survivals from the old direct-grant list.

### The Allocation Of and Take-Up of Places

It was sometimes assumed in early negotiations about the Scheme that participating schools would be making all their places available for means-tested assistance — or at least that they could do so if they wished. A few direct-grant and aided grammar schools remained willing to take that risk, only to have their offers contained within limits set by official caution. To prevent over-commitment to arrangements which might be ended abruptly by an incoming Labour Government, the DES insisted that not more than half a school's annual intake could be made available as assisted places. In contrast to this curbing of enthusiasm, it soon became obvious that insisting on *minimum* offers of at least ten places a year would deter many prestigious independent schools from participating at all. Between these extremes, many schools had to consider carefully how far they wished to dilute the social exclusiveness preserved by high fees, and how many places they felt obliged by their past traditions to make open to 'able children from less well-off homes' when they might have to support these places from their own funds if Government assistance was suddenly withdrawn.

The eventual outcome of all these school-by-school decisions was a predictable predominance of places in those day schools which were accustomed to recruiting from the maintained sector and well-practised in the paper-work required for pupils sponsored from public funds. At the sixth-form stage, the strength of LEA protests against worsening their own already formidable problems in maintaining viable provision produced a diplomatic limitation of new 16-plus places to not more than five a year in any school. At the main entry ages of 11–13, however, quotas ranged from none at all at nine boarding schools (for example, Stowe and Bedales) and only five each at eleven others (for example, Stonyhurst and Sedbergh), to forty-five a year at Dulwich and Latymer Upper, fifty at St Edward's Liverpool, and fifty-five at Newcastle Royal Grammar School. Of the thirty-seven schools which were allocated more than thirty assisted places a year to pupils aged 11–13, all but four had been direct-grant or voluntary-aided grammar schools — the kinds of schools most likely to regard the Scheme as an opportunity to return to familiar routines, familiar markets and familiar patterns of recruitment. Tables 5.3 and 5.4 show the large share of places which these schools took, and the largely 'token' participation of many boarding schools.

### Table 5.3 Initial allocation of assisted places, pupils aged 11–13

|  | Schools | | Places | |
|---|---|---|---|---|
|  | No. | % total | No. | % total |
| HMC boarding schools, not including direct-grant[9] | 48 | 21.9 | 398 | 8.9 |
| Other boarding schools | 13 | 5.9 | 166 | 3.7 |
| HMC day schools | 14 | 6.4 | 254 | 5.7 |
| Other independent day schools | 20 | 9.1 | 349 | 7.8 |
| Former direct-grant schools | 114 | 52.1 | 2962 | 66.1 |
| Former LEA schools | 10 | 4.6 | 351 | 7.9 |

*Source*: Aggregated School-by-School Statistics (England).

The generally smaller size of girls' independent schools, and their more limited access to funds sufficient to protect large numbers of assisted places against a sudden withdrawal of public support, were obvious obstacles to achieving even rough parity in the places available to boys and girls. Girls' schools provided 40 per cent of the 11–13 places available in 1981. The total number of places available to girls would have been lower if a similar scheme had been introduced after the Public Schools Commission made its *Second Report* (1970), because at that time only five of the 273 public schools and only two of the 174 direct-grant schools were coeducational. By 1981, 14 per cent of the schools offering assisted places were fully coeducational or in the process of becoming so. But even if these schools had been willing 'in the national interest' to

**Table 5.4  Allocation of 11–13 places to individual schools, 1981**

| | None below sixth form | 5–10 | 11–20 | 21–30 | 31–40 | Over 40 |
|---|---|---|---|---|---|---|
| HMC boarding schools | 8 | 25 | 13 | 2 | 0 | 0 |
| Other boarding schools | 0 | 8 | 5 | 0 | 0 | 0 |
| HMC day schools | 0 | 4 | 5 | 4 | 0 | 1 |
| Other day schools | 1 | 6 | 8 | 3 | 2 | 0 |
| Former direct-grant schools | 0 | 12 | 29 | 47 | 21 | 5 |
| Former LEA schools | 0 | 1 | 1 | 0 | 7 | 1 |
| | 9 | 56 | 61 | 56 | 30 | 7 |

*Source*: Aggregated School-by-School Statistics (England).

discriminate positively in favour of girls, it was only at the sixth-form stage that parity was readily achievable because of the large and rapidly increasing number of boys' independent schools (24 per cent in 1981, and 35 per cent in 1986) which admitted girls as sixth formers (Walford, 1983; 1986). Of the sixth-form places available in 1981, 66 per cent were in girls' schools, mixed schools or schools with mixed sixth forms. But at the main ages of entry the Scheme was unintentionally biased towards boys. The seven new schools joining it in the period 1981–4 made matters slightly worse, because five of them were boys' schools too. But the large addition to the list of schools (though not to the total number of places) which followed the 1987 election shows signs of positive discrimination in that twenty-three of the fifty-two are girls' schools and another eighteen are entirely coeducational.

Regional inequalities in the availability of assisted places were certainly less marked than they would have been in a simple revival of the old direct-grant list. They were nevertheless sufficiently marked to be an impediment to the main arguments used to justify the Scheme — that it constituted a substantial restoration of parental choice, a stimulus to state schools to improve their own standards, and a mobilization of academic talent in the national interest. Any engineering of places to match the main centres of population would have required either the creation of new independent schools at a speed which only the most fervent believers in an educational free market would think feasible; or the enticing into the private sector of far more aided grammar schools than actually made that move; or the provision of assistance for boarding education in the context of a much greater unsatisfied demand for it than seems to exist. In the absence of any of these conditions for an equitable 'network' of new academic opportunities, the erratic distribution of direct-grant and independent day schools around the country brought an inevitable concentration of assisted places in those urban areas which we identified in the first section of the chapter.

Table 5.5 shows that these regional inequalities are marked and have persisted. As we noted earlier, the need to solicit substantial offers of places from 'academically excellent schools' was a severe constraint on the 'fine-tuning' which some of the Scheme's advocates intended or promised — for example, the avoidance of wasteful competition with surviving maintained grammar schools or (presumably) with academically successful comprehensive schools. Efforts to even-out the distribution of places certainly led to some schools being admitted to the Scheme which would not have met the academic criteria if they had not been located in parts of the country where places (especially for girls) were in short supply. Despite these efforts, table 5.5 shows how far short the Scheme fell of being the national 'scholarship ladder' intended by its architects.

**Table 5.5 Examples of the allocation of 11–13 places in urban areas 1981 and 1988**

|  | No. of schools | | No. of new places available | |
|  | 1981 | 1988 | 1981 | 1988 |
|---|---|---|---|---|
| Outer London | 24 | 24 | 477 | 368 |
| Inner London | 18 | 19 | 470 | 457 |
| Manchester and Stockport | 10 | 10 | 271 | 258 |
| Bolton, Oldham, Bury | 6 | 6 | 206 | 206 |
| Liverpool and Birkenhead | 10 | 10 | 300 | 346 |
| Bristol and Bath | 13 | 13 | 199 | 225 |
| Newcastle | 5 | 5 | 157 | 145 |
| Birmingham, Wolverhampton | 3 | 3 | 122 | 117 |
| Hereford, Malvern, Worcester | 4 | 5 | 101 | 130 |
| Nottingham | 2 | 3 | 45 | 70 |
| Bradford | 3 | 3 | 58 | 63 |
| Leeds | 2 | 2 | 75 | 55 |
| Portsmouth and Southsea | 3 | 3 | 84 | 84 |
| Southampton | 1 | 1 | 35 | 35 |
| Sheffield | 1 | 1 | 40 | 16 |
| Leicester, Sunderland | 0 | 0 | 0 | 0 |

*Source*: Aggregated School-by-School Statistics (England).

Given the 'over-representation' of direct-grant and other independent grammar schools among the high-providers of assisted places, any substantial allocation of extra places once the Scheme became established would probably have made the overall distribution even more erratic. In fact, Treasury limits on total expenditure on the Scheme remained as tight as they could be when the amount of fee remission depends on the selection decisions of individual schools; the number of new 11–13 places was 4453 when the Scheme began and 4488 in 1987, while the number of new sixth-form places only rose from 984 to 1028. The former head of a school which had its 1981 application turned down has described the selection process as 'hit or miss', and doubts whether any serious effort was then made to recruit schools in under-provided areas like North Yorkshire (Wilkinson, 1986, pp. 54–5). His school, Scarborough College, is one of those which will be offering assisted places for the first time from September 1989. But while the extended list may do something to redress the gender imbalance, it will do little for regional inequalities. While none of the extra schools is in the well-provided area of Merseyside, and there is only one each in Greater Manchester and Avon, twenty-two of them are in London or the home counties. The omission of Leicester has been rectified, but the rest of the schools are too scattered to indicate much planning even if the number of places allocated to them were to be increased.

Treasury limits on its total budget made the reallocation of existing places the main mechanism for fine-tuning the Scheme. Inevitably, some schools overestimated their capacity to fill all the assisted places they had been given, or experienced persistent difficulty in recruiting the required proportion (60 per cent) from maintained schools. While the DES tolerated under-recruitment in the first years of a new scheme, a School's continued difficulty in reaching targets brought official enquiries. Some schools took the initiative by seeking reduced allocations; more schools had reductions forced upon them. Places given up have been redistributed to schools receiving more applications than they can cope with. But since these have tended to be schools to which large numbers of places were allocated from the outset, the redistribution has made regional differences slightly worse as is also apparent from table 5.5. Slight corrective action was taken in 1987, when a further small reallocation deliberately favoured strongly recruiting schools in Coventry and Worcester in the otherwise badly-provided West Midlands.

**Table 5.6 Reduced and increased allocation of 11–13 places, 1981–8**

|  | Reductions | | | | Increases | | |
|---|---|---|---|---|---|---|---|
|  | 1–5 | 6–10 | 11–15 | 15 + | 1–5 | 6–10 | 11–15 |
| HMC boarding | 7 | 0 | 0 | 0 | 8 | 2 | 0 |
| Other boarding | 1 | 0 | 1 | 0 | 4 | 1 | 0 |
| HMC day | 2 | 0 | 0 | 0 | 1 | 1 | 0 |
| Other day | 1 | 0 | 2 | 0 | 4 | 1 | 0 |
| Direct-grant | 13 | 15 | 3 | 4 | 24 | 7 | 1 |
| Former LEA | 0 | 0 | 0 | 0 | 1 | 2 | 0 |
|  | 23 | 15 | 6 | 4 | 34 | 13 | 1 |

*Source*: DES School-by-School Returns (England).

We turn now to the take-up of places, both regionally and in particular categories of school. Again, our evidence is taken mainly from the information which the DES collects annually from every school offering assisted places.

The final DES list showing what places were available from September 1981 was not published until January of that year. Many independent schools, as we describe in chapter 6, then made exceptional use of local radio and local newspapers to draw attention to these new opportunities, their national representatives arguing (unsuccessfully) that the Government should provide some of the money needed to publicize 'its' initiative. Good publicity was particularly necessary in areas where LEAs' opposition led to primary school heads being forbidden to provide information about the Scheme to parents, or information about individual pupils to the independent schools to which they were applying. More generally, Labour's declarations of intent to end assistance as soon as it was returned to power were intended to concentrate attention on the risks of ·participating in such insecure arrangements. For all these reasons it was expected in the DES, and accepted by some of the Scheme's advocates, that many places would be initially left unfilled. It was also expected that a high proportion of them would carry low levels of fee remission because schools and applicants alike would try to minimize the financial risks involved.

In these circumstances, the initial take-up of 82 per cent of the 11–13 places could be interpreted as evidence of successful publicity by the schools, and of a substantial latent demand for the academic opportunities which the Scheme was supposed to offer. When the 1983 Conservative election victory guaranteed at least a further four or five years of assisted places, and also made any subsequent removal much more difficult, the taking up of places at the main entry ages moved rapidly towards 'saturation'. Clearly, public methods of announcing the Scheme's existence and illustrating the diversity of social backgrounds from which place-holders came were soon supplemented for many interested families by personal example and word-of-mouth. Table 5.7 records how quickly the take-up at 11–13 rose to almost full capacity, but also shows the continuing shortfall at 16-plus.

At 16-plus, recruitment has remained well below capacity. It is at this stage that the private sector seems most obviously to exhibit its academic 'superiority', producing over a quarter of school leavers with three Advanced-level passes from its 6

### Table 5.7 Take-up of places, 1981–7[10]

|  | 1981 | 1982 | 1983 | 1984 | 1985 | 1986 | 1987 |
|---|---|---|---|---|---|---|---|
| New places 11–13 | 4426 | 4626 | 4761 | 4832 | 4506 | 4497 | 4488 |
| % places taken | 82.0 | 82.7 | 87.1 | 90.9 | 98.1 | 97.1 | 94.2 |
| New places at 16 | 984 | 996 | 1021 | 1032 | 1021 | 1020 | 1028 |
| % places taken | 53.4 | 61.8 | 73.0 | 79.0 | 80.0 | 76.5 | 72.0 |
| Total no. of places available | 5446 | 11058 | 15866 | 20699 | 25210 | 29295 | 33228 |
| % places taken | 76.9 | 77.9 | 82.6 | 84.0 | 84.9 | 83.6 | 81.0 |

*Source*: DES Statistical Summary, 1988 (England).

per cent share of pre-sixth-form pupils (Halsey *et al.*, 1984). But it is also the stage at which many independent schools lose pupils to the public sector, especially where sixth-form colleges and 'strong' sixth forms are competing with them. Pupils already in maintained schools are likely to feel reluctant to break the continuity of their schooling unless sixth-form opportunities are so limited that a move appears necessary. The LEAs' initial right to block transfers to the private sector at 16 years of age seems, even from ISIS evidence of what happened in 1981 and 1982, to have been used much less often and indiscriminately than Rhodes Boyson repeatedly claimed, although its existence for those two years may have deterred some parents from applying for sixth-form places at all. Once that veto was removed, Bob Dunn felt entitled to claim that the rise from an initially 'sluggish' 53 per cent to a relatively buoyant 79 per cent in 1984 was evidence of the Scheme's success in meeting a 'real demand'.[11] Yet there has been a fall-back since. And over the whole period 1981–7, some sixty schools consistently recruited below their sixth-form quotas. They include six which only offer places at that stage (Bradfield, Bedales, Charterhouse, Tonbridge, Stowe and St Swithun's), while another twenty are HMC public schools and seven are boarding schools for girls. It is also a notable contradiction of one of the Scheme's objectives — of creating new clients for private education — that almost two-thirds of those taking up assisted places for the first time at 16 are already fee-paying pupils in the same schools.

The high take-up of places at 11 and 13 is often taken as evidence of a Scheme so attractive to parents that it is pressing hard against Treasury-imposed limits on its scope and deserves to be substantially expanded. There has certainly been pressure from individual schools to be given larger quotas of places, and these requests have exceeded the number of places which it has been possible to redistribute from schools unable to fill their quotas. Indeed, the 260 additional places available from September 1989 might have been given to schools already well established in the Scheme rather than 'scattered like confetti' around generally less prestigious newcomers.[12] More generally, it can be argued by the Scheme's supporters that demand has followed supply, because areas relatively well provided with places have also tended to be areas where their take-up has been high. DES annual statistics give only regional figures, and these conceal considerable local variations. For what they are worth, they show that the take-up has been consistently highest in the north-west, the south-west and the West Midlands.[13] Our own more detailed analysis shows that the take-up of 11–13 places over the whole seven-year period 1981–7 was 99.3 per cent in the ten Merseyside schools, 94.7 per cent in nine Manchester schools, and 101.6 per cent in the nine Bristol schools. In contrast, the average in outer London schools was 82.2 per cent, while the 87 per cent average of eleven Surrey schools is produced from individual 'scores' which range from 56 per cent to 102 per cent.

Any averaging of take-up rates, especially within large regional groupings as is done in DES and ISIS published statistics, conceals wide differences between individual schools and to some extent between categories of school. The Scheme allows and has produced very wide variations in participation levels. By 1987 the average number of assisted-place pupils in the 226 English independent schools participating in the Scheme was 119. Excluding over 450 pupils who were then holding such places in the Newcastle-under-Lyme 'combined schools' (Newcastle High School and the Orme Girls' School), the numerical range extended from over 300 in St Edward's (Liverpool) and the Newcastle Royal Grammar School, and to nearly 300 in the Manchester Grammar School, Dulwich College, Latymer Upper School and Emmanuel School, to fewer than ten in each of three public schools and none at all in a fourth. By that time, with the Scheme fully in operation, there were twenty-eight schools with more than 200 pupils holding assisted places and seventeen with fewer than thirty. The contrast was between schools in which assisted places represented more than a third of their pupil numbers and schools which remained virtually untouched by their participation in the Scheme. Not surprisingly, all the schools with high numbers (except for Dulwich) were on the final direct-grant list or were former LEA grammar schools. Almost all those only marginally involved were boys' boarding schools in the public school tradition.

These differences make it hard to see how the Scheme could be substantially expanded on its own terms as a national scholarship ladder without markedly increasing those regional and local inequalities in provision to which we have already referred. As suggested by the figures we cited earlier, the schools which have met and even exceeded their targets are heavily concentrated in and around Liverpool, Manchester, Bristol and inner London. In contrast, there are clusters of schools in outer London and the south-eastern counties, where private boarding education is still prominent, which have had to leave many of their assisted places unfilled. In table 5.8 what we have called 'over-recruiting' schools filled more than their total allocation of assisted places over the whole period 1981–7; 'fully recruiting' schools filled between 95–100 per cent of their places; and 'under-recruiting' schools filled fewer than 70 per cent.

In the school year 1987/88, 36 per cent of pupils in HMC schools held assisted places. The proportion in equivalent girls' schools was also about a third. By that time there were many schools from the old direct-grant list and some others in which 40 per cent and more of pupils were holding assisted places. As has been pointed out from time to time, that constitutes both a potentially dangerous dependence on public funds for schools which are supposedly 'independent', and a level of financial support which is unaccompanied by 'that control which ratepayers would normally expect to have in a school which they fund'.[14]

The predominance of boarding schools among those which have been under-recruiting reflects the continued lack of assistance for boarding education among the Scheme's provisions, and the very limited help which most schools are able to give from their own resources.[15] But it is unlikely that all or even most of the boarding

**Table 5.8 Schools over-recruiting, fully recruiting, and under-recruiting assisted-place pupils aged 11–13, 1981–7**

|  | No. | 'Over' | 'Full' | 'Under' |
|---|---|---|---|---|
| Ex-LEA | 13 | 4 | 4 | 0 |
| Girls' direct-grant | 53 | 11 | 10 | 12 |
| Mixed direct-grant | 14 | 4 | 2 | 0 |
| Boys' direct-grant | 49 | 19 | 8 | 5 |
| HMC day | 14 | 5 | 3 | 0 |
| HMC boarding | 50 | 11 | 11 | 13 |
| Other day | 20 | 4 | 3 | 4 |
| Other boarding | 13 | 3 | 1 | 7 |
| Totals | 226 | 61 | 42 | 41 |

*Source*: DES School-by-School Returns (England).

places would have been taken anyway. Even at the time when the Public Schools Commission was becoming convinced by Royston Lambert's evidence of a widespread 'need' for publicly-assisted boarding education, it is very doubtful whether that evidence could also be taken as indicating a widespread 'demand' for it. Even in the late 1960s, many public schools were already experiencing difficulties in filling their places. Since that time the costs of boarding education have risen much more steeply than inflation, and the recent increase in the private sector's share of the secondary education 'market' is attributable to the rising popularity of independent day schools. Over the period 1981–7, the proportion of all assisted-place pupils who are boarders has not risen; it was 6.5 per cent in 1981 and 6.2 per cent in 1987. Those boarding (or largely-boarding) schools which have managed to fill most of their places are mainly situated in or near centres of population (for example, Mill Hill and Merchant Taylors in London, Wellingborough, Warwick School, Bedford School, Ipswich School and Clifton). Those whose intakes cannot justify their continued recognition as 'Assisted Place Schools' include some prestigious names. In 1987–8, for example, there were only thirty-three assisted-place pupils altogether in Bradfield, Stowe, Bedales, Charterhouse and Tonbridge. It will be interesting to see whether the many boarding schools among the fifty-two additions to the 1989 list will be any more successful in filling even their small quotas of places. In contrast, there were in 1987–8 more than 750 assisted-place pupils in the three former direct-grant schools which Mark Carlisle named when we interviewed him as illustrating the kind of Scheme he had in mind — Manchester Grammar School, Bradford Grammar School and King Edward VI School in Birmingham.

Marked under-recruitment by a significant number of girls' former direct-grant schools is much harder to explain than are the difficulties experienced by many boarding schools. They are situated in urban areas, they usually have well-established academic reputations, and they are accustomed to offering 'free' places to children from maintained primary schools. Given the relative overall shortage of places for girls, they would have expected little difficulty in filling their places. Yet of the twenty-four schools belonging to the Girls' Public Day School Trust, for example, twelve have had their quotas reduced. Some of the reductions have been substantial — for example, Sheffield High School from forty to sixteen, the Central High School in Newcastle from forty to eighteen, Croydon High School from thirty-five to nineteen, and Sutton High School from thirty to twelve. Eight other former girls' direct-grant schools have also had their allocations reduced, three of them by ten places. Taking these reductions into account, six have still filled fewer than 75 per cent of their allocated places while only six have 'fully' or 'over' recruited. Debbie Wall (1986) has identified from her interviews with heads of London GPDST schools some possible reasons for their difficulties. First is an initial overestimate of the demand for places. We described in chapter 2 the difficulty many governing bodies had in finding a balance between their sense of obligation to restore academic opportunities to 'able children from less well-off homes', their eagerness to take advantage of a renewed (or new) source of academically-able pupils, and their worries about the burden of school funds if the Scheme were to be ended abruptly. The Trust made the relevant decision for each of its schools. Given its long-standing claim to be offering academic education to girls 'irrespective of social class' (Kamm, 1971), a collective initial optimism about how the new Scheme would work is understandable. And for some of its schools, the initially high bids had to be further increased to cope with demand — for example at Birkenhead High School (thirty, increased to forty) — or have led to the places being filled without apparent difficulty (Nottingham High School and Norwich High School, each with thirty). Secondly, in London, where many of its schools are clustered, there is fierce competition for able pupils both from other independent schools and from the surviving aided and maintained grammar schools. In areas offering several alternatives within manageable travelling distance, multiple applications from parents create obvious difficulties for schools in managing the level of intake they want. Thirdly, the particularly strong opposition of the ILEA to assisted places certainly constrained many heads of primary schools from providing information about them, although outright non-cooperation has apparently been infrequent and diminishing (ISIS annual surveys, 1983–7; Wall, 1986). Finally, a general problem for schools in areas where salaries carry London weightings is that the parental income scales for assisted places make no allowance for such differentials. The Trust's policy of keeping its fees low relative to other independent schools in London may have placed it at an advantage in attracting fee-paying pupils, but at a disadvantage in recruiting applicants for assisted places insofar as it reduced the amount of fee-remission to which relatively better-paid parents were entitled to a level at which assistance might not seem worth applying for.

Some of these reasons for low take-up clearly extend beyond the particular group of GPDST schools. Also relevant to many girls' schools is the increasing number of mixed schools in the private sector, and the high (and rising) proportion of mainly-boys' schools which now recruit girls to their sixth forms. There is therefore a growing source of competition for pupils at sixteen-plus of which the heads of girls' schools are well aware and about which they often complain (Walford, 1983; Girls' Schools Association, 1987). While girls are in the majority among those who take up assisted places for the first time at the age of 16, many of them will neither be in girls' schools nor in schools which are mixed throughout their age range. More generally, we described earlier how the negotiations which preceded publication of the first full list of participating schools included efforts to increase the proportion of places available to girls beyond that indicated by the first trawl of offers. Neither the encouragement of some girls' schools to offer additional places, nor the acceptance of a few others which barely met the Scheme's academic criteria, made much difference to the initially unequal allocation and take-up. Of the first 1981 intake, 41.1 per cent were girls. That overall figure had risen to 45 per cent by 1987, but it has remained around 41 per cent for pupils entering at the ages of 11–13. We turn now to some other generalizations about the beneficiaries of the Scheme which can be supported either from the summary statistics issued by DES and ISJC, or from the school-by-school information collected annually by the DES.

### The beneficiaries of assisted places

In chapter 8 we discuss in detail the social and educational backgrounds from which our own sample of assisted-place pupils came, and compare that evidence with the findings of other recent studies. A main focus of our later discussion is whether places have gone predominantly to the kinds of pupils envisaged by the Scheme's advocates

**Table 5.9 Parental Income Bands of Assisted-Place pupils, 1981–7**

|  | 1981 | 1982 | 1983 | 1984 | 1985 | 1986 | 1987 |
|---|---|---|---|---|---|---|---|
| % annual intake entitled to free places | 37 | 39 | 40 | 41 | 42 | 40 | 40 |
| % all intakes from families with incomes below £8005* | – | 46 | 45 | 48 | 47 | 46 | 44 |
| % all intakes from families with incomes below £9204* | – | 57 | 57 | 59 | 58 | 56 | 53 |
| % pupils (all intakes) claiming free school meals | 5.3 | 6.2 | 7.6 | 8.9 | 9.6 | 10.1 | 10.5 |
| % pupils (all intakes) claiming uniform grants | 30.3 | 20. 9 | 22.1 | 33.3 | 33.9 | 33.1 | 30.7 |

*Note*: * Parental income bands are calculated in 1987 prices
*Source*: DES Statistical Summary, 1988 (England).

and highlighted in the rhetoric by which it has been legitimated. Yet despite its obvious relevance to that rhetoric, there has been no systematic monitoring of parental occupations, although (as we have noted) both the annual ISJC surveys and the pronouncements of ministers have regularly drawn attention to children of (for example) bus drivers and miners to illustrate the socially diverse backgrounds from which the beneficiaries come. The statistics cited most often are the high proportion of free places which have been awarded each year, and the fact that the majority of families benefiting from the Scheme have incomes below the national average.

These are the kinds of statistics on which ministers base their claims that the Scheme has indeed been reaching its intended beneficiaries. To illustrate the Scheme's success in reaching its intended beneficiaries, Bob Dunn, for example, noted that a scale which had been made deliberately ungenerous to middle-income families offered little assistance 'above the level of average earnings', and that this was 'precisely how it should be'. The Opposition was therefore 'manifestly wrong . . . in decrying the Scheme as a subsidy to the rich'.[16]

In 1987 the average 'relevant income' of parents of assisted-place pupils was £8516, compared with a national average household income for the equivalent year of £11,073.[17] The Scheme is certainly redistributive insofar as single-parent families have consistently been the 'largest single category of need' and unemployed parents have outnumbered any single occupational category.[18] On that evidence, it has been described as 'one Government scheme designed to help low income families which has not been hijacked by the wily, articulate middle classes' (Ayer, 1988). But the facts point less straightforwardly in that direction. Our main discussion of how widely this scholarship 'net' has been cast is in chapter 8, and it is open to the objection made by Sexton and many other advocates of assisted places that 'class' and occupation are irrelevant criteria for judging the Scheme's effectiveness. However, even on the grounds which have been used consistently to justify the Scheme — low income — it is worth noting that the parents of about a third of assisted-place pupils have above-average earnings. When evidence about the preponderance of professional and white-collar occupations is added to statistics about income levels, it is hard to argue that most of the schools offering places have given priority to their most disadvantaged applicants.

Above whatever threshold they set to determine the academic suitability of applicants, it is for individual schools to decide what weight to give to financial (or cultural) need and to academic merit. As we shall see in chapter 6, they may decide to recruit the ablest applicants, including those whose financial circumstances are such that they will receive little remission of fees. Or they may set an academic threshold and then give priority to those above it whose 'need' is seen as being greatest or whose presence in the school would do most to extend its social range. In short, how much weight should be given to 'compensating' for social and cultural disadvantage as the school perceives its applicants, and how far should places be treated simply as academic-merit awards to be given to the 'brightest' of those who are financially eligible? We will be exploring these issues in some detail in the following chapters. However, national statistics provide some initial insights into these questions.

DES statistics for individual schools certainly show wide variations in the proportions of pupils holding free places and in the average relevant income of parents. It is impossible to tell of course how far these differences reflect local economic conditions rather than school recruitment policies. Wall (1986), for example, cites a Merseyside girls' school with over 100 applicants for twenty-five assisted places in 1984–5; 95 per cent of those accepted came from maintained schools and a majority of them received full remission of fees. This is in an area of high unemployment, and high levels of long-term unemployment. But DES statistics only partly support expectations of more general regional variations. Schools with particularly high proportions of free-place pupils are geographically scattered, apart from the notable clustering in Liverpool where seven of the ten participating schools in 1986 were well above the national average of 40 per cent. Of the forty-eight schools which had recruited less than 30 per cent of their assisted pupils to free places in the period 1981–6, twenty-five were in London or the south-east. That is the nearest to a clear pattern which is apparent from these limited national statistics.

No decisive regional or other patterns emerge from the figures for average 'relevant' parental income. These show highly erratic differences even between schools in close proximity. Nor is there any general tendency for former direct-grant or LEA schools to recruit a higher proportion of pupils from the least well-off homes. In twelve schools, however, all but one in southern England, the average parental income for 1987 entrants was more than £11,000. In contrast, there were thirty-one schools — mainly ex-direct-grant but geographically scattered — in which the average was less than the free-place qualifying level of £6972. Although there is some tendency for average incomes of assisted-place parents to be higher in the south-east, table 5.10 suggests either significantly different 'catchment areas' within the same broad region or significantly different recruiting policies being followed by different schools.

Although participating schools are able to select pupils for assisted places 'in accordance with such methods and procedures as seem to them appropriate', they are

**Table 5.10 Average 'relevant parental income' of 1987 entrants with assisted places in schools in four regions**

| Region | £9000 + | £8–9000 | £7–8000 | £6–7000 | £5–6000 | Below £5000 |
|---|---|---|---|---|---|---|
| Manchester and Merseyside | 0 | 9 | 8 | 4 | 4 | 1 |
| Avon and Somerset | 4 | 6 | 8 | 0 | 1 | 0 |
| South-east | 16 | 6 | 4 | 13 | 4 | 2 |
| Greater London | 15 | 12 | 13 | 2 | 0 | 0 |

*Source*: DES School-by-School Returns (England).

formally constrained by the requirement that 60 per cent of those accepted should have spent the previous two years in maintained schools. We referred in chapter 3 to arguments within and around the DES about what the appropriate ratio should be when the Scheme's objectives included that of extending access to private education and creating new customers for it. Nationally, the proportion of all assisted-place holders recruited from the public sector has been well above 60 per cent from the start. For the whole 1987 intake it was 67.6 per cent. At 16-plus however, as we noted earlier, the required proportion has been virtually reversed. Until 1987, when the figure rose to 40 per cent, barely a third of new sixth-form recruits to assisted places came from maintained schools, and it is reasonable to argue that 'what the Scheme appears to be doing at 16-plus is to offer a final choice of a subsidised education to a few already in independent schools' (Tapper and Salter, 1986a, p. 324). This has forced many heads to take special care with their 11–13 entry in order to arrive at an acceptable figure overall, since failure to recruit in sufficient numbers from the public sector has been one reason for reducing schools' overall allocations of places. The difficulty many schools experienced in reaching this target, especially those lacking traditional links with the public sector, forced the DES to interpret the rules flexibly in the Scheme's first three years of operation. It is harder to understand the leniency still being shown to five public schools which failed to recruit even half their assisted-place holders from maintained schools over the whole period 1981–7.

We end the chapter by illustrating from DES statistics the very different scale on which individual schools are involved in the Scheme.[19] School A is a Catholic girls' school in northern England. In 1987-8 it had 143 assisted-place pupils of whom 38 per cent held free places and 70 per cent had been recruited from the public sector. Having over-recruited in the early years, it had its quota raised but still filled more than its designated places over the seven years 1981–7. For most of that period the average parental income of its entrants has been among the lowest in the country. School B is a former LEA grammar school in southern England, with 100 per cent take-up of assisted places producing 236 beneficiaries of the Scheme by 1987; 94 per cent of these had been recruited from the public sector and 46 per cent held free places. School C is a boys' public school in the north of England. It offers only sixth-form places. While almost all these have been taken up, there were still only twenty-four pupils with assisted places in 1987 and fewer than half of them had been recruited from maintained schools. School D is a former direct-grant school near London, with a high academic reputation and long practice in recruiting able pupils from a wide area. Over the period 1981–7 it recruited 229 pupils to assisted places. But since this was still an under-recruitment, it had its quota reduced by five in 1984. While it comfortably met its required 60 per cent intake from maintained schools, a very low proportion of free places (16 per cent) is reflected in an average parental income which was over £11,000 for 1987–8. School E, in contrast, is another large former direct-grant grammar school in northern England. It filled all the 175 assisted places available over the period

1981–7, 80 per cent of them from maintained schools and 45 per cent on free places. The average parental income of the 1987 intake was less than half that at School D. School F, a famous public school, offered the minimum of five places at 13 in 1981 and has not raised its offer since. Only five of its twenty-five assisted place pupils in 1987 held free places, and the average parental income for those pupils was close to the limit for fee remission. Finally, school G is a former LEA grammar school in London which recruited strongly from the start, had its quota raised by ten, and had almost 300 pupils with assisted places in 1987 — which was almost half its total roll. Average parental incomes close to the free-place qualifying level suggest something like the target group envisaged by the Scheme's main advocates.

Having limited ourselves in this chapter to generalizations which can be supported or inferred from officially collected statistics, we turn in the next four chapters to the schools from which we collected our own information, and to the evidence which our inquiries produced.

### Notes

1  In the press release announcing that fifty-two more schools had been invited to join the Scheme from September 1989, the 90 per cent A-level pass rate of assisted-place pupils is duly noted. It is surprising that this is not compared with the 70 per cent pass rate which has been one of the criteria used to select 'assisted place schools', because it suggests that such pupils have more than held their own (DES, 7 November 1988; ISIS, 16 December 1988).

2  Direct-grant schools certainly made strenuous efforts to raise money for scholarships, through direct appeals for special trust funds or by such indirect methods as 'levies' on fees.

3  These schools were generally the least academically selective on the direct-grant list, and less selective than most maintained grammar schools. In 1968, 60 per cent of all direct-grant places were free and 28 per cent of pupils paid 'full' fees; in those schools which were no longer independent in 1979, the proportion of free places had been 82 per cent with only 9 per cent paying 'full' fees (Public Schools Commission, 1970, Vol. 2, pp. 3-22).

4  The erratic distribution of direct-grant schools is set out in map form by the Public Schools Commission (1970, Vol. 1, p. 58) and by Bamford (1974, pp. 54-9).

5  These were Hampton Grammar School, Godolphin and Latymer School, Reigate Grammar School, Guildford Royal Grammar School, Colfe's School and Emmanuel School.

6  That generalization about price as evidence of quality is made with confidence in the Speakers' Notes on Independent Schools which the Conservative Independent Schools Committee produced for party candidates in the 1983 election.

7  The late exits were Marlborough, Lancing, Blundell's (Devon), Kimbolton (Herts), Bryanston (Dorset), Dover College, St. Leonard's (Sussex), Tormead (Surrey) and Queen Anne's (Surrey). The last three are girls' schools. The late entrances were Aldenham, Bradfield, Sutton Valence, Charterhouse, St John's Leatherhead, Epsom College, Bedales, Gresham's (Norfolk), St Swithun's Winchester, St Catherine's (Surrey) and Bramley (Surrey). Again, the last three are girls' schools.

8  These include fourteen boarding (or 'mainly-boarding') schools whose heads are members of the Headmasters' Conference. Two of them are boarding schools for girls.

9  As in other tables in this chapter, and following the practice of the Public Schools Commission, the 'boarding' category includes some schools with substantial proportions of day pupils; similarly, the 'day' category includes 'mainly-day' schools.

10  A press report in January 1989 suggested that the 1988 recruitment figures would be disappointing. See Hadfield (1989).

11  Commons Standing Committee on Statutory Instruments, 24 April 1985.

12  The reference to 'confetti' is taken from the *First Report* of the Public Schools Commission (1968) which, as we noted in chapter 2, was insistent that publicly-supported places in public schools had to be sufficient in number to force the schools themselves to change socially and educationally to accommodate them. Allocating a mere five places per school would have been deplored.

13. For example, the average take-up of places in the south and south-east for the seven years 1981-7 was 79.7 per cent; in the north-west over the same period it was 92.7 per cent, while in the south-west it was as high as 97 per cent.

14. Clement Freud, Commons Standing Committee on Statutory Instruments, 24 April 1985.

15. Of the 1665 assisted-place holders who were boarders in 1987, 1105 were receiving some assistance from their schools.

16. Commons Standing Committee on Statutory Instruments, 25 April 1985.

17. The comparative household figure is based on households with one or two adults with one or more children (DES Statistical Summary, April 1988).

18. Both these facts have been noted annually in the ISJC surveys of the Scheme, and in the ISIS press releases which accompany them.

19. We have deliberately chosen to cite schools here that do not figure in the sample of schools in which we carried out the fieldwork reported in subsequent chapters. We have, however, protected their anonymity, as these details are not published in identifiable form by the DES.

Chapter 6

# The Scheme in the Schools

Statistical analysis of the distribution and take-up of places was a necessary check on how far the Scheme, as judged by its own criteria, met the requirements of a national scholarship system intended to bring renewed academic opportunities to able children regardless of where they lived. But the limitations in the evidence being gathered by the Scheme's most obvious monitors, the DES and the private sector itself, made it necessary to go beyond the outlines they provided. As we noted in chapter 1, the impossibility of evaluating the Scheme's progress solely through national statistics presented at a high level of generality had been among the arguments used to support our own research proposal to SSRC. Our application had therefore emphasized the importance of following up the predictions made about its effects by interviewing those involved in or affected by the Scheme once it had got under way. Among other things, this involved focusing down on how the Scheme operated at school level. Only this type of data could help us answer questions about the extent to which the Scheme actually differed from the old direct-grant system, the social and geographical origins of the pupils involved in the Scheme and their similarities and differences to those of full fee payers, and the effects of the Scheme on a school's social and academic character and its relationships with neighbouring schools.

## Gaining access

Crucial to this part of our study was direct access to some of the schools taking part in the Scheme. Negotiating this proved to be one of our major preoccupations, both in the planning of the project and during the first year of its existence. As will become clear in chapter 7, we were concerned to explore not only the Scheme's operation in particular schools but also its impact on participating *and* non-participating schools, parents and pupils. We therefore chose to approach schools in three particular areas of the country rather than use a dispersed national sample, although we complemented these local studies by visiting several boarding schools elsewhere. Two of our main clusters of schools were chosen because they were near our 'home bases' and had a high concentration of schools offering assisted places. The third, which contained many of the schools most actively involved in the Scheme, was chosen because the enthusiastic cooperation of the head of one of them helped facilitate access to others. It was therefore an example of 'opportunity sampling', an approach which is especially common in social research where entry is difficult to negotiate and where 'gate-keepers' and 'sponsors' can exert a decisive influence over what evidence is collected (Burgess, 1984, pp. 32–4).

With a few exceptions, the most significant 'gate-keepers' for independent schools are their headteachers. We therefore sought interviews with individual headteachers and then discussed with those who agreed the extent to which they would assist in other elements of our study. In some cases they seemed very willing to meet us and to allow access to teachers, pupils and parents without any apparent consultation even with their governors. Some virtually 'sponsored' the research by writing letters to parents vouching for the seriousness of the investigation. Many were genuinely interested in what we would find out, the head of one prestigious former direct-grant school assuring us that should rigorously conducted research indicate that the Scheme was not fulfilling its objectives, he would personally feel obliged to abandon his advocacy of it. He was nevertheless confident that our research would provide a vindication of assisted places.

Inevitably, we encountered wariness as well as interest. A few heads of independent schools refused to answer repeated letters, while others expressed a willingness in principle to cooperate but claimed that our request had come at an inappropriate time. Some agreed to be interviewed themselves, but were not prepared for the research to move beyond their own offices. One head responded in a manner totally dismissive of the project, claiming that 'any academic research on the subject will be smothered by opinions which spring from emotional or political inclinations'.[1] This seemed to us, and indeed to some of his colleagues, to reflect an unwarrantably cynical failure to distinguish between research and propaganda; it would seem to deny even an attempt at objectivity to any investigation of controversial events. The doubts sometimes expressed by heads about the possibility of comparing systematically the opportunities offered by different kinds of school were better founded, especially in view of the controversy surrounding contemporary attempts to compare the effectiveness of academically selective and non-selective schools.[2] Yet a thoroughly sceptical stance towards making such comparisons, difficult though they are, seems untenable in relation to the Assisted Places Scheme when one of its explicit objectives is to meet the academic needs of pupils whose talents 'would not' be properly catered for in the maintained schools available to them. A more understandable objection to our request for cooperation stemmed from the fear of some heads that the conduct of the research might draw undue attention to assisted place holders as a category or as individuals, despite assurances that our methods were designed to avoid that outcome.

The response of heads was also influenced by the broader climate of opinion amongst their colleagues. We have already referred to the role of a local 'opinion leader' in gaining us access to one cluster of schools, and we were often aware that heads had made 'checks' on our credentials through their efficient local information networks before meeting us. Individual heads were also sometimes influenced by the stance of their representative organizations. In one case a head who in September 1981 had offered to help 'in any way that we can' wrote again in May 1982, when the Head-masters' Conference was urging caution, to tell us that he was unwilling to discuss the detail of the Scheme in his school because he had always felt that our research was premature.[3] Conversely, when HMC advised members that there was no reason not to cooperate with us, this considerably eased our access to some (though not all) HMC schools. Perhaps the most crucial moment in the entire project was a meeting at the end of its first year at which the project team was invited to meet the Assisted Places Committee of ISJC during one of its regular meetings at Queen Anne's Gate.[4] The 'interrogation' was courteous, but searching, and negotiations with individual schools certainly became easier after it. The national political climate was also a major influence on access. When we began the research the duration of the Scheme was uncertain. But as a likely second Conservative election victory made it seem much less politically precarious, the private sector became noticeably more relaxed about the Scheme being scrutinized.

Even so, it was individual heads who decided whether or not to meet us and how much access to grant. Altogether we interviewed the heads of twenty-five of the schools participating in the Scheme (sometimes alongside their bursars or the heads of their preparatory departments). These interviews usually lasted between one and two hours and included semi-structured and open-ended items. Factual questions about the school were followed by invitations to reflect on its relations with other schools in both sectors, on the selection of pupils, and on the detailed working of the Scheme. In most cases the interview transcripts were sent to the heads as an opportunity for second thoughts if they felt that they had misrepresented their schools or their own views — an opportunity which none of them took, though one commented on how 'turgid' he now thought he had been! Although perceptions of the Scheme amongst independent school heads are one form of evidence about its operation, and we present other perspectives in later chapters, we were repeatedly struck by the strong personal interest of many heads and by the extent to which an individual head's reputation and orien-tation influenced the climate of opinion about assisted places amongst colleagues, pupils and local parents. Heads therefore played a major role in defining the nature of the Scheme in the schools that we visited and in their localities, as we shall see in this chapter and the next.

Schools have been selected for 'assisted place status' on the basis of their high academic standing as indicated by their examination results, the size and range of their sixth-form provision, and their record of admission to higher education. Such schools actually constitute only a small segment of a highly diversified private sector, though it is a common practice to view the whole private sector through the halo provided by its leading exemplars. Yet even that 'elite' segment is itself diverse, despite the tendency of some proponents of the Scheme to characterize the academic quality of the participating schools as though they were all like Manchester Grammar School. In fact, the schools admitted to the Scheme vary considerably in size, character and traditions, and our own sample reflected many of these variations. Those where we interviewed pupils and parents ranged from a school with about 400 pupils to one with well over three times that number, and from schools offering fewer than ten assisted places a year to one offering over fifty. They included boys' schools and girls' schools, some of them with mixed sixth forms; day schools and boarding schools; former direct-grant grammar schools and voluntary-aided schools; and 'great' and more 'minor' public schools. Some took less than 20 per cent of their full intake from the maintained sector, others well over 70 per cent. Some sent about 90 per cent of their leavers on to higher education, others nearer 50 per cent. In view of this range and diversity and of the light control exercised by the DES over the operation of the Scheme, it is difficult to generalize about the way the Scheme is handled at school level. Nevertheless, we attempt here to pull together some of the main features and perceptions of the Scheme in those independent schools that we visited during the course of our study. In accordance with undertakings on confidentiality given to schools when we commenced the research, schools have been allocated pseudonyms which are used in the account which follows. A brief characterization of each school specifically mentioned in the text is given in the Appendix, though some details have had to be changed or omitted in order to preserve anonymity.

### Reasons for Entering the Scheme

The schools' declared reasons for entering the Scheme were largely consistent with its stated aim of helping individual children rather than schools, teachers or even parents. But the subsidiary reasons cited by heads often made reference to its benefits for the community or for the school itself. Most heads claimed that the Scheme was about maintaining, restoring or improving their social mix. In some ex-direct-grant schools it was admitted that there had been a loss of social diversity, not only after the 1976 withdrawal of the direct-grant regulations but rather earlier where LEAs had already begun to withdraw from offering free places. The headmistress of Brampton Girls' School therefore argued that the Scheme was 'simply a reversion to what we knew', while the bursar of Clifton Grammar School (formerly voluntary-aided) also saw it as returning 'part of the way to what we were'. And the head of a former direct-grant school that had functioned very much as a town grammar school commented:

I think we were in danger, we were just hanging on to our traditional market. But it was about to go . . . We saw ourselves as a school to educate the poor but bright boy in the area and we had insufficient resources to do that without being an assisted place school. (Milltown Grammar)

Such references to helping the 'poor but bright' child abounded in our interviews, especially amongst heads who had seen that as their schools' traditional role in the area. A typical justification for entering the Scheme was that it was a way of 'keeping up the inner-city grammar school tradition'. This was often presented as a form of 'service' to the community, through giving a particular type of child the experience of real academic education in a competitive environment as an alternative to being 'swamped by the peer-group pressures' of the neighbourhood comprehensive. This view of the Scheme as an educational rescue mission was, as we saw earlier described by one head as 'plucking embers from the ashes' of educational devastation in the inner cities, a striking metaphor that summarized a common attitude. The head of Sir James's Grammar School, however, hinted at the appeal of the Scheme in terms of institutional self-interest, as well as missionary zeal, when he admitted:

It gives us a quieter conscience, if you like. We feel we're helping more people and our ideals. I suppose it does give us some benefit in that there are some able boys who come here who wouldn't otherwise.

Nevertheless, few heads conceded the argument of critics that they had actually entered the Scheme to help them attract academic high-fliers and thus enhance their competitive edge. Ex-direct-grant school heads were particularly quick to quote statistics that showed that their O-level and A-level results had actually improved in the first non-direct-grant entry to pass through the school. However, the more candid admitted that they had not known this at the time of applying to enter the Scheme, when they had certainly had some worries about falling standards of entry. At Sir James's, the head admitted to a concern that the end of the direct grant had 'extended the bottom end of the ability range', while another head initially denied that the academic calibre of his intake was a consideration in entering the Scheme and then revealed some concern with it when drawing attention to the social value of the Scheme in helping those of modest means to enter the school:

When you look down the list [in order of academic merit] of the years when there was no assistance, it's easy to see the number of people that passed high and didn't come here . . . When there was any money to give [from a trust fund], that went to the first two or three and they came and then you get the list of those who didn't come — and now they do [come here on assisted places]. (Milltown Grammar)

For the traditionally independent schools, the argument was more that the

Scheme could help them to take in pupils from backgrounds which were different from those of their normal intakes. While this enabled the fortunate individuals to benefit from the style of education on offer, it was also felt to be good for the school itself to have a wider social mix. This was seen in turn to benefit the more traditional clientele, an argument that the matron of one highly prestigious public school put in the following graphic terms:

> It's good for them to realise that not everyone has three cars and two houses ... It's the old thing of the nobility freshening their blood by marrying pretty shop girls. I think it's the same principle really. Introducing fresh blood into the school. (Cathedral College)

For another major public boarding school, Bankside College, part of the reason for applying to join the Scheme was not only service to the community and the school, but also service to the Scheme itself. Its headmaster 'felt that for the Scheme to be shown to be important at a school of [this one's] status and prestige' would help to give it legitimacy, and it was felt to be incumbent on the school to offer at least a few places even if the DES decided not to take them up. For other boarding schools, however, the motives were less lofty. One had decided to join the Scheme because it felt it was losing pupils to a rival establishment, while the head of another which had been receiving barely more applications than it had places admitted frankly that:

> I think it was seen [by the governors] as something that might help a lot in our situation, with numbers — it being fairly hand to mouth ... (Weston School)

### Administering and Publicizing the Scheme

The purpose of the Scheme, as defined in the legislation which established it, is to enable 'pupils who might not otherwise be able to do so to benefit from education at independent schools'. Its target is intended to be 'academically able children whose parents cannot afford full fees',[5] and eligibility in terms of parental income is defined by an annually revised national income scale. Within very broad limits, it is up to individual schools to decide precisely how to recruit pupils under the Scheme. As reported in chapter 3, this had been regarded as essential by representatives of the independent schools during the negotiations of 1979–80, and it was agreed to very promptly by the DES. Some heads were highly appreciative of the loose rein upon which the Scheme was run by the DES. As the head of Nortown Grammar commented,

> They're remarkably decent ... saying 'here's the money, just tell us who you're giving it to and we'll take your word for it that they're up to standard'.

In most cases, admissions under the Scheme were incorporated into the schools' existing admissions mechanisms, often without those involved knowing whether a pupil was applying for an assisted place until after the academic selection had taken place. In any case, it was usually the school bursars who dealt with the financial paperwork and, in the case of certain foundation and trust schools, this was actually done away from the school itself. For those schools which had been part of the direct-grant system, the administration of the Scheme seemed entirely straightforward, even undemanding. As the head of Brampton Girls' School remarked: 'It's not an onerous task. It's really continuing largely what we've done before anyway.' Many such schools chose to adopt the assisted-place income scales as a basis for assessing entitlement to their own bursaries. There were others, however, including some traditionally independent schools with experience of offering free places or means-tested bursaries, which were more critical of the bureaucratic demands of the Scheme. In the view of the bursar of Cranmer School:

> It isn't a straightforward assessment by any means — much more time-consuming than our own schemes.

A few smaller independent schools without any tradition of means-tested awards regarded the administration of the Scheme as quite unnecessarily irksome. Even with a small number of places, the head of St Wilfred's High School reported that 'the workload has proved more than we expected', and similar comments were made elsewhere. When we put this point to the head of Nortown Grammar, a school with a large number of assisted places and a long previous tradition of 'free places', he remarked dismissively that the work 'could all be done in an afternoon!'. Nevertheless, the problems encountered by the less experienced schools were reflected in the nature and tardiness of their annual AP10 returns to the DES, though it is fair to add that the bursars of most schools were themselves critical of the DES's own tardiness in sending them information about the annually updated income scales.

There were heads who felt that certain elements of schools' autonomy in administering the Scheme were counter-productive. Some argued that time was wasted processing the applications of pupils who had been entered for a large number of schools in the same area, and that this sometimes led to places being left unfilled. The idea of group decisions or even of a common application form for the Scheme asking parents to express preferences between schools was rejected because other heads regarded it as a 'restrictive practice' which would interfere with parental choice. However, schools in some areas effectively forced parents into early choices anyway by agreeing common application dates, examination dates and decision dates. A few schools also cooperated by agreeing on common marking standards, thus preventing any academic 'undercutting'. In the early days of the Scheme it seemed to the head of Clifton Grammar School that a few parents were playing the market by 'shopping around and waiting for the best offer in terms of fee remission' — a practice rejected as contrary to a Scheme based on a common income scale and common regulations. It was perhaps understandable that bursars made different assessments on the basis of parents' initial AP1 applications for an assisted place, but the more detailed final AP2 form should not have produced such discrepancies. Some bursars therefore got on the phone to colleagues, to discuss the financial eligibility of pupils who had applied to more than one school, before making their offers. Despite such local arrangements, however, the way the Scheme is administered has remained primarily in the hands of the individual schools. This autonomy allows a measure of head-hunting, as we found in one family where a very able boy had been tempted (unsuccessfully) away from a place he had accepted at Milltown Grammar by an offer elsewhere of a school bursary on top of his assisted place.

However it chose to tackle these matters, the first task for a school which had entered the Scheme was to make its existence known to prospective candidates for admission. Virtually all schools included references to the Scheme in press advertisements for their entrance examinations and in the prospectuses and publicity material they sent out to parents. In many cases these references were relatively discreet, but a few schools marketed the Scheme much more aggressively. One head claimed that his school had spent £2000 on special advertisements proclaiming 'There's a free place waiting for your son at . . . ', comparing that sum to the £60 it normally spent on advertising its entrance examination. Some heads publicized the Scheme by appearing, either individually or in conjunction with other local heads, on local radio, in some cases as part of the station's news or public service output and in others through buying commercial advertising slots.

Few heads were happy that their own advertising was entirely successful or cost effective and some felt that more should be done nationally by the DES. However, a deputation to Sir Keith Joseph had failed to produce any money for this. Some local groups of schools joined together to place group advertisements and most schools took part in regional ISIS promotions of the sector, which also gave publicity to the Scheme. Some schools initiated, and all probably benefited from, a series of news stories and features in local and national newspapers about the attractions of the Scheme both generally and in terms of individual 'success stories'.[6] The overall need to advertise to attract applicants diminished as the Scheme became better known, though advertising was still considered important by particular schools and for particular target groups. When it began, many schools used only conventional means of recruitment because they had no experience of anything else. Others deliberately tried new strategies, such as distributing handbills to local filling stations and take-aways. We found some evidence of increasing sophistication in marketing as time went on. In at least one case a change was inadvertently triggered by a member of the research team when a school secretary had expressed puzzlement at the lack of assisted-place applicants in response to advertisements placed in the school's usual quality-press advertising outlet. As a result of that conversation, which touched on issues such as the income-levels of the readers of that paper in that area, the school advertised the following year in more local and down-market media. During our interview with the head of Milltown High School, she spoke of her growing sense of obligation to try harder to reach a group that the Scheme was not yet attracting:

> I mean I have been toying with the idea, although like a coward I have crept back from it, I think perhaps I had better go on local radio . . . They tell me that a lot of the parents that perhaps ought to know about this Scheme are the sort that put on Radio [BBC local station] or Radio [local commercial station] from six o'clock in the morning, and that's where I ought to go.

On yet another occasion, advice was actively sought from us by the head of school about how to interest members of the local black community in the Scheme, again providing evidence of a will to attract a new clientele but little practical conception of how to go about it.

In terms of the overall market, though, people progressively got to know about the Scheme through word of mouth, and although few schools seemed to keep records of the source of enquiries, one that did found that less than 10 per cent of enquiries originated in press advertisements. Far more effective was what the head of Stoneyford High School called the 'parental bush telegraph'. Increasingly, recommendations also came through primary school teachers. When we first wrote to all the primary heads in one of our study areas, at a time when recruitment of the first cohort of assisted-place pupils had already taken place, a significant minority of them had not heard of the Scheme or confused it with earlier LEA-funded 'free places'. A year later the Scheme was much more clearly understood, and within two years there was some evidence that it had been accepted by primary heads as a normal feature of the educational land-scape.[7] Most schools sent out information about the Scheme to their local primary schools and some had regular meetings with local heads. Nevertheless, few of the schools circulated all local primary schools and many of them only contacted schools that had sent pupils to them in the past. Even though this sometimes amounted to about fifty primary schools (and in a few cases up to 100), it was a somewhat odd strategy to use in support of a Scheme designed to produce new clientele. However, those schools that tried for blanket coverage found some areas 'which we are just not getting through to any more', guessed at certain schools where their letters just ended up in the wastepaper bin, and recognized that there were primary heads who actively dissuaded pupils from applying to them because of their own belief in the state system.

A few heads of participating schools reported particularly enthusiastic cooperation from primary headteachers even if it sometimes had to be given in such a way as to avoid the wrath of antagonistic local authorities. Recalling the occasional unauthorized message about a promising pupil, the head of Sir James's Grammar School described how:

> Some primary heads send us reports irrespective of any ban, others politely
> tell us they're unable to meet our request — some add that they wish they
> could.

Many heads told us that their primary colleagues were 'very helpful over the phone,
but not on paper' and the head of Brampton Girls' remarked sympathetically: 'Who
can blame them, poor things, the difficulties they have to face.' Overall, independent
school heads seemed to agree with Bob Dunn's claim to a parliamentary standing
committee in 1985 that 'many maintained school headteachers, whatever their initial
reservations about the Scheme, are now prepared positively to encourage the
individual pupil who could benefit from it to apply for an assisted place'.[8] This is an
impression also reported by Wilkinson (1986) and in the annual ISIS surveys of the
Scheme's operation, though, as we shall see in chapter 7, some secondary heads in the
maintained sector were extremely bitter about what they regarded as 'talent spotting'
by their primary colleagues on behalf of the private sector. Surprisingly, though, in
view of the arguments about reaching a new clientele, only one independent school
head was prepared to say that the Assisted Places Scheme had definitely increased the
number of applications to her school, while the others said either that it appeared not
to have to done so or that its effects could not be distinguished from other factors that
had led to an increase in demand for private education.

### Allocating the places

The extent to which schools relied on advertising or outsiders to assist in recruitment
was partly related to their traditions and to the spirit in which they had entered the
Scheme. The same was true of the ways in which they administered the Scheme and
selected pupils for it. For some schools the Scheme was in practice a means of offering
assistance to traditional applicants whose parents or grandparents had hitherto had to
make 'unwarranted sacrifices' to purchase independent education for their children. In
these schools, parents it was thought might qualify for assistance under the Scheme
had it drawn to their attention at the time of their application for a fully fee-paid place
or when a place was offered. In some cases the parents of children already in the school
who might qualify were also approached. As we saw in chapter 5, this was a particularly common strategy in the case of sixth-form places, where there were often
insufficient outside applicants for the places available even after the LEAs' right of veto
was removed and where the result has been a preponderance of internal recruitment.
However, in offering places to pupils already in the system, schools had to limit this to
years in which there were already assisted-place holders and to bear in mind the
required ratio of those from a maintained school background. Even so, some schools
have consistently failed to conform to this requirement even as liberally interpreted by

the DES.[9] Most accepted that they ought to try to achieve the 60:40 ratio in favour of maintained school entrants. But the head of Nortown High School argued twice during our interview that it ought to be changed to permit more eligible pupils already in the independent sector to benefit, the head of Dame Margaret's High School regarded it as 'unfair to the preparatory schools', and the head of Cranmer School wondered

> ... whether it's actually necessary bearing in mind the means test ... It seems to me not to matter a hoot from what kind of school they come — it isn't about schools, it's about children — and providing there is a stringent means test (which there is) I'm not quite sure, apart from political considerations, why we need to keep this.

As we have seen already, however, many heads entered the Scheme as a way of attracting new categories of pupils into their schools beyond those already in them or those from outside who would have applied to the school without even the possible benefits of an assisted place. While recognizing that there were pupils already in their own schools or elsewhere in the independent sector who might need help, some heads felt uneasy about using the Assisted Places Scheme for this purpose. In these schools, ensuring that at least 60 per cent of the intake came from the maintained sector was as much a matter of principle as of avoiding an annual letter of rebuke from the DES. Some of them actually managed to keep the percentage well over 80 per cent and this included a few schools where this was not typical of its entry as a whole. It proved easier to maintain the balance at 11-plus and even those schools most committed to taking entrants from the maintained sector experienced great difficulty in filling, let alone achieving the appropriate balance within, any 13-plus and 16-plus entries they had been allocated. They were therefore relieved when the DES agreed that the calculation should be based on the total entry under the Scheme.

Some schools had difficulty in awarding the total number of places allocated to them. As we indicated in chapter 5, this was particularly though not exclusively true of boarding schools, and of girls' day schools in certain parts of the country. Because demand was less than the number of places available, these schools were able to offer assisted places to all those applying for them who passed over the threshold of the normal entrance examination provided the outcome was roughly in line with the 60:40 ratio. Choosing between qualified applicants was not therefore an issue. As the head of Stoneyford High School remarked:

> If we had more than thirty-five qualified for admission, then we'd just work an ability preference. But so far, I've not had to.

Responding to a similarly hypothetical question, the head of Smythe School said that if she had to sift through more than forty eligible applicants:

> I don't know what I'd do, but I think after that I would probably give the Assisted Place to the parent who was most in need.

There were many other schools in our sample, particularly the boys' grammar schools, that had already had to make this kind of choice between offering assistance according to academic merit or balancing merit against financial need. We have already seen in chapter 3 that flexibility on this issue had been regarded as essential by representatives of the independent schools when the details of the Scheme were being drafted. As a result, when the Scheme was implemented, there were wide disparities between the practices adopted by different schools. Some schools used the order of merit to offer assisted places to all who had applied for them up to the maximum number of such places available. In these cases no account was taken of the amount of assistance each child would get, and in some cases no attempt was made to calculate this in advance of the offer. Sometimes, though, the strict order of merit had to be varied in order to ensure that at least 60 per cent of assisted-place holders were from the maintained sector. Other schools felt that they should offer assisted places to those most in need and therefore offered places to those passing the entrance procedures who would qualify for maximum fee remission under the Scheme. This meant that some pupils higher in the order of merit were not offered assisted places because the level of assistance they needed was small.

Because, unlike its Scottish equivalent and unlike some schools' own bursary funds, the Scheme is not cash-limited, it made sense to some heads to take this course of action in order to get as much out of the Scheme for parents as was possible. This strategy was cited in interviews as evidence that schools were responding to social need and also to show that they were not necessarily creaming-off the academically most able via the Scheme. However, heads who operated a different system pointed out that it could equally well be seen as a way of maximizing entry, since those higher up the order of merit but needing less assistance would probably come to the school anyway, whereas this was less likely to be true of those who qualified for maximum fee remission. Also, it was said, some schools used their own limited bursary funds to help those needing limited assistance and concentrated assisted places on the most needy. To many heads, though, this was entirely consistent with the spirit of the Scheme. The headmistress of Oaklands High School seemed convinced that:

> As the Assisted Places Scheme is intended to help those most in need, it seems to be the only principled way of doing it.

Furthermore, the headmaster of nearby Nortown Grammar, while acknowledging that there were other acceptable ways of proceeding, shared the view expressed by Lady Young while the Scheme was being planned[10] that the greater the number of pupils on maximum fee remission the more legitimate the Scheme would appear in political terms. As far as his school was concerned, they

. . . wanted to be able to say 'This is what the Scheme was intended to do and, look, every assisted place, or nearly every assisted place, has gone to someone who warrants maximum remission of fees'.

Nevertheless, it was recognized that political realism could also be used to justify the opposite approach. Some heads, and more particularly bursars without large foundation or appeal funds to draw on, were wary about the potential plight of a school with many pupils on maximum fee remission in a situation where the Scheme was terminated at a stroke in the manner threatened by the Labour Party. It was felt that parents receiving limited help would probably find ways of keeping their children in the school, but those receiving high levels of assistance would either have to leave or be dependent on the school itself for assistance. One headmaster confessed that his governors had discussed the idea of giving assisted places only to those needing limited fee remission but had eventually rejected it, while another claimed that a school 'not too far from here' had actually adopted that strategy. A headmistress in another area was candid enough to say that she hoped that the school's financial position did not enter into her decisions about whom to give places to, but she was aware that it might be colouring her judgment. In practice most schools in our sample found that 35–55 per cent of their assisted-place pupils received full fee remission, though we pointed at the end of chapter 5 to some significant differences in this percentage and in the average parental earnings of assisted-place holders between different schools across the country as a whole.

The treatment of schools' own bursary funds after the advent of the Assisted Places Scheme varied quite considerably amongst the schools that we visited. A few schools had suspended their own schemes entirely, leaving the capital to accrue interest for future contingencies. Some boarding schools were using bursary funds to help assisted-place holders with boarding fees. Other schools had substituted assisted places for bursaries at the point of entry and were now using the bursary fund purely to help pupils already in the school. Still others were operating both systems side by side, sometimes for different levels of need as described earlier, with those needing maximum assistance being given assisted places. But whatever strategy they adopted, most schools were very much aware in the early days that they needed to conserve at least some of their own funds in case the Scheme was abruptly terminated and the school had to bail out pupils in need. One bursar said he would only abandon this caution if the Scheme went on 'for another government, another two governments possibly', though his head felt ready to take the risk after only one. Some schools have anyway found the Assisted Places Scheme sufficient to meet their needs and are continuing to hold their bursary funds in abeyance 'for a rainy day'.

How assisted places were awarded was often related to the stance a school took on the measurement of academic ability. Most schools used a combination of mathematics, English and Verbal Reasoning tests to produce an order of merit and made a further selection on the basis of interview. Especially in the boys' grammar schools like Clifton, there was some evidence that assisted-place holders were 'significantly above the cut-off point for other candidates' in the order of merit, though that did not mean that they were by any means alone at the top end. The head of Stoneyford High, a former voluntary-aided girls' school, also told us that half her assisted-place pupils were 'very able' and thus 'helped the school'. At other girls' schools and at many boarding schools, though, assisted-place holders tended to be lower down the list:

> No assisted place girl is of outstanding ability or a 'gifted child'. Some are academically sound though. (Nortown High)

> Places . . . appeared to have been able to spread quite a long way down our intake list and I can only assume from that that a fair number of girls in the upper and middle ranges of our intake were too wealthy to qualify. (Oaklands High)

In some schools, the question then arose of whether assisted places should be awarded to any pupils who were further down the order of merit than other applicants. Some heads regarded it as a matter of principle that there should be absolutely no difference between the academic criteria used to select assisted-place holders and those used for other entrants. In such schools the same academic cut-off point seemed to have been used for full fee-payers, assisted-place holders and other award holders, except for scholarships explicitly linked to academic merit. Even though, as a result of this policy, he had just failed to allocate all his assisted places in each of the first two years of the Scheme, the head of one of the few boys' day schools not to reach its target justified his action in these terms:

> Even though I haven't filled the places, I haven't dropped standards. Had I filled them all in the situation I'm in, I would have been having two standards. So I had the same academic standards. I think this is very important, because one would not be being fair to fee-paying parents if I was taking in assisted place pupils below the level of the last fee payer. (Forsyth School)

While largely sticking to their normal definitions of academic merit, some schools did make special allowances for the educational background of the applicants. Some took into account the fact that children from maintained primary schools were less likely to have been specifically coached for entrance than those from preparatory schools. For 11-plus entrants, this meant making an adjustment of a few marks on the entrance tests, while those few schools with a 13-plus intake from outside the independent sector did not generally find the Common Entrance system appropriate for these candidates and preferred to use other methods of assessment. One such head said:

> Some assisted-place holders are behind in certain subjects when they come in, but they'll be fine in the end. (Cranmer School)

A few heads made more subjective adjustments based on their reading of the influence of a child's social background. Thus, for example, one told us:

> What we are prepared to do is give some benefit of the doubt to an assisted place candidate academically. He's got to be, we reckon, capable of coping, but, because we are very often comparing him with the kind of rather thrusting professional parents or the child of such parents, I think we are often prepared to say 'well, his marks are a bit lower than we would have liked to have taken, but because he is clearly a deserving case, we're willing to give him a place'. But, generally, they've got to get in on academic merit. (Christchurch)

This approach was not necessarily inconsistent with normal entry practices, since some schools always make subjective judgments on whom to take within a broad band below those who self-evidently qualified as academically outstanding.

A few schools, though, used the social need argument to go further down the order of merit to offer assisted places than they did to offer other places. Nevertheless, as Wall (1986) also reports in her study of London GPDST schools, heads sympathetic to such arguments still found themselves having to reject financially eligible pupils on academic grounds, even at the expense of leaving places unfilled. However, one head apparently felt that she had to fill her assisted places, come what may, rather than take more highly qualified fee-payers. As a result, far from enhancing the academic quality of her intake, her view was that the Scheme was actually depressing it:

> The trend has been that they are disappointing. We have a few able girls, but I think they probably would have come anyway and the general level has been below the level of our fee-payers, so the school is actually suffering by having to take these children. (St Wilfred's High School)

This does appear to be the exception and it is, of course, based on a misconception about the Scheme. Indeed, another head told us that he thought this was about the only practice that was contrary to the spirit of the Scheme and one that might eventually lead to trouble with the DES. Most schools have preferred not to allocate assisted places than take academically questionable pupils and the Scheme places no absolute obligation on schools to fill them. Yet in this particular school the head felt obliged to take pupils who, in some undefined sense, had reached a 'minimum standard', even though her normal cut-off point of a Verbal Reasoning score of about 110 was itself significantly lower than that of most other schools we visited.

Within the sector as a whole, though, the general view was that there was little clear difference in academic quality between assisted place and other entrants and that they certainly did not constitute the academic elite of the schools. The range of practices that produced this overall effect was seen by one of its leading advocates amongst the heads of entirely consistent with the spirit of the Scheme:

As long as you're not admitting them below the level at which you admit your other pupils, then I don't think it's a matter of concern to the Government whether you give an AP to the chap who comes first or who comes bottom of your entry list, as long as you're not fudging the list dramatically to give an assisted place. (Nortown Grammar)

## Financial Eligibility and Class Background

However they allocated the places, most heads seemed satisfied that the Scheme was reaching its target in academic terms. They also felt it was largely, though not exclusively, reaching its target in financial terms and that it had gone some way towards attracting pupils from socially disadvantaged backgrounds who would not otherwise have attended their schools. A few heads said that they occasionally adopted various forms of positive or negative discrimination to select particular sorts of pupils on other than financial or academic grounds. Even within a Scheme quintessentially 'meritocratic' in conception, there was some appreciation of the sociological argument that 'what schools define as merit is principally the advantage of having literate parents, books in the home, the opportunity to travel, etc.' (Reimer, 1971, pp. 29–30). As a result, some preference might be given to pupils from home circumstances that they regarded as putting the child at a disadvantage, the most common example being children from one-parent families. The head of Brampton had taken an Asian girl on her 'own say so' without consulting the staff or even putting her through the normal entrance examination. But we also encountered some concern about taking too many children from backgrounds substantially different from that of the majority of pupils for fear of their 'not fitting in' and upsetting the social 'character' of her intake. The head of Dame Margaret's reported that she had 'turned away some whom I might have taken if they'd given more indication that they would fit in', and this seemed largely to do with their willingness to participate in the school's extra-curricular activities.

Not all heads were prepared to discuss the character of their assisted-place intake in social class terms, one stating that he was 'colour-blind as far as class is concerned'. Most seemed to acknowledge, however, that the rhetoric initially used to justify the Scheme, and which we explored in earlier chapters, meant that at least one of the tests of its success ought to be its ability to attract working-class or 'inner-city' pupils. We return to this issue in chapter 8. Perhaps the major reservation about its success in these terms, as it emerged during our interviews with heads and other senior staff, was about the role of the self-employed within the Scheme. Indeed, many heads had severe doubts about the eligibility of some of the children of the self-employed. One went so far as to say that she would always offer a place to the daughter of someone with a verifiable income, like a teacher or a policeman, in preference to the child of someone who was self-employed. Another headmistress told us quite categorically that 'the self-employed are not honest'. Yet another, while accepting that few of the self-employed were actually 'cooking the books', felt that too many of them benefited from the services of 'clever accountants' — a view which was echoed by the bursar of the neighbouring boys' school.

Although we did not encounter examples of bursars 'snooping' on the homes of assisted-place applicants, as has been reported in the press,[11] a few heads had backed their 'hunches' about parents' real need for assistance. These heads felt that they could spot abuses, one of them suggesting that her bursar was 'well used to doing that, of course, from the old days' and that she herself took a hard line with some parents:

> The hairdressers, the ones who send their children to prep schools and then send them here and say their income is £3000 or £4000, and you know it's not. Well, we don't offer a place. We say she can have a full fee place but not an assisted place. (Brampton School)

Parents who paid the balance of a child's fees in cash aroused obvious suspicion. And while some of the views we recorded undoubtedly reflected a measure of cultural disdain towards people in certain self-employed occupations, they also reflected a concern that the Scheme might be brought into ill-repute if people with too ostentatious life styles were seen to benefit from it. Many had particular examples or worries to quote:

> Some of the occupations given by the parents worry me a lot . . . The solicitor surprises me and, I mean, the widowed mothers are probably all right, I don't know, they all seem to dress so well . . . (St. Hilda's)

> You see a man driving a Rover three and a half who is extremely well-dressed for an Assisted Place . . . It's unbelievable. (Clifton Grammar)

> One of ours waited until it was all signed and sealed and then they all went off to Australia for a holiday. And he is paying nothing. (Dame Margaret's)

However, even though suspicion and unease about the declared income of the self-employed was very widespread, most schools took the view that there was little they could do except feel 'irritated'. The bursar of one school felt moved to contact the DES about the issue but was told there was nothing they could do either. The general view was therefore that, whatever the rights and wrongs of the situation, it was up to the Inland Revenue rather than independent school bursars to deal with abuses:

> One can only check up so far and I think that if you talked to bursars you would find the vast majority of them feel that justice is not being done for some people . . . But in practice it's impossible for the school to probe about this. We're not tax inspectors. (Clifton Grammar)

Much the same sense of resignation accompanied equally 'aggravating' suspicions about the real family income of some 'single-parents' who were benefiting from the Scheme at the same time as receiving considerable support either from the other parent or from another co-habiting partner.

Such reservations apart, most heads were reasonably happy that their own schools were reaching the Scheme's intended targets. Typical responses to questions about the backgrounds of assisted-place holders referred to the 'quite noticeable number of manual working-class parents among assisted-place holders on parents' evenings' (Brampton), or to 'the majority of boys that we have taken on assisted places' being describable as working class (Christchurch School). Little evidence was offered in support of such impressions. Where it was, the impressions were sometimes contradicted. Christchurch, for example, had twenty-one assisted places available each year, of which five were allocated at 13 or 16 years of age. Its head felt that these should be disregarded in the calculation and then went on to say:

> So, we're talking about sixteen places at 11, but not all those places go to children in maintained schools to start with, so we're talking about a dozen children. And I am saying that my impression is that you wouldn't have any doubts that six or seven of those were genuinely working class.

Even that rather curious arithmetic barely produced a working-class majority among those admitted under the Scheme. Other heads offered us lists or examples of parental occupations for assisted-place pupils, sometimes from the actual returns but more often from memory. Sometimes these were full lists, delivered with a grimace or a comment when coming upon unlikely occupations. A typical list, provided by the head of Cranmer School, was:

> Postman, one or two that are unemployed, there's usually a single-parent family, wine trade, teacher, pastor (not quite sure what that means), pharmacist, musician, secretary, housewife, graphic design work, banker...hmm...I also have a vegetable wholesaler — that could be fabulously wealthy, but in fact he's actually running a small little shop and he is a nil contribution...

Other lists consisted of parents with unambiguously working-class occupations, reminiscent of those offered in ISIS and DES publicity and in press stories about the Scheme, and often similarly designed to refute popular criticisms of the Scheme:

> We have a town hall cleaner, we have dinner ladies, post office workers, that sort of thing. They are not all single-parent families who are poor because they are divorced. (Brampton)

> I don't think you'd find a postal worker or a herdsman sending their sons here if they hadn't got an assisted place. (Weston)

We have a laundry delivery driver who said to me 'I've driven my van past [your school] for years and always said — ha, ha, if only I could get my little lad in there'. And he has done. (Christchurch)

A few heads admitted that they had not really attracted the core target group in the first couple of years of the Scheme, but were now beginning to get applicants who might enable them to do so. As the head of Milltown Grammar commented in the interview:

I'm trying to decide who will get the last five assisted places this year, and it's awful trying to weigh one up against the other . . . but the occupations we are talking about are . . . we've got a lorry driver, a British Rail guard, window cleaner, school meals assistant — that's a single parent family — van driver, textile worker, unemployed, and two of these boys are actually . . . both sons of first generation Pakistani immigrants who work in textile firms as operatives. So overwhelmingly our application this time is certainly bringing in poor children from inner cities.

Like the authors of the ISIS annual surveys, heads seemed particularly fond of quoting lorry drivers' children as examples of the Scheme's egalitarian character! But as we shall show in the next chapter, such occupations appeared infrequently in our own sample of assisted-place pupils. They were also infrequent in the full lists of place holders provided by some of the schools. It remains to be seen whether a significantly different picture will show up in national statistics in future years.[12]

Some heads took a view closer to that argued by government ministers and based their claims to success on the fact that, whether or not the Scheme was reaching working-class or 'inner-city' pupils, it was certainly helping families with very limited means — especially the unemployed, single parents by divorce or widowhood, and those in middle-range white-collar occupations. Even those sceptical about certain other categories of beneficiary were very ready to acknowledge the special difficulties of single parents. There was also considerable concern that some worthy applicants were being excluded by the nature of the income scale. London schools in particular felt that candidates who ought to qualify were losing out because of the higher level of gross salaries in the south-east and that the basis of income assessment should be changed to disposable income to take account of the heavy mortgage commitments of many families. The head of Smythe School, a school which has had persistent difficulty in filling all its assisted places, explained the problem in this way:

A friend of mine who's got assisted places in Liverpool tells me that they can fill them without any difficulty. And people here who appear to be relatively affluent in terms of the Assisted Places Scheme, because of the price of housing and so on in this district, don't feel as rich as the Assisted Places Scheme think they are. It's the high cost of housing that cripples people around here.

Another common, though by no means universal, theme in our interviews was the plight of white-collar workers with a number of children who were felt to be disadvantaged by the operation of the scale. Many heads complained that there was 'too steep a cut-off' on the scale, a point which (as we noted in chapter 3) had been argued by Stuart Sexton and some representatives of the independent schools at the time of the Scheme's inception. This could also affect pupils already in the schools when such parents received even modest pay increases. The head of Brampton told us the distressing story of a university lecturer who was going to have to withdraw his daughter from her school

> because they've gone off the scale. And he came to see me and he was desperate about it, but they have three little ones and he's paying a mortgage. You know what university promotion prospects are . . . and he said 'this £1,000 a year rise is family income that I must spread amongst the babes as well as this bright elder girl'. And so I'm afraid I am going to lose a very bright girl.

Nevertheless, some concern was also expressed by heads that those with particular cultural resources were benefiting at the expense of others, a view that echoed the comment of Tapper and Salter (1986a, p. 327) that the Scheme had provided 'real financial assistance to relatively impoverished but educationally aware members of the petite bourgeoisie'. These heads were not entirely convinced by the official claims, noted in the last chapter, that the high level of fee remission meant that the Scheme was reaching its target:

> [It attracts] generally people who sort of made their own way to a certain extent . . . who want something better for their children and who have learnt to push a bit in business. You see I think the people that we're missing out on completely are those who allow themselves to be buffeted by everything and everybody in life, are told 'you do this, you do that' and, if it's not employers, it's their unions . . . (Dame Margaret's)

> I think our impression is that they are the kinds of people for whom the Scheme was intended. The only qualification I would make is that you do get certain categories of people who are in a sense well-positioned to know about something like the Assisted Places Scheme. I am thinking of single-parent middle-class families, right? That's one category. And teachers and clergy, you know, I mean, they spring to mind. And immigrants . . . There's no doubt that the local Indian community has got on to it. (Christchurch)

It will be clear from the evidence we present in chapters 8 and 9 that most of these groups, described by one head as a 'kind of ambiguous category . . . with, if you like, culturally middle-class standards', were indeed well-represented or even over-represented within the Scheme. However, although a few other heads also made the point about considerable interest from the Asian community, we ourselves found no evidence that many pupils from that background had actually entered the schools under the Scheme. The particular head who had made the remark about 'immigrants' quoted here skilfully avoided a question about how many such children were actually admitted, while the head of Stoneyford remarked revealingly that the Asian community was 'very, very keen. Lots and lots of applications and *some* are very successful' (her emphasis). In another part of the country, one headmistress told us that she was resisting 'blackmail' from a primary head who wanted her to take an Asian pupil on an assisted place, because her school did not need to exercise positive discrimination as it already had a proud record of taking Asian pupils even though they were mainly from the families of doctors or lawyers. If the evidence about the number of pupils of Asian origin participating in the Scheme was ambiguous, both the heads' comments and our own evidence agreed that the Scheme had had very little impact at all amongst the Afro-Caribbean community at the time of our interviews.

### Assisted Pupils in the Schools

Whatever their backgrounds, once the assisted-place holders were in the school, most heads were concerned to protect their anonymity and treat them in exactly the same way as other pupils. In some schools, no mention of the assisted place was made on files available to staff and only the head, the bursar and perhaps the head of lower school knew the identity of assisted-place holders. Free meals and grants for incidentals were also treated discreetly. In some cases the form tutors knew the identity of assisted-place pupils, and in others there was some indication given to staff that certain pupils, including assisted-place pupils, might need financial assistance for field trips and the like.

It therefore proved very difficult to get any view of how assisted-place pupils were faring in their schools and what impact, if any, their presence was actually having. Some clues were certainly gathered from the pupil interviews which we report in later chapters. As far as the heads were concerned they had mainly fitted in well. Especially in schools where participation in the Scheme was seen as a way of maintaining their existing clientele, they were 'invisible' in the sense of being indistinguishable from other pupils in every respect except their possession of an assisted place. In most schools in our sample, they were also present in sufficiently large numbers not to be isolated even if their distinguishing characteristic was known; and some of these schools had substantial numbers of other pupils receiving various forms of assistance. In Nortown Grammar, for example, the fact that other pupils also needed financial assistance was quoted by the head as part of the reason for not undertaking any special monitoring of the assisted-place holders:

> We've never monitored a particular category. And an analysis of the AP pupils here is in one sense artificial because really if you want to identify a group it's all those who get help to come here because they couldn't afford it ... But would you expect the AP pupils to be at the top end in attainment? As we don't stream ... every boy coming in is potentially a university entrant.

In schools with only a small number of assisted-place holders in a large intake, most heads were also optimistic that they had fitted in, though at least one head felt that 'social and personal' integration had been easy and that it was academic integration which had 'taken time'. By and large, they felt that they had avoided stigmatizing assisted-place holders as 'guinea pigs', a traditional fear that Carlisle had identified as applying with particular force to boarding pupils.[13] Nevertheless, comments from boarding school heads that 'it has brought us some interesting characters' (Weston) and 'they're the salt of the earth and they're doing jolly well' (Cranmer) suggest that assisted-place holders were actually far from socially 'invisible' in these settings and that they were even perceived as somewhat exotic. In some cases this was welcomed since, as we have seen, some of these schools had entered the Scheme to change the social mix of their intakes. In general, the numbers involved were thought to be too small to have a significant influence on the character of the schools, though the head of one boarding school expressed disappointment that the presence of such 'characters' among his assisted-place holders had not had a greater effect:

> It's not been a sort of great magic thing for this school. It's something that I now feel fairly lukewarm about in terms of its effectiveness ... There are occasions when I think 'We give a lot for that character', but there are few occasions when I've thought 'That character did a lot for us'. (Weston)

In general, of course, it was early days to judge the effects of the Scheme on the schools and some heads were understandably reluctant to make judgments, particularly about academic quality. Even schools where the assisted-place pupils had been 'well up the ability range' on entry rarely claimed that they were high-fliers or attributed to them a rise in the overall quality of their year group. One, possibly in a defensive response to accusations of creaming, even reported with apparent satisfaction that:

> Our head of physics, it may be an old man coming up to retirement, but he told me this term that the set he's teaching in the third year, of whom a lot of boys are on assistance, is the worst set he's ever taught in twenty-nine years of teaching. (Milltown Grammar)

Such caution may also have reflected a wish not to pre-judge examination performance, since the Scheme places an obligation on participating schools to publish their examination results in the same way as maintained schools. However, any coyness in the private sector about the academic performance of pupils admitted under the Assisted Places Scheme quickly disappeared by the time ISIS made available national figures for the first cohorts of such pupils to enter public examinations. In 1985, 55 per cent of sixth-form assisted-place holders went to university and 74 per cent into all forms of higher education, compared with 44 per cent and 61 per cent of all HMC sixth-form leavers and 26 per cent and 44 per cent of those leaving GSA/GBGSA sixth forms (quoted in Walford, 1987). In 1987, ISIS reported a success rate of 91.2 per cent amongst assisted-place holders taking A-levels and an 87 per cent success rate at O-level including 34 per cent of passes at A-grade.[14] In 1988, the figures quoted were two-thirds entering higher education, 90 per cent gaining A-level passes, and 66 per cent gaining grades A and B in GCSE examinations.[15] Specific cases quoted in that year included one school where thirteen assisted-place holders each achieved three A-grades at A-level and two others four A-grades. Oxbridge successes also featured prominently in the reports. Such publicity carried at least the strong implication that these pupils would not have achieved these results had they not attended independent schools on assisted places. Thus Lady Johnston, chair of the Assisted Places Committee of ISJC, was quoted in the ISIS press notice as saying:

> Naturally we are delighted with the high performance of assisted place pupils. In particular it is gratifying to see the number of socially disadvantaged children who are benefiting from the Scheme. It is clearly fulfilling its aim of enabling academically able children to make the most of their talents.[16]

The evidence of these early results[17] also offers some credence to Wilkinson's conclusion that 'it is disingenuous to argue that the scheme just helps children' even if 'it is equally dishonest to pretend that it only helps schools' (Wilkinson, 1986, p. 59). It has certainly reinforced the fears of those state school heads reported in the next chapter, who feel that the Scheme is drawing away from them some of the very pupils who could have helped to establish or sustain the academic success of their own schools.

Amongst the independent school heads we interviewed, though, there was an overwhelming feeling that the Scheme was a success and that its continuation could be fully justified. As far as virtually all these heads were concerned, the benefits at least balanced the costs and probably significantly outweighed them. Even so it was clear that it was the successors of the group that originally thought up the Scheme, the Direct Grant Committee of HMC, who still regarded it with the greatest favour. This was especially true of heads of the former direct grant boys' day schools we visited. The girls' former direct grant schools had, in general, been less successful in implementing the Scheme, while in the traditionally independent schools (especially boarding schools) the Scheme remained marginal and there was some disappointment that it hadn't 'taken off' more strongly. Many heads felt that the Scheme still needed some fine tuning on issues like the appropriate ratio to be recruited from maintained schools, the cut-off point at the top of the income scale, the effect of higher earnings and a higher cost of living in the south, and so on, and some heads felt that the Scheme should be extended to new categories of assistance including meeting boarding need. Our own observations also prompt questions on other issues, such as the equity of a Scheme partly conceived as a national academic scholarship ladder being administered significantly differently in different areas and in different schools within the same area. However, the strengths and limitations of the Scheme cannot be judged just on the basis of evidence gleaned from within the participating schools, and in the next chapter we therefore look beyond the schools themselves to explore the impact of the Scheme on the local 'economy' of schooling in the three areas of the country that we selected for detailed study.

### Notes

1 Letter to one of the research team dated 16 September 1981. This school had one of the largest allo-cations of assisted places in the country, yet its head regarded the evaluation of a Scheme involving the use of public money as both unnecessary and impossible. Fortunately, most heads adopted a more responsible approach to the Scheme and a more open-minded attitude towards our own endeavours.

2 See, for example, the conflicting evidence on this issue in Marks *et al.* (1983) and Steedman (1983), and the discussion of it in Gray *et al.* (1984) and Cox and Marks (1988).

3 Letters to the research team dated 18 September 1981 and 26 May 1982.

4 Meeting with Assisted Places Committee of Independent Schools' Joint Council on 20 January 1983.

5 Education Act, 1980, Section 17; DES Press Release.

6 See, for example, *Daily Express*, 6 February 1985. See also note 10 to chapter 8.

7 *Times Educational Supplement*, 16 December 1983.

8 Standing Committee on Statutory Instruments, 24 April 1985.

9 The 60 per cent rule was not applied with any degree of rigour until 1984, and even thereafter sanctions do not appear to have been applied against all schools which have failed to conform to it.

10 Report of meeting, 13 August 1980.

11 *Times Educational Supplement*, 12 October 1984.

12 Even in January 1989, a number of heads were reported by Hadfield (1989) as concerned that publicity was not getting through to some of the core target groups.

13 Interview with Mark Carlisle, 16 November 1982.

14 *Times Educational Supplement*, 6 November 1987.

15 ISIS press release, 16 December 1988, p. 1.

16 *ibid.*, p. 2.

17 We hope to be able to monitor the actual results and careers of our own sample of pupils over the coming years.

Chapter 7

# *The Scheme in Three Localities*

Many of the competing claims about the likely effects of the Scheme had raised questions about its potential impact on the local 'economy' of schooling. Had the Scheme disturbed a previously peaceful coexistence of maintained and independent schools? Was it creaming off talent from a few local comprehensives or spreading any loss more widely? From what kinds of family were assisted-place pupils typically drawn, and what distinctive opportunities did their families see the Scheme as offering? Why did other families choose not to take advantage of the Scheme? In order to follow up these sorts of questions, we needed to complement our data from the independent schools with similar information from state schools nearby, and in concentrating our field work in three separate areas we were able to examine the Scheme's impact in three different educational settings.

The independent schools we visited had overlapping catchment areas, most of which straddled several LEAs and which were sometimes very wide indeed. It would therefore have been inappropriate to limit our studies of the state schools to single LEAs. But since we lacked the resources to undertake detailed research in all the schools in an area, we used our local knowledge, augmented by information solicited by letter from primary school heads, together with our fieldwork amongst independent school teachers, pupils and parents, to develop a broad understanding of school networks in the three areas. We then identified state schools where interviews with heads, teachers, pupils and parents, on a scale similar to those carried out in the private sector, could help us to add texture to our developing picture of the impact of the Scheme on schools and school choice in our three chosen areas.

Gaining access to schools in the maintained sector was obviously essential if we were to be in a position to 'consider the Scheme not only on its own terms but for its effects on the maintained sector'. Even though that statement appeared regularly in our letters to chief education officers and to heads of maintained schools asking for permission to interview as many pupils and parents as were providing our evidence from the private sector, gaining access to the public sector presented its own difficulties. This was partly because headteachers were by no means the only 'gate-keepers'. Outright refusals of cooperation from several Labour-controlled LEAs opposed to the Scheme ruled certain areas out of our study altogether. As we noted in the opening chapter, disliking the Scheme was sometimes used as a reason for not cooperating in an investigation which might give publicity to an initiative which the LEA preferred to ignore. Nevertheless, we eventually gained cooperation from LEAs controlled at the time by both Labour and Conservative administrations, although some of the latter came under Alliance control during the course of the study. But even when an LEA was willing for schools to be approached, we had several reminders that the support of a well-disposed chief officer can leave a head's resistance entirely intact. However, no head of a maintained school declined to cooperate on principle, although some failed to reply to our letters. Of those that did decline, the main reasons given were that their schools had been over-researched, that hard-pressed staff had no time, or (in the later stages of the project) that the teachers' industrial action made it impossible to add any further complication to already delicate relationships with colleagues or parents.

Nevertheless, we were able to conduct research in fourteen primary schools, fourteen maintained secondary schools (eleven of them comprehensive) and one tertiary college. As in the independent schools, the extent of the cooperation varied. But our sample of pupils of high academic ability and their parents was comparable in size to that obtained from independent schools in the same areas. In addition, we had a further sample of pupils across the ability range.[1] Because they were not directly involved in administering the Scheme and because it offered state schools no tangible benefits, the heads of maintained schools as a group understandably took rather less personal interest in the research than their independent school colleagues and, with a few exceptions, the facilities and hospitality offered to us were more frugal.

It was, however, noticeable that those heads who took most interest in our work were also those whose approach to marketing their schools to parents most resembled that of the other sector. Our interviews with heads were particularly important in this context because heads are often the 'organic intellectuals' of their own schools and of their sector more generally. It is they above all who publicly articulate the 'ethos' of their schools and the meaning and importance of the education they provide. In describing and explaining to us what the curriculum of their schools embodied, they also revealed something of their approach to the public justification of their educational practices and their capacity to mobilize governors, parents, pupils and fellow professionals behind their work.

We now use data gathered from our three areas, and particularly from some of those independent and maintained schools in which we carried out our most intensive fieldwork, to explore the impact of the Assisted Places Scheme on real patterns of choice, cooperation and competition between schools in the mid-1980s. As in the previous chapter, the schools have been allocated pseudonyms and certain other details concerning the areas and the schools have been disguised in the descriptions of them offered here.[2] The three areas we term Dilston, Riverside and Scotsdale.

### Dilston

Dilston is a large conurbation with a very mixed social character, ranging from areas of traditional heavy industry now experiencing very high levels of unemployment, through to affluent leafy suburbs housing the professional and managerial classes. It spans ten LEAs containing about eighty maintained secondary schools and twenty-five independent secondary schools. Of the latter, the fifteen that now participate in the Assisted Places Scheme were nearly all on the last direct-grant list. Many of the independent schools have a long tradition of awarding free or subsidized places, and continued to do so even after some LEAs withdrew their support during the 1960s and 1970s. A local trust fund offered alternative financial support to pupils for all but two of the years between the ending of the direct-grant system in 1976 and the introduction of the Assisted Places Scheme. This, together with a continued take-up of places by a few LEAs, enabled many of those schools to retain part of their role as town grammar schools. Only one LEA in the area still maintains its own grammar schools. We use our study of this area to focus particularly on the operation of the Scheme in schools which were formerly direct-grant grammar schools and we consider its significance for other schools with which they ostensibly compete. The schools to which we pay particular attention in our analysis of the dynamics of schooling in this area are briefly characterized below under their assigned names.

*Nortown Grammar* is a large ex-direct-grant grammar school for boys with an outstanding record of university entrance. It draws its pupils from a large number of primary schools spread over a very wide area and is academically highly selective. Nearly 50 per cent of its intake receive some form of assistance, but the school was awarded rather fewer assisted places than it had hoped for — presumably because the whole area was certain to be well catered for. In accordance with its long tradition of catering for 'poor scholars', it claims not to be socially selective. Its intake of assisted-place holders however, let alone of fee payers, seems not to bear out this claim even to the limited extent that it was justified in its earlier direct-grant days. Nevertheless, the headmaster and many other staff of this school had a missionary zeal about the school's involvement, seeing it as a way of 'rescuing' bright working-class pupils from neighbourhood comprehensives in inner-city areas.

*Nortown High School* is a girls' independent school, formerly direct-grant, with a total of nearly 500 pupils, including 160 in the sixth form. It also has its own preparatory department. It offers a traditional curriculum and a highly academic ethos; 90 per cent of pupils stay on in the sixth form, 80 per cent of whom go on to degree-level courses in higher education. Its pupils are drawn largely from the affluent suburbs and commuter-belt to the south of the conurbation. The school has about twenty assisted places per year at 11–13 and a handful in the sixth form. The headmistress claimed that these Assisted Places Scheme pupils were not amongst her 'high-fliers' and that the maintenance of her school's academic reputation rested with affluent middle-class pupils who had received free places in the days of the direct-grant system but whose parents now chose to pay for them.

*Milltown Grammar* is another former direct-grant school, but with a more local intake of 650 boys in the main school. It also has its own preparatory department. Like the girls' school of the same foundation, it is still perceived as 'the town grammar school'. Many of the parents we interviewed prefer not to acknowledge that it is now a private school and resent the fact that it can no longer be selected as a choice on the LEA transfer form. At the same time some of the parents, including a few who have traditionally been Labour voters, feel betrayed that the Labour Party has taken away a route to social mobility, even if it is one that they did not take advantage of themselves. For such parents, the Assisted Places Scheme is a welcome restoration of perceived opportunities for their children and it has a potent appeal in a town with a notoriously poor record of entry to higher education and a comprehensive system which, on the evidence of our own home interviews, has so far failed to instil confidence among the aspiring classes.

*Milltown High* is the girls' school of the same foundation, with just over 500 girls and its own preparatory department. It appeared from our sample of pupils that both its fee payers and its assisted-place holders were drawn from higher social groups than those in the boys' school and it seems to benefit from the non-availability of single-sex education, as well as grammar school education, within the state system in this part of the conurbation. It had also felt tangible benefits from the recent ending of selection in a neighbouring authority. The school has a significant number of ethnic minority pupils, though they are mainly from upper middle-class Asian backgrounds rather than the daughters of millworkers.

*Redland Comprehensive School* is an up-market comprehensive of about 1600 pupils, located in a part of Dilston which has many of the characteristics of an 'urban village' and in which many of the staff of the local university and polytechnic have their homes alongside members of other 'new middle-class' occupations. Three of its nine forms of entry are treated as being of grammar school standard. Though the head points out that the school includes large council estates in its potential catchment area, other staff have told us that it draws predominantly from the owner-occupied areas and that most of the children from the council estates go to another local comprehensive. This seemed to be confirmed by the parental occupations we came across at this school. Unlike many schools in this particular LEA, Redland had successfully resisted an attempt to remove its sixth form, largely as a result of well-organized articulate parental opposition to the proposal. The sixth form is academically selective and concentrates almost exclusively on A-levels.

*Cherry Tree Comprehensive* is a mixed comprehensive of 1500 pupils in a nearby authority, formed from two secondary modern schools in the early 1970s. It seemed very much a neighbourhood school, most of its intake coming from three large primary schools and two smaller ones. The catchment area is divided into distinct housing areas including 1930s middle-class estates, working-class terraces and a substantial council estate. However, its reputation is such that it attracts a few pupils from further afield. The school's facilities were designed for dual school–community use and the site is heavily used until late at night. The school offers a wide range of extra-curricular activities, especially in music, drama, sports and outdoor pursuits. Just over two of its eight forms of entry can be considered of traditional grammar school ability, but just over 40 per cent of its fifth years normally achieve five O-level passes. About 60 per cent of pupils stay into the largely conventional sixth form and about 75 per cent of A-level leavers go on to further or higher education. It was therefore far from being the kind of academically unsuccessful neighbourhood comprehensive that featured so markedly in the early justifications for the Assisted Place Scheme. The authority had invested £1 million in new science and technology facilities in the 1970s, but the school has chosen to retain its conventional curriculum structure rather than participate in the authority's pilot TVEI project, partly because the head felt that the latter might limit the school's appeal to academically-orientated parents.

*Moorside Comprehensive* is also a mixed comprehensive school of 1500 pupils, located in rural surroundings outside Milltown, but drawing upon both urban and rural catchment areas. It has a good reputation in Milltown as the local comprehensive school most likely to succeed, and its head was confident about its capacity to attract children of middle-class parents committed to comprehensive education. It has become increasingly popular since it developed a large sixth form and this has been particularly attractive to parents who were denied free places at the Milltown grammar schools after 1976. But we found noticeably fewer children here from the kinds of university-educated professional and managerial backgrounds which featured at Cherry Tree and were especially prominent at Redland. This suggests that the Milltown grammar schools still exert a strong pull on that group of parents, many of whom are still determined to obtain a traditional grammar school education for their children. Indeed, the head of Moorside took the view that, if a purely academic education was what they wanted, their choice was probably appropriate.

*Highgrove County School for Girls* is an LEA grammar school for nearly 1000 girls. The LEA has twice changed hands politically in recent years and the school has been subject to rumours both of comprehensivization and of merger with the boys' grammar school. Despite the headmistress's view that its intake is academically but not socially selective, the social composition of our sample of pupils is at least as skewed towards the service class as that of most of the local independent schools in which we worked.

There is no doubt that independent schools are a highly significant feature of the educational landscape of the Dilston conurbation. The Assisted Places Scheme is also becoming significant, both in terms of the number of places available and the fact that the schools offering them have generally been successful in filling their quotas. Historically, the direct-grant schools took substantial numbers of pupils on LEA free places, some schools drawing pupils from right across the conurbation (and beyond) and others acting as town grammar schools for various parts of it. Although this distinction between the elite grammar schools and more local ones remains, and this is reflected in the number and geographical spread of the primary schools from which they draw, one effect of the withdrawal of LEA free places was to make the more local schools look further afield for a fee-paying clientele. This pattern appears to have been continued with the assisted places intake, which means that fears that the Scheme would heavily cream the intake from particular local schools apppear to have been unfounded. It might even be argued that making an independent school a real choice for parents has been further extended by the Scheme. Nevertheless, a lot of the attraction of the schools in the independent sector in this area derives from their history as grammar schools and it is their academically selective nature rather than their independence that has the strong market appeal. When this is combined with media images of 'rough' comprehensive schools run by 'extremist' local authorities, or with ill-thought-out or politically contentious LEA reorganization plans, independent schools are also seen by parents with academic aspirations for their children as a haven of tranquility where traditional conceptions of education still prevail.

Some of these parents clearly have the means to pay for private education. The involvement of schools like Nortown Grammar in the Scheme is not manifestly a matter of self-interest, since their reputations are such that they have no substantial difficulty in filling their places with academically able and well-motivated fee paying pupils who will keep them high in the league table of academic distinctions. In the case of less prestigious schools like Milltown Grammar, however, the Scheme has enabled them to retain more of their traditional grammar school character than had looked possible at the time of the abolition of the direct grant. Unlike Nortown Grammar, neither Milltown's own bursary scheme nor the incomes of its traditional clientele looked sufficient to compensate for the huge loss of free places that that policy change brought about. While probably facing no substantial threat to its viability as an independent fee-paying institution, the school had faced an uncertain future and one where the rigours of the market were likely to bring about a significant change in its social and academic character. In a situation of falling rolls, elite grammar schools like Nortown Grammar and Nortown High School could continue to attract well-motivated and academically able pupils whose parents were able to afford to pay fees, but Milltown Grammar had been in danger of losing those very pupils whose academic success brought it prestige in the days of the direct grant.

Indeed, prior to the advent of the Assisted Places Scheme, it was beginning to have to fill its empty places with pupils whose parents had money but little interest in the particular style of education that the grammar schools had traditionally offered. In the view of some of the staff at the school, such parents merely wanted the cachet of having provided an independent schooling for their children and, in so far as they had views on what the school should offer, it was often at odds with that which their children were actually to receive. The tensions which this brought about, and the extent to which the Assisted Places Scheme offered a lifeline to schools like Milltown Grammar, was colourfully brought home to us in the following remarks of its senior history master. In contrasting his working life with that of colleagues in Nortown Grammar, he pointed out that the intakes of the two schools were socially and culturally worlds apart and had been in danger of becoming more so:

> They're a different group this lot here . . . They're all irredeemably plebian. Pub owners and filling station owners, haulage contractors and the like. Call themselves 'managing directors', of course [laugh]. But you can see what their values are. You organise a ski trip for £250 and you can't keep them away. And they arrive with another £250 hanging out of their back pockets to spend — they never bring any back. But you organise a visit to the [local symphony] orchestra and they just don't want to know — you can't even fill a minibus . . . What these parents know about higher education, you could write on the back of a postage stamp. Half of them couldn't even spell 'university', let alone tell you what one really is. The ignorance is appalling . . . .

So, by providing a continuing intake of 'worthy' and well-motivated lower middle-class and, to a lesser extent, skilled working-class pupils, the Assisted Places Scheme was protecting the school from the worst excesses of a market that was increasingly being dominated by the *nouveau riche*. The incipient existence of that group in the school was graphically described in the following terms by Mrs Honey, a stalwart of Milltown 'society' whose husband was an old boy of Milltown Grammar and whose children were currently in the school:

> There are different sets of boys in the school now, you know. The bright fee payers, the bright boys getting some kind of help, the not so bright boys getting some kind of assistance, but then those who are quite rich but really thick. I mean how do you really describe boys who get 20 per cent in exam subjects? How did they get there anyway? Did they pass the entrance exam? Well, when you see the parents — you know we meet at parents' evenings and social events — well they stand out a mile. The *nouveau riche*

> — young businessmen dripping in gold, you know, thick gold bracelets, chains around their necks and her dripping in diamonds, and you think good Lord!

The availability of an alternative clientele through the Assisted Places Scheme, more closely aligned culturally and academically with the school, was thus protecting the academic reputation of Milltown Grammar in a way that reinforced its capacity to compete with local state schools for the sorts of pupils who would continue to bring it the academic success that it had enjoyed when it was more legitimately regarded as the town grammar school. As we saw in chapter 6, the head himself conceded that, with the ending of the direct grant, Milltown Grammar had lost some academically bright potential pupils, who were now once again coming to the school on assisted places. Another local independent school, regarded with derision by most educated observers, was left to pick up the lucrative but professionally unrewarding market that lay in the children of the *nouveau riche* — a school described by Mrs Honey as 'the rich man's comprehensive' which would take anyone with 'a gold bracelet and a personalized number plate'. For Milltown Grammar then, there is little doubt that whatever the declared intentions of the Assisted Places Scheme the school, as well as individual place holders, has been a distinct beneficiary.[3] To the extent that some of the assisted-place holders would otherwise have gone to local comprehensive schools, the maintained system as a whole, and perhaps particular schools like Moorside, could be considered the losers.

However, as we shall demonstrate in more detail in chapter 8, even schools like the Milltown grammar schools were not attracting many working-class and inner-city children and they did not, by and large, appear to be competing with the sort of inner-city neighbourhood comprehensives whose shortcomings were part of the original rationale for the Scheme. Rather, it was schools like Moorside, Cherry Tree and Redland Comprehensives, or maintained grammar schools like Highgrove, that were the alternatives for those assisted-place applicants who would not otherwise have entered the independent sector. Indeed, the parental choice and appeals provisions of the 1980 Education Act — and this will be even more true of the 1988 Education Reform Act — have made it unlikely that the sort of parents who have so far showed up so prominently among beneficiaries of assisted places would otherwise have found their children confined to an inner-city comprehensive. It was particularly unlikely during the period of falling rolls in maintained schools which has accompanied the Scheme's growth towards 35,000 places. As in all the areas in which we worked, there was considerable evidence of the role of primary heads and fourth-year junior school teachers in directing academically able pupils away from particular schools, both into the independent sector and to suburban comprehensive schools. In Dilston there was particular pressure to keep such pupils out of the 11–16 schools. One head told us 'Some of the inner-city schools . . . find it hard to give more than a handful of kids an

IQ rating over 105'. Another primary head told us that the archetypical target pupil for the Assisted Places Scheme would probably not figure in the Scheme anyway 'because, generally speaking, poor people are not interested in that [kind of education]. Nor are they capable of passing the examination'. Whether such perceptions were accurate or not, they were likely to have had real effects given the key role of primary heads in identifying pupils who might be interested in the Scheme.

It therefore appeared to us that the main competitors with the independent sector in this area for pupils of an academic ability that would qualify them for the Assisted Places Scheme were well-established 11–18 schools, especially those with traditional selective sixth forms. Even so, the extent to which their own headteachers believed in their capacity to compete varied considerably. The headteacher of Moorside did not believe that his school could really compete academically with the Milltown Grammar Schools, let alone with Nortown Grammar, and he would not encourage parents whose sole aspiration for their children was academic to choose his school in preference to them. However, the heads of Cherry Tree and Redland did feel that their schools could meet the needs of academically able pupils, but differed in the way they viewed competition from the independent sector. Cherry Tree is located next to a mixed independent grammar school and loses a few pupils each year to this and to other independent day schools within the conurbation. Even so, the head told us that the loss of the half dozen or so pupils that he knew about each year ever since he had been in the school was 'something I have ceased to worry about — it's nothing to do with me'. Though he did feel that the Assisted Places Scheme was drawing some able pupils away, he remained philosophical about the loss even when the chair of his governing body chose to send his younger son to an independent school on an assisted place rather than allowing him to follow his elder brother into Cherry Tree.

The head of Redland Comprehensive, the most academically successful comprehensive school we visited in the area, took a much more critical view of the creaming of his intake by independent schools and was especially hostile towards the Assisted Places Scheme. To date, he had been successful in persuading many service-class parents who could probably afford to pay fees that his school could offer a sound academic education and a wide range of extra-curricular activities. He nevertheless resented the fact that half the pupils leaving some local primary schools went into the independent sector and he was particularly critical of primary school teachers who encouraged it. He declared himself 'outraged at some of the kids who haven't come here this year' and he believed that half the pupils leaving one local primary school to go into the independent sector would be on assisted places. Despite the obvious academic success of his school over the past few years, he thought that it had not yet succeeded in attracting either that group of professional parents for whom Oxbridge entry was their prime goal or those aspiring working-class parents who regarded grammar schools as the best or only route to social mobility. While the school had plenty of pupils in the IQ range 117–130, it appeared to have less than its share of those over 130, and it might now lose some of these through the wider availability of financial assistance through the Assisted Places Scheme.

If, in fact, the real impact of the Scheme is to deprive academically successful comprehensive schools of more of their most able pupils, this will of course make it even more difficult for them to compete successfully with the independent schools in the future. The alternative notion, espoused by some advocates of the Scheme, that the less successful comprehensive schools would somehow be stimulated by the Scheme to better themselves was treated with derision by the head of Redland. In what he described as 'radical middle-class Redland' his own school's capacity to attract the full range of ability might just be maintained because:

> . . . there are sufficient bright children whose parents make a conscious decision, as it were, to send them here; that certainly won't be true of my colleagues in other schools [in the area] . . .

For those schools, he felt, the Scheme might even make a downward spiral inevitable. In practice though we found that few, if any, holders of assisted places in this area would have attended the sort of inner-city schools to which he was referring if they had not been admitted to independent schools. Indeed, so striking was this finding that we returned to the area just before this book went to press to investigate whether the situation had changed as the Scheme had become better known. Both the heads of inner-city 11–16 high schools that we approached warned us over the telephone that our journey would be wasted if we thought the Assisted Places had any relevance to their situation. Even so, we persisted with the interviews which provided us with the following explanations of their reactions:

> When you rang was the first time the Scheme assumed any significance here at all . . . Most children from the local primary schools come here, though it varies from school to school. We lose a few each year, mainly for geographical or religious reasons. But some go to other schools of the sort that appeal to your more middle-class sort of parent, especially from one of the primary schools . . . I firmly believe we could cater for them if they let us, but we don't ever see them. They go to safe and secure, er dull and predictable schools without excitement or innovation, schools which are dragging their feet on TVEI, for instance . . . So the odd pupil from the local primary school who goes to one of the independent schools wouldn't have come to us anyway, they'd have gone to another high school . . . (Thomas Darby High School)

> We don't lose many really. Those that we do lose want single-sex education and they go to one of the other high schools. A few go across the border to other LEAs and a couple have gone to what I call private venture schools run for profit . . . I don't know of any who have gone to the mainstream

independent schools — even though Nortown Grammar is actually our nearest school . . . [consults colleague] Oh, sorry, I'm told two did go this year. I'd have to check whether they were assisted places — but they were from a primary school that probably wouldn't have sent them here anyway . . . (Knotley High School)

Even allowing for the fact that these heads might have been ignorant of a few more children who went into the private sector, the total number doing so from the inner-city parts of their catchment areas seems to have remained negligible. The heads' perception that any assisted-place holders would not have attended their own schools suggests that the Scheme is not, in fact, exerting any direct competitive pressure on those schools to improve and there is no evidence that the Scheme itself poses any direct threat to the existence of these particular inner-city schools. In one of the schools there had been no children with Verbal Reasoning scores that would suggest they were potential candidates for the Scheme for many years. But, although the alleged failure of such schools has been used to justify the Scheme, it has apparently had little impact on them for either good or ill, although the head of Knotley High did consider it had contributed significantly to a loss of morale in the state sector as a whole.

What is perhaps especially disturbing for the maintained sector in the longer term, though, is the judgment on the part of the head of a relatively successful school like Redland that his own school's capacity to compete may be weakened by a combination of the loss of a few more pupils to the independent sector and other developments that sap public confidence in the state sector. Nor, in his view, was this necessarily directly related to the academic quality of the schooling on offer in the two sectors. Though he could understand the motivation of parents who sent their children to Nortown Grammar School rather than to Redland, he had little time for those who patronized some of the 'dreadful private schools that will take anyone'. But, like other heads of successful comprehensive schools, he viewed with foreboding the effects that prolonged teacher action might have on the perceptions of those parents who currently support the school. And a feeling of being 'the nut in the nutcracker', between Nortown Grammar School and a 'Marxist city council', illustrates the kind of tension that might make a school consider grant maintained status in the future.[4] This would, in turn, further stigmatize the schools left in the LEA system as inappropriate destinations for pupils with academic aspirations. Even the head of Cherry Tree seemed worried that this was already happening to some of the other schools in his LEA, and was unhappy about the overly vocational orientation being adopted by the inner-city schools that were participating in the pilot TVEI programme. The disadvantage in resource terms of not participating was, in his view, balanced by Cherry Tree's retention of a curriculum structure that was recognizable to parents seeking an academic education for their children.

In this situation, it might be expected that the one LEA retaining selection would be particularly well placed to resist the attractions of the independent sector. With up to 30 per cent of the age cohort receiving grammar school education in this borough, the availability of maintained grammar schools was certainly one of the selling points employed by local estate agents. Primary heads told us that pupils who, in other circumstances, would have sat the independent school entrance examination chose not to do so. As one such head put it:

> We have children now who in our opinion would probably do very well, they are very able and capable, who have not even bothered to sit these exams, because they are quite happy with the education that is provided by our local grammar schools.

Some parents we interviewed, several of whom are cited in chapter 9, expressed this view strongly. Even so, the LEA had until fairly recently awarded fifty free places in local independent schools, partly to top-up its own provision of grammar school education (the traditional function of such purchased free places) but partly perhaps as an indicator of a perceived quality difference between maintained and independent grammar schools. In this, there seem to be differences between the various grammar schools within the authority and between girls' and boys' schools. All the local boys' grammar schools were considered very much in the second division compared with Nortown Grammar, though some were seen as well capable of competing with other schools in the Assisted Places Scheme. As one primary head in the area put it:

> I do think that Nortown Grammar has a fantastic reputation and it does take the very high-fliers. [Other Assisted Place schools] have boys go there who, in my opinion, are not all that good. I mean, I've sent far better material to our local grammar schools. So I'm not terribly impressed by those particular schools.

However, Highgrove County Girls' school is in much more direct competition with Nortown High School and similar elite schools. While this may partly reflect differential parental perceptions of the needs of boys and girls, it is also clear that the quality of education at Highgrove has attracted parents who can see little point in paying fees or even seeking an assisted place when a service of at least equivalent quality is available within the state system. One primary head suggested that Highgrove might actually be doing a better job than Nortown High given its intake:

> The two independent girls' schools [including Nortown High] are very small and they too only accept the very most, the ablest of pupils ... Our local grammar schools have all abilities to cater for, the good ones and the lot who are not as able. I think if children are prepared to work hard and their homes are the right kind of encouraging background, then they can achieve a great deal at our local grammar schools. Past children have

done . . . It's just that there are more of the more able at these [independent] establishments. So they ought to get better results, shouldn't they?

Highgrove Girls' seems to be particularly attractive to so-called 'new middle-class' families, where the parents themselves have achieved high levels of education and professional occupations through attending maintained grammar schools. Yet in the north of the conurbation, where the maintained system is now fully comprehensive, these very parents might well have opted for the independent Milltown Grammar School. It is also clear that Highgrove Girls' benefits substantially from being a single-sex school, and the headmistress feels that she has lost more girls to the independent sector whenever there has been talk of amalgamation with the boys' school, whether or not this has been linked with comprehensive reorganization.

Another measure of the extent to which the public and private sectors interact is the extent of professional and social contact between teachers. We have already seen that there was a variation in the extent to which primary heads cooperated with independent schools both in sponsoring pupils into them and in supplying information about prospective recruits. In one part of the conurbation, the Labour-controlled local authority had taken a very strong line against contact, though even here some primary heads had successfully circumvented the ruling by informal means. Some other LEAs were also hostile to the Scheme and it was suggested by one independent school head that primary heads cooperating with the Scheme jeopardized their chances of further promotion. Elsewhere, however, relations seemed to be much closer and not a significant matter of contention. Contact between independent school teachers and other secondary school teachers also varied between the LEAs in the area. Liaison between grammar school teachers in both sectors was common, while in Milltown the independent grammar schools hosted the heads and teachers of the local comprehensive schools at SHA and subject group meetings much as they had done in the old direct-grant days. In other authorities, though, contact between comprehensive school teachers and independent school teachers was described to us as virtually non-existent. This was particularly true of an authority with a radical left-wing council. However, whatever the views of elected members, there was often a degree of informal contact between independent and state school heads. The head of Redland confessed to meeting his independent counterparts in the 'Redland gin-and-tonic circles', though he claimed never to discuss education with them. But the head of Brampton School, an independent girls' school just to the north of the conurbation, felt that such contacts actually influenced the ways in which the two sectors related, claiming that there was no problem about transfers at 16-plus in one LEA because the Director of Education and most of the secondary heads sent their daughters to her school. After all, she told us, 'it's very much local conditions that alter cases, don't you think?' The fact that those running the maintained system had an interest in the success of the independent sector was, of course, particularly disturbing to members of left-wing LEAs trying to instil confidence in the comprehensive system. Certainly, some of the parents we interviewed in this area justified their choice of the independent sector on the grounds that so many state school teachers did just the same.

### Riverside

This is a mixed suburban area, although it borders on to the inner city and has a sizeable ethnic minority population. It has light industry but is predominantly an area of commuting and non-manual local employment. It contains about fifteen secondary independent schools, excluding specialist schools. Eleven of these participate in the Assisted Places Scheme, five are ex-direct-grant schools and three have been voluntary or special agreement schools in the maintained sector within the past twenty years. All these schools draw some pupils out of the public sector and one of the six LEAs in this area has amongst the highest participation rates in the country for private education. Most movement into the private sector occurs at 11-plus, which is also the normal age of transfer between state schools in most of the six LEAs. There are about fifty maintained secondary schools in the area, though some of the pupils attending the independent schools come from much further afield. One of the LEAs maintains selection at 11-plus and one has reorganized its 16-plus provision into a tertiary system. In the discussion which follows, we focus particularly on the interaction between maintained schools and those schools in the Scheme that were traditionally independent or (in one case) had opted for independence as an alternative to becoming comprehensive within the maintained system. The following independent and state schools are those that figure prominently in our discussion of this area.

*St Hilda's Girls' School* is a highly prestigious girls' independent school. It draws pupils from an extensive catchment area and its intake of about 600 girls is highly selected, both academically and socially. Unlike many of the other independent day schools in the area, it did not have direct-grant status prior to 1976. Nevertheless, it had admitted up to a third of its intake on LEA free places or bursaries in the 1960s, although by 1975 this had dwindled to a handful as the various LEAs involved withdrew their support. A high proportion of the schools' pupils go on to higher education and the school has recently pioneered developments in the technological education of girls. The head adopts a high public profile and, as a particularly well-practised advocate of her school and of independent education generally, she is a prime example of a head who acts as an organic intellectual for the sector.

*Dame Margaret's High School* is also an old-established girls' school with about 550 pupils, which moved to a new greenfield site in the 1930s and became fully independent after the Second World War. It has its own junior school. Our parental interviews suggest that it tends to attract a *nouveau riche* clientele as much as one traditionally associated with independent education. Though never a direct grant school, it received about 20 per cent of its pupils on free places from its LEA until the 1970s and its solid, though not outstanding, A-level results and record of entrance to higher education was highly dependent on this group.

The nearby *Clifton Grammar School* is also an old foundation and, as a voluntary school, it had served as the local maintained grammar school for boys before the LEA went comprehensive in the early 1970s. It now has a Common Entrance intake at 13-plus as well as its 11-plus entry. The school has 800 pupils, a strong academic sixth form entered by 90 per cent of pupils and a good record of university entrance, together with a strong sporting tradition. The head of this school was a member of HMC even in its voluntary-aided days and was active in the campaign to ensure that former voluntary schools were included in the Assisted Places Scheme.

*Parkside Girls' School* is a maintained girls' school of about 950 girls, aged 11–16. Its recent history has been heavily affected by two LEA reorganizations during the past fifteen years. It occupies a building that was originally a mixed grammar school and subsequently a sixth-form college, but the present school emerged from an amalgamation between two girls' comprehensive schools, one based on a grammar school and one on a secondary modern. Its appeal as a single-sex ex-grammar school made it over-subscribed in the early years of comprehensivization, but its reputation now seems to be declining. Some parents who in the past would have regarded this school as a viable alternative to local independent schools no longer do so. Nevertheless, its headmistress still sees the school as mainly being in competition with the independent sector and she feels that even more would go into that sector if her own single-sex alternative was not available. Even so, some parents now preferred to send their children to attend other state schools in the area, including a former boys' school now becoming coeducational.

*Vicarage Road Comprehensive* is a mixed 11–16 comprehensive school with about 950 pupils, unpromisingly located next to two independent day schools, Clifton Grammar School and Dame Margaret's School, both of which participate in the Assisted Places Scheme. It lies between an area of post-War council housing and an affluent tree-lined estate of large detached owner-occupied houses. As a secondary modern school in the 1950s and 1960s, it was regarded locally as a 'sink school'; as a comprehensive school in the 1970s, its reputation was little better, with a poor record of examination results compared with other local schools. However, the appointment of a new headteacher, together with substantial investment from the LEA in refurbishing its buildings, has brought about a distinct change in its fortunes.

*Archbishop Ambrose's Grammar School* is an old-fashioned voluntary controlled grammar school for about 850 boys in an affluent traditionally Conservative LEA. The headmaster of the school is a long-standing member of HMC. The school has the ethos of a traditional-style grammar school, and a strong academic record at least equal to that of the now independent coeducational ex-direct-grant grammar school across the road. Pupils are allocated to the school on the basis of the LEA's 11-plus examination and the entry amounts to about 15 per cent of the age-group across the borough. The intake of about ten out-borough pupils each year is even more academically selective. The school has a sixth form of about 300 and it sends about two dozen boys to Oxbridge each year. Its buildings are in the poorest state of repair of any encountered during the project.

*York Road County Secondary* is a nearby secondary modern school for just over 1000 boys, whose previous headmaster ran it on almost public school lines with a strong emphasis on sport allied to academic achievement. It has a thriving sixth form and prefects in gowns. Like Archbishop Ambrose's Grammar in the same LEA its physical plant is decidedly sub-standard.

*Riverside College* is a tertiary college, which takes all pupils from its LEA at 16-plus. It replaced an earlier scheme in which the authority had two sixth-form colleges and a technical college and it now occupies the site of the latter. It attracts pupils from other local authorities, as well as a few from local independent schools.

The take-up for the Assisted Places Scheme in Riverside has been patchy. Part of this has to do with the high average level of incomes in the area which excludes from eligibility children who in other areas might have entered the Scheme, a point we noted earlier with regard to the London GPDST schools.[5] Additionally, it is an area in which a sizeable proportion of families are already using or are familiar with private schooling on offer, and that pool was unlikely to be significantly enlarged by the Scheme. In this situation, the character of the intakes of traditionally independent schools like St Hilda's and Dame Margaret's does not seem to have been significantly affected by their participation in the Assisted Places Scheme, but Clifton Grammar School has been successful in winning back some of its former maintained grammar school clientele, as have the ex-direct-grant boys' schools in the area. However, the ex-voluntary-aided and ex-direct-grant girls' schools in the area have found it quite difficult to allocate all their assisted places.

The comprehensive schools in Riverside were very conscious of the competition from the independent sector, but not specifically troubled by the Assisted Places Scheme. The socio-economic character of the area is such that, although the independent sector takes as many as a quarter of one borough's children out of the state system, many maintained schools still retain what one head described as 'a critical mass of well-motivated, able, middle-class pupils'. Unlike Dilston, where only a few schools such as Redland could claim this 'critical' mass, many schools here claimed to be able to cater for academically able children and some had a good track record in this respect. In the area as a whole there was a substantially higher rate of entry into higher education serviced by both sectors. Even the effects of major secondary reorganization programmes, and a change to a tertiary system in one LEA, did not appear to have had the same effect on morale in the maintained sector that we had encountered in Dilston, though some heads felt that prolonged industrial action by teachers might tip the balance firmly in favour of the independent sector.

For the moment, however, many of the maintained schools in Riverside were confident not only that they could meet the needs of academically able children, but also that they could persuade sufficient parents of such children that they were able to do so. Particularly noteworthy here was the confidence of Vicarage Road, which in the past had had many of the disadvantages of the 11–16 schools in Dilston. Its recent renaissance had resulted partly from the extensive investment in the school by the LEA but mainly from the considerable public relations skills of its new headteacher. From being a school which was never a serious competitor for the local independent schools, Vicarage Road has, in the past few years, occasionally succeeded in attracting the siblings of pupils attending those schools. It has mainly gained at the expense of other LEA schools like Parkside Girls, although it also attracts pupils from the neighbouring LEA, despite that authority's long-established and successful system of 11–18 comprehensives — though this is partly because unlike those schools its intake is over-whelmingly white.

Yet far from being stimulated by the Assisted Places Scheme, the success of Vicarage Road was arguably the result of a headteacher exploiting the other parental choice provisions of the 1980 Education Act to compete successfully with other maintained schools both inside and beyond the borough. There was a marked change in the ethos of the school, followed by a significant improvement in the Verbal Reasoning scores of pupils entering it. From being a school to which pupils who did not get into their first choice were allocated, it had recently become a school for which parents (including a senior education officer of the LEA) appealed if their children were allocated elsewhere. But it was not the existence of independent competition that had stimulated Vicarage Road's success, though its headteacher certainly shared some of the attributes of the most articulate and image-conscious independent school heads we interviewed.

The neighbouring independent school heads acknowledged Vicarage Road's success with a degree of patronizing admiration. Yet it was certainly not regarded as posing a threat to their schools, since they were aware of a large pool of clients who would never consider any maintained school, certainly if it were comprehensive, as a potential alternative. Nevertheless, our parental interviews suggested that some of those who had paid for elder siblings to go to Clifton Grammar or Dame Margaret's at the time of comprehensivization were beginning to question whether there was now any need to spend money on sending their younger children to these schools. On the other hand, the existence of the Assisted Places Scheme allowed other parents to consider Clifton Grammar and Dame Margaret's without the disincentive of cost and, in at least some of these cases, the longer-standing academic traditions of those schools (and particularly the existence of their large sixth forms) had helped them retain a balance of advantage over Vicarage Road and other non-selective schools. The number of pupils drawn from Vicarage Road in this way by Dame Margaret's was small, but the number drawn by Clifton Grammar was rather more significant. However, two pupils we encountered who had declined assisted places to attend Vicarage Road showed that the conclusion was not a foregone one even for those successful in independent school examinations.

In a neighbouring borough which retained selection, we found further evidence that the existence of selective schools in the maintained sector gave that sector a better chance of retaining its more able pupils even against competition reinforced and extended by the Assisted Places Scheme. The headmaster of Archbishop Ambrose's Grammar School welcomed us on our first visit with the words, 'assisted places, eh? We don't like them here, you know!'. Yet there was little evidence that his school was being significantly creamed by the independent sector. Both academically and socially this school was not readily distinguishable from its neighbouring ex-direct-grant competitor. Indeed, one parent told us that she had accepted an assisted place at the neighbouring school because it had less of a 'hothouse' atmosphere than Archbishop Ambrose's, which she also claimed was more of a 'snob school'. Though it clearly creamed the local non-selective schools of virtually all of the top 15 per cent of boys in the borough, and also creamed the comprehensive schools of the surrounding boroughs of very bright children, this school's major networks were with the private sector. Not only was the headmaster a member of HMC, the school's strong rugby club pitted its A team against independent school opposition while its B team played the local comprehensives. The school's quarrel with the Assisted Places Scheme had little to do with the two or three pupils it might attract away from the school into independent schools, but more to do with the general implication that high-quality academic education was not already available in the area. The head's view, like that of some Conservative critics of the Scheme such as Matthew Parris,[6] was that there was 'absolutely no case for assisted places' in this area and that, in allocating some to nearby schools, the government had gone back on its initial pledge to concentrate places in areas where the state system was not making adequate provision for able youngsters.

However, it would be simplistic to conclude that the maintained sector as a whole can compete better with the private sector if it maintains academic selection. It was also the case in Riverside that the non-elite part of the private sector benefited considerably from the existence of selection. With only 15 per cent of pupils qualifying for the maintained grammar schools, some parents preferred to buy their children out of what were perceived as secondary modern schools. Indeed, the new head of York Road described his school in these terms and, in abandoning some of his predecessor's attempts to attract pupils by offering them the trappings of an elite education, had already provoked some parents into moving their children into the private sector. It is possible that the existence of genuinely comprehensive schools in the LEA might win some of those pupils back into the public sector schools. However, this gain might be offset by the increased attractiveness of the private sector and the Assisted Places Scheme to those parents who believed that *only* grammar schools could cater for the academically able. It looked as if this might be put to the test right at the end of our research when local government elections led to a change of control on the LEA and a proposal to reorganize schools on comprehensive lines, but a by-election prevented the plan proceeding.[7]

Parkside Girls', in another LEA, provided some evidence of the problems faced by a former grammar school trying to adapt to comprehensivization at the same time as competing with the independent sector. The head regarded her school as in direct competition with independent girls' schools, ranging from St Hilda's through Dame Margaret's to a local convent school whose traditional clientele had included middle-class girls who had failed the 11-plus. Parkside was characterized by the head of nearby Riverside College as 'very caring, very studious, very scholarly' and, despite some recent bad publicity, it still sought to provide a high-quality academic education for girls. Its strengths had traditionally been on the arts side, though this had very recently been balanced by some of the innovations brought in with TVEI. One of its problems was maintaining its appeal in relation to the local independent girls' schools at the same time as competing successfully with the rising Vicarage Road and with a highly-regarded maintained boys' school that had recently gone coeducational. Though perhaps successfully retaining one set of clients, it was losing another in the process. Comprehensive schools like Parkside are faced with a problem not encountered by highly academic independent schools — the need to maintain their market appeal in a diverse, and to some extent segmented, market. Responding to the competitive pressure exerted by independent (or indeed maintained) grammar schools can bias the curriculum and a school's distribution of resources in ways that conflict with its overall philosophy of providing a comprehensive education.

Parkside Girls' was experiencing some tension in this respect at the time of our visits and it might well have lost more of its traditional clientele had it not been the only remaining single-sex school in the borough. The head was certainly strongly of the view that many more parents would send their daughters into the private sector were the single-sex option of Parkside not available to them in the maintained sector. For boys in the same borough there was no longer the option of a single-sex maintained school. However, parental preference for single-sex education for boys in this area seems anyway more strongly associated with a preference for selection and independence than it does in the case of girls. This had meant that Clifton Grammar

School's market appeal was only marginally increased when the last boys' comprehensive went coeducational.

Another issue that we considered in analyzing the dynamics of schooling in this area was the impact of tertiary reorganization on the interaction between the maintained and independent sectors. One of the arguments used by Stuart Sexton[8] to justify the Assisted Places Scheme had been that 11–16 schools could not attract the quality of academic staff available in schools with sixth forms and that they were therefore inappropriate for exceptionally academically able pupils. They were also seen by Sexton as particularly vulnerable to neighbourhood peer-group pressures on working-class pupils. On the other hand, it is often claimed that sixth-form and tertiary colleges attract academically able pupils away from the sixth forms of independent schools. Within the one LEA in this area that was organized on a tertiary basis, neither claim appeared to be strongly sustained. Although interviews with headteachers and parents indicated that the two successive reorganizations that had produced the present system had provoked some parents to move their children from the borough's 11–16 schools into independent schools or into 11–18 maintained schools in neighbouring boroughs, it was also the case that many parents were more than happy with the academic quality of the 11–16 schools. Indeed, in the case of Vicarage Road, it was clearly improving. Of course, as one head pointed out, the retention of well-qualified staff was easier to achieve in 11–16 schools with that 'critical mass of intelligent, well-motivated pupils' thought to be typical of this borough than it would be in 11–16 schools in inner-city areas. Nevertheless, our evidence from this area would suggest that the existence of 11–16 schools cannot in itself reasonably be used as a justification for the Assisted Places Scheme.

With regard to transfer between the sectors at 16-plus, there appeared to be as many pupils moving into the sixth forms of independent schools from 11–16 comprehensives as were moving from independent schools into the tertiary college. Furthermore, the principal of the college was frank enough to admit that his pupils from independent schools were not amongst his most academically able students and often came because, for various reasons, they had not fitted in well at their previous schools. Some independent school parents told us that they would have been more attracted by a sixth-form college than a tertiary college. The principal claimed that there had been a marked reduction in the number of transfers at the time when the Assisted Places Scheme was introduced and he felt that 'that must have been the effect of the Scheme'. However, neither he nor the LEA were particularly concerned about this, since in other respects the college was becoming increasingly popular and its A-level results had improved dramatically during the same period.

The variation of LEA response to the Assisted Places Scheme was as noticeable in Riverside as it was in Dilston. In the normally Conservative borough in which Archbishop Ambrose's School was located, the Scheme was seen by officers and, indeed, some members as an unnecessary irrelevance which posed little threat to the borough's own provision. The later suggestion that Archbishop Ambrose's Grammar School might apply for grant maintained status was seen as far more likely to threaten the quality of the service. In a neighbouring Conservative borough, officers expressed a certain amount of antagonism to the Scheme, but felt that they had to cooperate with it because it was the brainchild of the party of their political masters. But even when the Alliance parties took control of the council, it remained possible for some of the primary schools around Clifton Grammar School and Dame Margaret's High School to measure their success in terms of the numbers of pupils they got into these schools — a performance indicator intensely irritating to schools like Vicarage Road. In a nearby Labour borough, which had no significant independent schools within its boundaries but had traditionally sent many pupils into direct-grant schools just beyond them, there was some evidence that the political preferences of the council influenced headteachers' orientations towards the Scheme and towards our own research. From the Director of Education downwards, our letters went unanswered, though persistence eventually gained us permission to approach local heads. Promises to contact us were frequently broken and, when we eventually did get access to schools, this was on a very limited basis. Heads seemed unusually defensive, and one deputy head parried virtually every question with answers like: 'I can't tell you that', 'I'm not supposed to know that, so I had better not tell you' and 'I really don't think my personal opinion enters into it'. Yet, even in this borough, we found evidence that primary school teachers were encouraging particular children to take entrance examinations for independent schools elsewhere in the Riverside area.

### Scotsdale

Our third study area centres upon another large city. This city, which is the region's 'capital', has a considerable number of independent schools, reflecting its historical importance in trade and industry and the presence of a large professional and business middle class. Five of these independent day schools are in the Assisted Places Scheme, four of them having been on the final direct-grant list. At the time of the Public Schools Commission, there were five other direct-grant schools which have since been absorbed into the public sector or closed, and a sixth which is now fully independent.[9] There is one boarding school among the wider region's alternatives to public education, but in the city itself the tradition is entirely of independent grammar schools.

The conurbation which surrounds the city contains a number of LEAs which display considerable diversity in how they organize their schooling. For example, while the independent secondary schools remain traditionally 11–18 (they are also traditional in being single-sex), they are at least notionally in competition with middle schools, 11–18 comprehensive schools, 13–18 high schools, and 11–16 high schools 'topped' with various forms of 16-plus provision which include a sixth-form college. Even the city itself contains both two-stage and three-stage patterns. In one sense, then, it is the public sector rather than the private sector which offers wide-ranging parental choice. However, before discussing the local 'system' more fully, we need once again to characterize the particular schools from which most of our own information has been drawn.

*King Henry's Grammar School* is the largest and oldest of the city's independent schools, and is (in the head's words) 'bursting at the seams'. It has about 1000 boys, a 95 per cent entry into its sixth form of 300, and more than 80 per cent of its entrants go on to higher education. The head regularly emphasizes the importance of having a 'critical mass' of academically able and academically ambitious pupils large enough to create powerful peer-group pressures to stay on and do well. But he is also disinclined to claim too much credit for the school for its excellent examination results; its capacity to attract so many 'high-fliers' means that its results are 'about as good as they ought to be'. As a direct-grant school it had reserved about 35 per cent of its places for two local LEAs while another 20 per cent of its pupils held scholarships or paid reduced fees. It received one of the highest allocations of assisted places in the country, and has filled most of them. Like its other direct-grant neighbours, it has taken particular pride in its claim to have offered opportunities to many able working-class children.

*The Queen's High School* has about 550 girls in its main school of whom some 120–130 are in the sixth form. It also has a lower school for pupils aged 4–11, from which about half its annual secondary entry is drawn. In 1983 it had an A-level pass-rate of 92 per cent and a similar proportion getting 'good passes' at O-level. In many respects it represents the kind of traditional academic girls' school which is sometimes seen as countering gender bias in education. In particular it has a notably strong 'science side', and the headmistress reported a significant trend for the ablest girls to take science or mathematics. Occasional proposals that the school should move to a less cramped green-belt site had been firmly resisted by governors proud of its city character and traditions, and the head referred in a typical direct-grant fashion to the 'wide social mixing' of children from industrial and 'county' areas. 'Once they're in our uniform', she said, 'they're all our children, and that's it'. As a direct-grant school, it had offered about thirty 'free places' a year to the same two LEAs as King Henry's, and filled them without difficulty. Initially, it asked for a larger number of assisted places in the belief that the new means-tested scales would make these revived academic opportunities more widely available. Serious under-recruiting of assisted-place pupils in each of the three years 1981–3 led to its quota being halved, but the school has no other recruitment difficulties.

*Sir James's School for Boys* has 450 pupils. It was allocated the equivalent of a one-form entry in assisted places, and filled those places easily enough to have that quota slightly increased. The head's previous teaching experience had been entirely in grammar schools, both direct-grant and maintained, and he had moved into the private sector simply because that is where almost all the grammar schools now were. He told us that he saw the Scheme as directed entirely and properly towards 'a certain kind of child who will benefit from a certain kind of distinctively academic education'.

*Rowton Comprehensive School* had been built as two secondary modern schools, then transformed on opening into the city's first comprehensive. It had 1600 pupils aged 11–18 at the time of our interviews, 150 of them in the sixth form. Although rolls have fallen elsewhere quite sharply, Rowton has kept its own numbers partly because of population growth in the immediate area and partly because its reputation has led to parents opting-in from beyond its main feeder schools. The head still regards the sixth form as too small, and the rate of progress to higher education as disappointing. Improvements on both fronts are among her priorities. Apart from having 'very few children with foreign names, let alone foreign origins' (a form of relative homogeneity which it shares with the other city schools), she described its intake as being 'truly comprehensive, ranging from the affluent middle-class districts of [Rowton] to the deprived northern estates'. It certainly has the widest social mix of any school in our sample. Its immediate neighbourhood includes quite affluent suburban housing and a conspicuously impoverished council estate, and the school has been allocated several additional teachers on the basis of the LEA's own 'index of deprivation'.

*Frampton Comprehensive*, in another LEA, is the kind of renamed secondary modern school which is common in discussions of comprehensive reorganization. At the time of our work there it had 800 pupils aged 11–18, of whom only about twenty were in the sixth form. That very low figure reflects its actual secondary modern origins, the almost entirely working-class character of its intake, and traditionally low academic aspirations in the locality. The area generally has one of the lowest staying-on rates in the country, and how best to organize its post-sixteen provision has been a continuing headache for the LEA. Although Frampton itself was seen by many of the parents we interviewed, and by most of the pupils who actually attended it, as the only school available to them, it has faced competition for pupils with an ex-grammar school on one side and a comprehensive with a more socially 'select' intake on the other.

In marked contrast, *Shirebrook School* exemplifies in some ways the kind of middle-class 'colonization' of state schools described by Hatton (1985) in Australia. That is, although it recruits a socially-mixed intake from a large, predominantly rural area, it also has a sufficient proportion of academically-able and ambitious children to reassure those anxious about their children's 'chances' and to attract parental 'strategists' into the area. Formerly a grammar school, its O-level and A-level results have recently matched and then exceeded those of its selective days while its 'output' of academically-qualified pupils is now considerably larger. It has 1000 pupils aged 13–18, with about 250 in the sixth form. In recent years, it has moved a long way in curriculum and organization towards being 'truly' comprehensive. However, the head has been careful to retain some of the more traditional features of the school in order not to lose the confidence of middle-class parents (especially in academic and professional occupations) who, in other circumstances, might have experienced strong peer-group pressure to opt out of public education. In fact, such groups were as strongly represented in our sample from this school as in those from the independent schools and, as we shall see in chapters 8 and 9, they figure prominently in discussion of our parental interviews.

*Sandgate School* in the city is another 13–18 high school with a strong academic reputation and a 'very mixed intake' which the head nevertheless described to us as having 'a higher proportion of middle-class commuters than many comprehensives do' and as being 'skewed towards people with perhaps more positive attitudes to education'. Its pass-rates of 70 per cent at A-level and of 55 per cent getting 'good passes' at O-level (or equivalent) were comparable to those at Shirebrook School. Indeed, both schools have the size of sixth forms and array of academic subjects which would have qualified them for 'assisted-place status' if they had been in the private sector. Neither they, nor Rowton, seemed the kind of school from which able pupils needed to be 'rescued' in the terms defined by advocates of assisted places.

We now consider briefly what the schools in the two sectors may have gained and lost by the operation of the Scheme. Although it has a national reputation and normally had had a high place in the annual 'league tables' of Oxford and Cambridge awards, King Henry's School shares with the other four independent schools the characteristic noted earlier in Milltown — that of being regarded essentially as a grammar school. Indeed, the strongly Labour education committee retains nominees on its governing body. These schools are seen primarily as academically selective, their independence being valued less for its own sake than as a necessary condition of that selectiveness. Under the direct-grant arrangements, as we mentioned earlier, the schools drew their free-place pupils mainly from the city itself and from a neighbouring shire county. The new Scheme, being 'administered centrally rather than tied up with local affairs' (as the headmistress of the Queen's High School put it), has brought more geographically-dispersed intakes of assisted pupils. For example, half the assisted-place pupils entering St James's School in 1981 and 1982, and two-thirds of those entering King Henry's School, came from outside the city's administrative boundaries. Since they also came from homes located in six different LEAs, the quantitative effects on particular schools have obviously been diluted. Their distribution, however, is uneven enough to make the direct effects of the Scheme appear very differently in different schools.

The head of Frampton, for example, who has 'had to work damned hard even to stand still' and has still seen his numbers fall by 25 per cent in four years, regards the region's independent schools as essentially irrelevant to his problems. In this respect he is like some of the heads in Dilston. The competition facing his school has come mainly from a neighbouring comprehensive, regarded locally as more academic and more socially selective. Certainly the independent school statistics referred to earlier show some recruitment of assisted-place pupils from his LEA, but none from his main catchment area. On the other hand, the head of Rowton estimated that her school lost altogether a dozen 11-year-olds a year to independent schools, with some further loss at 16 to comprehensive schools with larger, more established sixth forms. However, while the area in which Shirebrook School is located provides a stream of pupils for independent schools which are a convenient train journey away, this school makes a significant net gain at 16 from pupils recruited out of the private sector. The head of Sandgate identified three comprehensive schools with which his own was in competition, but also noted that the particular 'pull' of independent schools would already have had its effect:

> Well, the fact that we receive pupils at 13 means that in the normal way parents who are going to sent their children to private schools have already made that decision, and so leakage from the system happens at the middle-school stage. Now, prior to your visit I rang up the middle schools . . . We seem to have lost to the private sector something like twenty pupils. Now that isn't an enormous number, but they were twenty pupils we would have preferred to have.

They were also likely to be twenty able pupils who would produce 'a very substantial crop of examination results, sixth-formers, and ultimate transfers to higher education'.

As in Dilston and Riverside, we found no clear evidence that would support a justification of the Assisted Places Scheme on the ground that it would lead to a rise in academic standards in the public sector. Its existence might encourage some comprehensive schools to intensify their efforts to retain the support of academically-ambitious parents by improving and publicizing their own results. But it was more likely to draw off able pupils whose own 'substantial crop' of passes would otherwise have contributed to a state school's record. In a school like Frampton, of course, even a very few high achievers may be enough to announce possibilities which other parents had previously thought beyond their children's and the school's reach.

The heads of the independent schools approved of the Scheme, not only for lessening their dependence on fee-paying parents but also for having raised the academic quality of their intakes. All three independent schools we have referred to in this section had tried to offset the worst effects of the Labour Government's withdrawal of direct grant by establishing their own trust funds to support scholarships and means-tested bursaries, a main objective being to resist too great a narrowing of their social range. But, like some of the heads quoted in chapter 6, they were also conscious of the potential academic gains that would arise from extending this provision via the Assisted Places Scheme. The head of King Henry's School, for example, described his first intakes of assisted-place pupils as 'bulking large at the top end of the 11-plus field', and expressed his particular pleasure that the school was again able to recruit 'brainy and often bookish youngsters' from a wide range of backgrounds. From his own records, though, very few indeed of these were from manual-working backgrounds. But, for schools whose market appeal rested so heavily on academic results (especially at A-level) and high rates of entry to higher education, it was the academic as much as the social gains that made the Assisted Places Scheme especially welcome.

From the other side, it seemed an unjustified slur on the public sector which was having evidently damaging results. As the head of Sandgate put it:

> The extent to which the state sector is creamed of able pupils is the extent to which it is disadvantaged by being unable to show what it can do for them, and simply has the odds loaded against it because able pupils, by and large, will always flourish academically wherever they are. And in the natural course of events the private sector appears to be very successful, but then it should be very successful.

The head of Rowton, with experience as a pupil in a public school and as a teacher in a direct-grant school, made the same point in similar terms:

> I resent any political will that seeks to cream off pupils from the state system and then judges the state system to have failed academically when pupils have in fact been removed who might have proved that state schools are capable of the same quality of education, of standards of education . . . In a city like [this] we cannot provide models of good practice in comprehensive schools because we are compared all the time with schools set up for different purposes.

Thus, although perhaps not on the scale evident in our first study area, the Assisted Places Scheme has certainly been a significant feature of secondary education in Scotsdale. In broad terms, the competition from independent schools had already spread throughout the region before the arrival of the Scheme, even if, as we have seen, it remains today unevenly distributed between schools. At the start of the Scheme there were over 150 places available in the area for new 11–13 entrants, together with another twenty-five at the sixth-form stage. Even in the Scheme's first year, 135 pupils took up assisted places. Although there were slightly fewer new entrants in 1987–8, the total number of assisted-place pupils had then reached 830. That figure represented almost a third of all pupils in the five schools, and illustrates the extent to which parts of the private sector would now be affected by the Scheme's abandonment. All except the Queen's High School have filled most of the places allocated to them, and Queen's itself has been meeting its reduced target since 1984. Private primary education in the city is not extensive, and all five have met the requirement that they should recruit more than 60 per cent of their assisted-place holders from maintained schools. The scale of what seems to LEAs to be a Government-sponsored exodus from the public sector at the secondary stage has therefore been considerable.

It is hardly surprising then that there is strong LEA opposition to the Scheme. Apart from exercising their initial right to veto transfers from the public sector at 16, most LEAs in the region have tried to constrain primary school heads from encouraging applicants or even publicizing the Scheme's existence. Part of this opposition derives from a principled objection to a Scheme so manifestly based on the assumption that state secondary schools cannot cope with able pupils. But there are also obvious practical objections at a time of falling rolls, possible amalgamations, and intensifying difficulties in 16-plus provision which have been especially marked in the city itself and in the most urban of its neighbouring LEAs.

### Conclusions From the Local Studies

While there are some clear differences between our three study areas, in terms of both history and current practice, the Assisted Places Scheme has very quickly become an established feature of the 'economy of schooling' in each of them, apparently regardless of the attitude of particular LEAs towards the Scheme. Even though there are some contrasts in the fine details of the Scheme's impact in Dilston, Riverside and Scotsdale, some of which relate to traditional patterns of provision and parental choice in the different areas, a number of common features stand out.

Firstly, the Scheme does not appear to be drawing pupils from the sorts of inner-city neighbourhood schools that were central to its rhetoric of justification, a point we discuss in detail in the chapter which follows. While this may be partly to do with the lack of academically able pupils living near these schools, it is also the result of the established role of parents and primary school teachers in directing such pupils to other schools, in suburban or mixed catchment areas, perceived as more likely to cater for their needs. Though the Assisted Places Scheme may now provide an additional option for such pupils, it has not apparently tapped a significant new clientele within any of our study areas. This is broadly consistent with the views of independent school heads which we reported in chapter 6.

The second point is that, although we found no single secondary school that had been substantially creamed by the Scheme, it has attracted enough additional pupils away from good comprehensive schools to raise questions about the long-term capacity of some of them to compete for academically able pupils. This is because the removal of a few more of their potential three-subject A-level candidates, including some who would traditionally have been sent to them as an escape from 'sink' schools, has in turn weakened their own appeal to other parents concerned to send their children to schools where there is a 'critical mass' of such pupils. Thus, the suggestion in the Headmasters' Conference journal, *Conference*, that 'a Scheme designed to attract working-class children who would otherwise go to a poor neighbourhood comprehensive may simply attract middle-class children who would otherwise go to a good comprehensive'[10] appears to be rather closer to the truth in our study areas than the claim that the Scheme is 'plucking embers from the ashes'.

Thirdly, although for most good comprehensive schools the Scheme is as yet an irritant rather than a serious threat, it is likely to make it more difficult in future for other state schools to produce the sort of 'turn-round' in their fortunes that has occurred at Vicarage Road. Just as such schools were gaining some success in attracting pupils away from local independent schools, the Assisted Places Scheme has intensified the competition. Critics of the state sector, and especially advocates of cross-sector voucher schemes, would argue that this merely proves that independent schools have the competitive edge when competition with the state sector is put on equal terms by the removal of the financial disincentive posed by fees. However, given the widespread social perception of the superiority of independent schools, it might equally be claimed that the Scheme is denying 'improving' comprehensive schools the opportunity ever to prove their worth.

The fourth point that arises from our findings is that comprehensive schools that do successfully compete and retain the confidence of parents of academically able pupils sometimes find themselves doing so at the expense of serving other market segments. We found some evidence that those state schools, apart from the maintained grammar schools, that were most successful in retaining academically able pupils were those that had a public image closest to that of an independent school.[11] Furthermore, the headteachers of these schools were also frequently similar in background and style to those we encountered in the private sector. Yet, unlike their independent school colleagues, they face the difficult task of maintaining their appeal to a wide range of pupils and parents, not all of whom aspire to academic success. An emphasis on academic success was sometimes seen as incompatible with curriculum innovations in other areas, including those being urged on schools by the Government. To this extent, the 'pull' of the private sector may distort the market in other services that the public sector alone is currently expected to provide. In Dilston, for example, there was evidence that the heads of those schools that sought to compete with the private sector were wary of TVEI on the grounds that it might not appeal to those parents who wanted an academic education for their children. Although Vicarage Road in Riverside appeared to have had some success in avoiding this danger, it was only

Shirebrook School in Scotsdale that seemed entirely confident of its ability both to compete successfully with independent schools for academically able pupils and provide a worthwhile education for all the others.

Finally, it is clear that, even if the Assisted Places Scheme itself has had limited and somewhat uneven effects on the maintained sector, it has played a role, alongside other influences that coincided with it, in sapping the morale of that sector and in boosting the confidence of the independent schools. This was a development that was particularly disturbing to the head of Redland, the most successful of the comprehensives in Dilston, who was somewhat less confident than the head of Shirebrook about his own school's immunity to this danger. The extent to which it has already influenced patterns of parental choice is an issue we return to in chapter 9, while in chapter 10 we speculate about some of its longer-term consequences. Meanwhile, in chapter 8, we explore some of the characteristics of the pupils who have entered independent schools through the Assisted Places Scheme and compare them with full fee-paying pupils in those schools and with their peers in the maintained sector.

### Notes

1 The extension of the sample to pupils across the comprehensive ability range was designed to provide us with some insight into the broader dynamics of school choice in our study areas. See chapters 8 and 9.
2 See Appendix.
3 Wilkinson (1986), himself now the head of a school on the assisted places list, argues that the *majority* of schools in the Scheme will have benefited considerably from its existence. 'Many schools will be "sick" if the APS is withdrawn — sick financially and in terms of the loss of children of ability' (p. 59).
4 The idea of allowing parents to vote to opt out of LEA control was floated during the 1987 general election campaign and translated into legislation in the 1988 Education Reform Act, which established this new category of grant maintained schools.
5 See Wall (1986).
6 Letter to Mark Carlisle, 29 October 1979.
7 When their future was uncertain, the grammar schools within this LEA considered the possibility of avoiding comprehensivization by applying for grant maintained status.
8 Sexton stressed this argument during both his interviews with us.
9 This school is due to join the Assisted Places Scheme in September 1989.
10 Editorial in *Conference*, February 1980.
11 The public image of a school is not necessarily a reliable indication of its practices. In curriculum terms, some of the activities which parents described as 'gimmicks' in comprehensive schools in the Dilston area were actually an established part of the curriculum in some of the local independent schools. To this extent, academically-oriented comprehensive schools may feel constrained by parental wishes to offer a curriculum that is actually more traditional than the *reality* of what is currently offered in some of the competing independent schools.

# Chapter 8

# Pupils and Parents:
# The Beneficiaries of Assisted Places

The Assisted Places Scheme involves direct contractual agreements between individual schools and the Government. The schools themselves depend on attracting direct applications from financially-eligible families. How such families perceive the opportunities being offered is therefore critical to the Scheme's evaluation. Having described how the Scheme operated in some of the schools offering places and how it was perceived in other nearby schools, we now focus down on the beneficiaries themselves and on comparable groups of fee-paying and maintained-school pupils and parents. In doing so, we try to answer some of the questions which guided our collection of evidence.

The most obvious of these questions was whether assisted places were reaching the intended target groups. In chapter 5 we analyzed the limited national statistics available for answering that question. From that source, information about the social backgrounds of pupils is almost entirely confined to broad categories of income. Whatever may be inferred from those statistics is insufficient to test the confident predictions which were made when the Scheme was introduced about who its principal beneficiaries would be. It is true that, since the Scheme has become established, ministers and other advocates have regularly insisted that low income is the only relevant social criterion for access to an assisted place. But, as we have seen, it is also true that the image of the 'ideal client' which appeared in much of the supporting rhetoric when the Scheme was first mooted was that of an able boy or girl from a working-class inner-city home being 'rescued' from the academic inadequacies of local comprehensive schools. Critics of the Scheme, on the other hand, were convinced that such pupils would not figure extensively among its beneficiaries. Have such children been attracted in large numbers? And to what extent are they being 'rescued' from maintained schools evidently unable to cope with them?

In this chapter we compare the social and educational backgrounds of assisted-place pupils with those of contemporaries paying full fees in the same schools,[1] and of pupils of the same age attending maintained schools. In the chapter which follows we examine in detail the complex relationships between family situations and choice of secondary school, the processes through which the eventual decisions were made, and pupils' and parents' perceptions of the schools which had eventually been chosen. What relative advantages did assisted-place pupils and their parents see in being sponsored to attend independent schools, and what benefits did fee-payers see themselves as buying? Were their perceptions of relative advantage accepted even by those who had followed other routes? Did the three groups differ significantly in their views of secondary schooling, and of the opportunities available to them?

Our attempts to answer those questions required extensive interviewing of pupils and their parents. Before reporting the evidence, we therefore need to describe briefly how it was obtained.

### Interviewing Pupils and Parents

The pupil interviews were intended to make comparisons possible between fee-paying and assisted-place pupils in the same schools, and between pupils in independent and maintained schools. They gave a pupils' perspective on the relative attractions of different schools and kinds of school, and some indication of how far their present school had been positively chosen rather than passively accepted.

The interviews took place in the schools. We used the same schedule of questions throughout, taking about twenty minutes to ask them. Assurances of confidentiality were always given, and most pupils talked readily despite the inevitable formality of the encounter.[2] Nevertheless, we recognize that situational constraints (including no doubt the interviewers' continuing resemblance to the teachers they once were) are likely to have encouraged safe answers and softened criticisms. At least two of us were involved in interviewing in each school, so making it possible to compare impressions and to discuss any themes which emerged as the interviews progressed. There were opportunities around the interviews themselves to talk informally with staff about some of the matters which pupils had raised and to check on local facts.

Given the different size and character of the schools willing to cooperate, and our dependence on parental consent for the interviews, it is unlikely that any sampling of pupils could have been tidily systematic. There was, however, some strategic planning. Sixth-formers were likely to be highly unrepresentative of the Scheme's beneficiaries because of the high proportion of recruits already in independent schools, so that focusing on 'mainstream' entrants in the most active fieldwork years 1983–4 limited us largely to pupils who were aged 12–14 at the time of being interviewed. This in turn determined the age of the comparative samples of fee-payers and pupils in maintained schools. Apart from two small groups of 11-year-olds at Cathedral College and Weston School, and first-year pupils at Shirebrook (a 13–18 high school), our sample were all in their second or third year of secondary schooling. Unlike some recent studies (for example, Fox, 1985; Walford, 1986), we wanted equal numbers of boys and girls. The preponderance of boys in our private sector sample is an unintended consequence of the schools being single-sex and the boys' schools being larger. The preponderance of girls in the public sector sample is partly a 'balancing act', partly the reflection of which parental permissions were received first. The 'academic ability' of most of those interviewed was determined by our starting-point in a Scheme explicitly intended to revive opportunities for grammar school education. Assisted-place pupils are 'able' by definition, and their fee-paying contemporaries were drawn from the same classes. Because the Scheme is supposed to offer academic opportunities unlikely to be available in the public sector, we initially asked maintained schools to identify children who 'would have qualified for grammar schools' if that option had still been available. The effect of that requirement produced a marked over-representation of middle-class pupils. Although this sample was appropriate for most of our purposes, we also needed a wider sample to help us interpret our findings. As indicated in chapter 7, we therefore extended our sampling to embrace a wider range of ability. The number of pupils involved are shown in table 8.1, which records the scale of our interviewing.

## Table 8.1 Number of Pupil Interviews

|  | Boys | Girls | Total |
|---|---|---|---|
| Full fee-payers | 83 | 62 | 145 |
| Assisted-place holders in the same schools | 90 | 67 | 157 |
| Pupils in maintained grammar schools | 28 | 33 | 61 |
| 'Academically able' pupils in comprehensive schools | 95 | 153 | 248 |
| Other pupils in comprehensive and secondary modern schools | 31 | 33 | 64 |
| Total | 327 | 348 | 675 |

The sample was large enough for us to make detailed comparisons of the social background of pupils, and of some of their attitudes and aspirations. It gave us information about the network of local schooling, and about the information and prejudices on which a choice of school had been based. It highlighted instances where parents had clearly been drawn into the private sector by the existence of assisted places, and where parents had hovered between sectors — often in prolonged indecision. Nevertheless, the sample falls short of the representativeness for which we had hoped. In one area, for example, the independent schools remained resistant to any interviewing of pupils, although they provided a good deal of information themselves. In general, the sample reflects the inevitable compromises which had to be made in an investigation which was entirely dependent on schools' willingness to cooperate and which concerned a Scheme about which many schools (in both sectors) felt very defensive.

The primary purpose of the pupil interviews was to explore perspectives on local educational provision. Our early questions focused on why the school they now attended had been chosen, whose choice it had mainly been, and what other schools (if any) had been considered. The aggregated responses threw light on the rank-ordering of schools in local opinion, and what the available alternatives seemed to have been. There were also enough indications of talent-spotting for the private sector at some primary schools, and of systematic coaching for entry to particular independent schools, to introduce a theme into our analysis which we had not fully anticipated when the interviewing began. We asked about pupils' 'best friends' at their previous school, which secondary school those friends now attended, and whether contact had been maintained. These questions were relevant to whether the Scheme was having the socially-divisive consequences which its opponents often predicted. They also enabled us to identify those schools in the public sector which assisted-place pupils were most likely to have attended if a place in an independent school had not been sponsored from public funds. Further questions about pupils' hopes of extending their schooling beyond 16, and about any occupations they might already have in mind, were a basis for some tentative comparisons between sectors in the nature and firmness of these early ambitions. While we were cautious about pupils' identification of their parents' occupations, these were generally confirmed by the parental interviews and by school records. There was, however, significant under-reporting by pupils of single-parent households, though this was partly because some of those who appear in statistics as single parents cohabit with partners who act as parents even though they have no legal responsibility for the children involved. The distinction between single parents and lone parents raises questions about the appropriateness of the means test applied in the Scheme, but this was clearly not something that could be pursued in the context of pupil interviews.

Finally, pupils were asked what they liked and disliked most about their present school, what was 'most important' to them about being there, and how they thought it compared with other schools. As we report in chapter 9, strong criticisms were rare and most responses could be placed on a continuum from grudging loyalty to outright enthusiasm.[3] Prejudices about particular kinds of school however, especially private sector myths about comprehensives, were often conspicuous. What might be called the 'folkloric' aspect of familial orientations to secondary schooling is a theme which we explore later.

Conducting the home-based interviews was the most time-consuming part of the research. It was also the most enjoyable. Indeed, as other researchers have found, it became at times almost addictive! The attraction lay in the variety of homes we visited, and the willingness of most parents to talk freely about their own backgrounds, their hopes for their children, and the often difficult decisions they had made about the 'right' secondary school. Very occasionally we had been made to feel like intruders when the interview was being arranged, only to find ourselves actively engaged in conversation once it had begun. Much more commonly, we were welcomed from the start, often being turned into confidants in the way that strangers can. Table 8.2 shows the number of parental interviews conducted.

#### Table 8.2 Number of Parental Interviews

| Status of child | No. of interviews | Mother only | Father only | Both |
|---|---|---|---|---|
| Full fee-payers | 82 | 39 | 12 | 31 |
| Assisted-place holders | 90 | 55 | 17 | 18 |
| Able state school pupils | 147 | 70 | 21 | 56 |
| (25 attended grammar schools) | | | | |
| (122 attended comprehensive schools) | | | | |
| Total number of interviews | 319 | 164 | 50 | 105 |

The interviews lasted at least an hour, some two hours or more. Initial contact with parents was made by letter, written by the researchers but usually sent out by the school, outlining our purposes and asking for permission to interview their child at school. They were also asked about their own willingness to be interviewed. The involvement of the schools in the sending out of these letters, and in receiving the replies, undoubtedly reassured some parents about the inquiry's legitimacy.[4] We hoped to interview the parents of half the pupil sample at each school, and this objective was broadly achieved. No category of parent was any more elusive than the others, and only two parents (both with children holding assisted places) after first agreeing refused to be interviewed.

The interviews were organized in three parts. First, we asked questions about the parents' own schooling, their occupations, the occupations of their own parents, and their present family circumstances. The second stage of questioning then focused on their choice of secondary school for the child we had interviewed previously, with some additional questions to independent school parents about assistance with school fees (whether from the Scheme or from other sources). Finally, we asked more general and open-ended questions about their perception of educational and occupational opportunities, their attitudes to selective secondary education and other aspects of schooling, their political affiliation, and their views of the 'openness' of British society.

Where it was practicable and appropriate to do so, answers were pre-coded or re-coded for computation using the SPSS program; other kinds of information were noted in detail during the interviews, including verbatim recording of opinions. Parents were often given a copy of the interview schedule at the start of the interview, to facilitate more conversational responses than if the interviewer was tied mainly to an interrogating role and to reassure them that there were no hidden questions. We decided against tape-recording, mainly because the labour of transcribing such long interviews would have been unmanageable. As soon as possible after leaving each home, we wrote a 'narrative' of the setting, the character of the exchanges which had occurred, and any preoccupations which the parents themselves had highlighted. We found the Connell study (Connell *et al.*, 1983) helpful as an example of 'listening to people talking about their own life histories', compared with (for example) Irene Fox's (1985) study of parents' expectations of private schooling, in which we missed hearing similar 'voices'.

The interviews were predominantly enjoyable as well as instructive. Many parents made considerable efforts to see us — changing busy work schedules, interrupting domestic arrangements (including one instance when they had only just returned home from the funeral of a close relative and insisted that the interview go ahead), or putting an evening aside when free time was obviously scarce. Most parents were self-assured on their own ground, but there were some who were clearly apprehensive and on their best behaviour — like the mother who kept wishing that her husband was not away and who later admitted that she 'hadn't slept all night' for fear of making a fool of herself in front of 'the man from the university'. That latter response raises two methodological issues we discuss below and which we intend to develop more fully in subsequent publications. They concern the class and gender of the researchers.

Except for the first few months, all the interviewing was done by males whose academic status placed them as unmistakeably middle class in the eyes of those being interviewed. Although relics of London, Welsh and Australian speech may have helped to ease some encounters, there was no mistaking the occasional smart dress in mid-afternoon or the best china. Especially in some working-class and lower middle-class homes, the interview was obviously being treated as an event — in contrast to the many occasions when they were clearly being fitted into a hectic schedule and treated more casually. There is evidence that working-class informants, especially perhaps women, are more likely to treat interviews as formal events. Many parents were prepared to challenge questions, use them to explore and clarify their views, or debate their responses. In contrast, a few of the working-class mothers seemed to respond to the more general questions as though they were part of an examination, occasionally apologizing for 'not knowing anything about that'.

The second issue relates to general difficulties of cross-gender research, and particularly to the interview dynamics of male researchers interviewing women (Roberts, 1981). We were conscious of the problems, especially as in our research more than half the interviews were with mothers only. This was partly because they were more likely to be at home during the day, partly because the child's education even at the secondary stage was still seen as primarily their business, and partly because over a third of our assisted-place holders came from households headed by single-parent mothers. There were also some occasions in joint interviews where the woman's contributions seemed constrained, and where trying to contain a male conversational dominance was a considerable problem for the interviewer. There were several striking instances of a mother beginning the interview on her own, being joined by her partner, and then virtually vanishing as the respondent! We tried in such joint interviews to direct questions to each partner in turn — a practice which sometimes revealed clear boundaries around 'his' and 'her' domains of family knowledge, and which sometimes uncovered differences in opinion or strength of opinion which came as a complete surprise to both! There were certainly many instances of parents turning parts of the interview into a debate between them, or even into a three-way 'seminar'. Dr Rees, for example, a university scientist with a daughter at Shirebrook, was forced to withdraw a series of assertions about the 'known' superiority of independent schools by his wife's insistent demands for 'evidence'![5]

Generally, most of our informants seemed to find it illuminating and enjoyable to reflect on the factors which had fed into their choice of school, and were often prepared to elaborate well beyond the scope of the questions about their own social origins and educational histories. There were expressions too of continuing pain in recalling (for example) 11-plus failures even thirty years before, or of evident distress at the loss of a partner or at some other upheaval in family arrangements. There were a few occasions when the interviews edged towards therapy sessions, usually where death or separation had disrupted the family, and many more when parents tried to elicit information or reassurance about decisions relating to their child's schooling which they had found or were finding difficult. We certainly had to consider seriously the notion of reciprocity in research interviews of this kind. In what Lather (1986) calls 'post-positivist research', it is argued that people's life histories should not be wrenched out of them and then mangled into aggregated form. Instead, the research act should resemble an exchange in which the researcher gives something in return. Our interviews were not exchanges in that full sense. But although clearly committed to maintaining confidentiality, we did not aspire to neutrality. If challenged directly about our own attitudes or experiences, we made them known insofar as this was necessary to maintain what we hoped would be seen as essentially conversational encounters. We would argue that to elicit 'life-stories', it is often necessary to tell something of one's own. In the course of the interviews we were struck by the fatalism of some families about the situation they found themselves in, where local bureaucracy or lack of material or cultural resources seemed to them insuperable obstacles to having any choice at all about their children's education. It was also difficult not to feel sympathy for those single parents, and other parents in difficult circumstances, who were conspicuously proud that their child was attending an 'elite' independent school. There were many more who clearly felt educationally dispossessed by the disappearance of the grammar schools, and many others who displayed an evident enthusiasm for the opportunities offered by their child's comprehensive and for its humane atmosphere compared with the secondary schools they had attended themselves. Although the rest of this chapter is predominantly about generalizations from our evidence of assisted-place pupils and their contemporaries, we hope that the diversity of family circumstances also shows through.

### The social origins of assisted-place pupils

Has the Assisted Places Scheme enabled participating schools to recruit, as intended, children from social backgrounds not traditionally associated with fee-paying education? Has it extended parental choice? Has it provided a route to selective academic education for academically able working-class children thought to have been lost with the demise of direct-grant and maintained grammar schools? Or have most places gone, as some research has suggested, to the children of 'distressed gentlefolk', or to families made 'artificially poor' by death, divorce or unemployment (Tapper and Salter, 1986a, p. 325; Douse, 1985, p. 215)? In the rest of this chapter, we describe the backgrounds from which our sample of assisted-place pupils came, and how they differed from their fee-paying contemporaries and from the academically 'able' pupils we interviewed in maintained schools.

In their 'interim evaluation' of the Scheme, Tapper and Salter use published statistics to deny that places are going largely to children from culturally disadvantaged backgrounds, and therefore to deny that the schools offering those places are having to adjust to a significantly new kind of client. They conclude that assistance has not been concentrated where 'need' is greatest, even as the Scheme itself defines need, and that a high proportion of beneficiaries are the children of 'relatively impoverished but educationally aware members of the petite bourgeoisie' (1986, p. 321). Douse (1985) came to a similar conclusion about who the beneficiaries were, but denied that his evidence constituted a criticism of the Scheme because its architects had defined prospective beneficiaries by parental income and not by class. That evidence, drawn from postal questionnaires to 110 schools offering places and interviews with 199 assisted-place pupils, showed that very few came from 'unambiguously working-class backgrounds' and also that a large minority were from families 'already within the independent school frame of reference' because (for example) a parent or sibling had attended an independent school. Heads' responses suggested that 30–40 per cent of their assisted-place pupils would have gone to the school even if the Scheme had not existed. Our own preliminary report (Fitz *et al.*, 1986) noted a high proportion of such pupils from 'submerged middle-class backgrounds already well-endowed with cultural capital', and contrasted our evidence with the particular concern for able working-class children 'denied' academic opportunity which many architects of the Scheme had expressed. If most places were undoubtedly going to children of parents with low or at least 'modest' incomes, they were rarely going to children from 'manual working-class families, especially where the fathers are in semi-skilled or unskilled employment' (1986, p. 185). Wilkinson (1986, p. 61) points out that even in income terms the Scheme tends to appeal to the 'deserving fairly poor'.

Before looking at our own evidence on the social backgrounds of the assisted-place holders, we need to say something about the categories that we have employed to classify our data. We have used stratified categories of occupation as the means of describing and analyzing that data though we are aware of the limitations of this mode of analysis. We return at the end of the chapter to some specific criticisms of the use of such categories in research on the Assisted Places Scheme and confine ourselves here to some broader issues in the study of 'social class'. While occupational status is obviously not the equivalent of social class, it provides a commonly understood means of talking about groups differentiated by the kinds of work they do, and by the broad differences in education, income and social status which that differentiation makes probable. There is a continuing debate about the relative merits of 'occupational class' (as used in most official statistics, and in the 'political arithmetic' research tradition) and 'social class', derived from the Marxian conception of the social relations of production (Duke and Edgell, 1987). Classifying occupations by their status or standing gives priority to the division between manual/non-manual occupations, while neo-Marxist categories are differentiated broadly by reference to the ownership/non-ownership of the means of production (Duke and Edgell, pp. 48–9). Most British mainstream analysis of 'social class and educational opportunity' has employed versions of stratification theory (for example, Heath, 1980; Heath and Ridge, 1983). Researchers like Connell and his colleagues (1983), however, have used a 'two-class model' (working class/ruling class) to explore different forms of 'articulation' between Australian families and schools by emphasizing the market relationship of middle-class parents with the schools they pay for, and the bureaucratic relationship of working-class parents with schools 'provided for them'. We found these categories too broad for our purposes. We also wanted to facilitate comparisons with other recent British investigations of public and private schooling, although we have also tried to give equal attention to the occupations (and educational experience) of men and women. We also collected such information about the parents' own parents.

The Hope–Goldthorpe classification (Goldthorpe and Hope, 1974), which we have used to analyze our data, employs thirty-six categories of occupations which have then been combined, following Goldthorpe *et al.* (1980), into seven groups and three broad 'classes':

*Service Class*

I   Higher-grade professionals, administrators, managers, proprietors, e.g. doctors, lawyers, accountants, dentists, surveyors, architects, engineers, stockbrokers, senior civil servants, managers in large commercial and manufacturing enterprises, local authority senior officers, working owners of large shops and service agencies.

II   Lower-grade professionals, administrators and managers; supervisors; higher-grade technicians — e.g. police officers, computer programmers, draughtsmen, managers in small business, industrial and construction enterprises, primary and secondary school teachers, civil service executive officers, social workers, supervisors of clerical workers.

*Intermediate Class*

III   Clerical, sales and rank-and-file service workers — e.g. cashiers, commercial travellers, cooks, stewards, hairdressers, shop assistants.

IV   Small proprietors and self-employed artisans, the 'petty bourgeoisie' — e.g. farmers, smallholders, working owners of small shops and service agencies, small builders, hoteliers, painters and decorators, carpenters, publicans.

V   Lower-grade technicians and foremen, the 'aristocracy of labour' — e.g. electrical and electronic engineers, auto-engineers, foremen in construction and mining, transport and distribution.

*Working Class*

VI   Skilled manual workers in industry — e.g. fitters, tool-makers, sheet metal workers, other ranks in Armed Services, bricklayers, miners, riggers, furnacemen, butchers, bakers.

VII Semi-skilled and unskilled manual workers in industry — e.g. machine tool operators, food process workers, bus drivers, postal workers, dock workers, gardeners and groundsmen, factory labourers, office and industrial cleaners, agricultural workers.

For our particular purposes, we added the categories of unemployed, houseworker, student and handicapped/invalid/disabled. But as a way of registering structural inequalities in life chances, we found the classification difficult to use in relation to women's jobs because of the predominance of routine non-manual occupations which are ostensibly 'intermediate' but which might reasonably be regarded as 'working-class' jobs for women — for example, dinner ladies, domestics, or lower-grade office workers (Murgatroyd, 1982). More generally we were also aware of the debates about the application of class analysis to conjugal families, and the treatment of women in conventional stratification theory (Delphy, 1981; Goldthorpe, 1983; Stanworth, 1984; Heath and Britten, 1984). The critics of the conventional approach have argued that it takes insufficient account of the high proportion of women in paid employment outside the family, disregards the nature of the work they do, and gives inadequate consideration to the woman's contribution to the social class location of the family. As our own study progressed it was inevitable that this debate influenced the way we approached our data analysis. As a consequence we were convinced of the necessity to record and take account of the employment, paid and unpaid, of the mothers in our sample.

As is clear from tables 8.3 and 8.4, most parents in our total sample were employed in occupations categorized as 'service class' or 'intermediate' occupations. A minority were self-employed, or ran small businesses employing one or two other workers. A few had been made poor by long-term unemployment, disability, chronic illness or a recently failed marriage. A very small number appeared to be wealthy, with considerable property. Largely absent from the sample, in comparison for example with Fox's (1985) public school study, were landowners, corporate tycoons, people doing that mysterious 'something in the City', and people who did not have to work for a living at all.

Table 8.3 reveals several notable features about our sample. Firstly, most fathers of fee-paying pupils were in well-paid, high-status occupations in the service class. In fact, our evidence shows that over 60 per cent of them were in the 'higher-grade' (often self-employed) professions such as medicine, law, architecture and engineering, or in senior management positions in industry, commerce and the public service. Those figures are unsurprising, given the fact that tuition fees alone in our sample schools ranged in 1984 from £1431 to £3264 (the national average for assisted-place schools then being £1730). More significant from our perspective, however, is the high proportion of service class occupations in the assisted-place sample, and the conspicuous absence of 'unambiguously working-class' occupations not only in that sample but in the maintained grammar schools as well. A marked skewing towards 'middle-class' occupations is apparent throughout table 8.3, a feature related to the fact that the comprehensive school sample shown here came from the upper ability bands of those schools. Nor does the picture change in table 8.4, which is derived from a smaller number of parental interviews. While children are often found to be vague or 'over-optimistic' about the work their parents do, the distribution of occupations recorded from our own pupil interviews is broadly similar to the data produced by parents.

Taken together, the two tables show very few children of working-class parents among the assisted-place pupils. Less than 10 per cent of those pupils had fathers who were manual workers, compared with 50 per cent with fathers in service class occupations, while almost all the employed mothers were in white-collar employment. While it can be argued that overall these pupils were less socially-selected than their fee-paying contemporaries, on this evidence they are not clearly from socially or culturally disadvantaged backgrounds, despite the relatively low incomes of their parents. The social composition of our sample of assisted-place pupils resembles that described by Douse (1985). It also resembles the composition of direct-grant schools in

**Table 8.3 Occupational status of parents (as reported by pupils)**

| | Service Class | | Intermediate Class | | | Working Class | | Not in paid employment |
|---|---|---|---|---|---|---|---|---|
| | I | II | III | IV | V | VI | VII | |
| **Father** | | | | | | | | |
| Full fee-payers | 65.3 | 20.7 | 0 | 12.0 | 0 | 0 | 0 | 2.0 |
| Assisted-place pupils | 11.9 | 38.1 | 10.2 | 15.3 | 8.5 | 6.8 | 2.5 | 6.8 |
| Grammar school pupils | 54.3 | 34.7 | 0 | 6.5 | 0 | 0 | 2.2 | 2.2 |
| Able comprehensive pupils | 24.5 | 34.0 | 7.5 | 11.2 | 6.6 | 6.6 | 6.2 | 3.3 |
| **Mother** | | | | | | | | |
| Full fee-payers | 7.6 | 30.5 | 16.6 | 5.6 | 0 | 0 | 0 | 39.6 |
| Assisted-place pupils | 0 | 22.2 | 36.8 | 2.8 | 1.4 | 1.4 | 2.8 | 32.6 |
| Grammar school pupils | 2.0 | 46.0 | 28.0 | 4.0 | 0 | 0 | 0 | 20.0 |
| Able comprehensive pupils | 1.2 | 29.0 | 32.8 | 2.3 | 1.5 | 0 | 6.2 | 27.0 |

*Note:* Figures are shown as percentages (N = 611).

Table 8.4 Parents' occupational status aggregated into broad 'social class' categories (as declared by parents)

| | Service | | Intermediate | | Working Class | | Not in paid employment | | Missing data | |
|---|---|---|---|---|---|---|---|---|---|---|
| | Fathers | Mothers | Fathers | Mothers | Fathers | Mothers | Fathers | Mothers | Fathers | Mothers |
| Full fee-payers | 85.4 | 40.3 | 12.2 | 19.5 | 0.0 | 0.0 | 1.2 | 40.2 | 1.2 | 0.0 |
| Assisted-place pupils | 54.4 | 28.9 | 27.8 | 41.2 | 6.6 | 0.0 | 7.8 | 28.8 | 3.4 | 1.1 |
| Grammar school pupils | 84.0 | 48.0 | 8.0 | 28.0 | 4.0 | 4.0 | 4.0 | 20.0 | 0.0 | 0.0 |
| Able comprehensive pupils | 65.6 | 28.6 | 18.0 | 42.7 | 9.0 | 0.5 | 4.9 | 27.8 | 2.5 | 0.4 |

*Note:* Figures are shown as percentages (N = 319 households).

the 1960s when, despite their claims not to be socially selective, some 60 per cent of their intake came from professional/managerial families compared with 8 per cent from the manual working class (see chapter 2). Neither those schools, nor the more recent embodying of the 'direct-grant principle' in assisted places, constitute that 'unique social mix' claimed by advocates to be the consequence of offering opportunities based solely on academic merit. In both cases there has been a marked tendency for advocates to cite evidently working-class instances as being more representative than they are.

Our data also show a significant under-representation of working class children in the sample of 'able' comprehensive pupils. It was not unusual to find 50 per cent or more of these pupils coming from service class backgrounds. At Moorside, 53 per cent of fathers and 33 per cent of mothers were in service class occupations; at Parkside Girls' it was 67 per cent of fathers and 23 per cent of mothers; at Cherry Tree it was 54 per cent of fathers and 22 per cent of mothers, while at Vicarage Road the comparable figures were 55 per cent and 22 per cent. And at Shirebrook High School, 81 per cent of fathers and 35 per cent of mothers were in service class occupations — a proportion almost as high as in any independent school in our study, even amongst fee-paying parents. While these proportions partly reflect the social composition of the areas in which the schools are located, and the well-documented preponderance of middle-class children in upper-ability bands, they also suggest that many professional and managerial families have identified and are prepared to use maintained schools with a good local reputation. Moreover they have developed strategies (especially of house-buying) which have maximized the chances of their children securing a place at a 'good' comprehensive. In her recent Australian study, Hatton (1985) reports how residential segregation allowed middle-class families to use their 'cultural power' to 'capture' local state schools. In those schools, curriculum, teaching styles and staffing were profoundly influenced by middle-class families working through 'parents and citizens' committees. Even in the absence of such overt pressure groups in our own three study areas, schools like Shirebrook go to considerable lengths to look after 'the top end' and they are under considerable parental pressure to do so. In effect, they are reassuring parents seeking — in that phrase often used by independent school heads when publicizing the attractions of their own schools — a 'critical mass' of children they hope will be as able and ambitious as their own.

This is one reason why the Connell (1983) 'two sector' model of 'ruling class' and 'working class' schools does not fit the comprehensive schools in our study. Even in areas traditionally associated with manufacturing and light industry, and near large council estates, many families who in other circumstances might have done so had not bought their way out of the state sector. In Frampton, the most working-class of our schools, the range of occupations is still quite broad. While mothers mainly worked in shops, the school meals service or as secretaries, the fathers' occupations included electrician, miner, car sprayer, fitter, screen printer and bus driver, and five in the service class including the manager of a large gas plant and an engineer working for a large ship-building firm. At Rowton, a school in the same conurbation with a similar catchment, the presence of pupils from service class families is enhanced by our sampling from only upper ability children at that school. Here twenty-two out of forty fathers and thirteen out of forty-five mothers were in service class occupations. Four of the fathers had occupations classified as higher grade professional or senior management. The heterogeneity of social backgrounds in some comprehensives is a strong defence of their claim to be egalitarian institutions. Certainly some of the interviewees regarded that social mix as a positive inducement, valuing it in contrast to the narrow social and academic stratum they thought populated the independent schools.

We turn now to the apparent discrepancy between the undoubtedly high proportion of low-income families among the beneficiaries of assisted places, the fact most often cited by Ministers and other defenders of the Scheme to demonstrate its success, and the high proportion of 'middle-class' occupations. It is partly explained by the presence in considerable numbers of professional parents earning around the average national income — notably, clergymen and teachers. But the main explanation, in national statistics and in our own sample, has been the substantial presence of single-parent families. Generalizing across all 319 homes in which we carried out interviews, most resembled the conventional 'cereal packet' family, in that over 80 per cent were headed by married couples, 88 per cent of the marriages were first marriages, and 90 per cent had between one and three children. They were also families in which both parents were likely to be in paid employment. Of the mothers, over 40 per cent had full-time paid employment (a figure which was consistent across all four categories), and another 27 per cent had part-time jobs; of the fathers, 90 per cent were in full-time jobs. The only significant categorical differences here were that more of the fee-paying mothers were not employed at all — 39 per cent compared with 24 per cent of mothers of assisted-place and comprehensive school pupils — and that a higher proportion of assisted-place fathers were unemployed. Much more significant was the fact that no less than 40 per cent of the assisted-place families were headed by a single parent, compared with less than 10 per cent in the other pupil categories. At the time of our fieldwork such families accounted nationally for 4 per cent of all households, with 29 per cent being composed of married couples with dependent children. The ratio between these family types was therefore 1:7. For our own complete sample, it was 1:6. For the families of assisted-place pupils, it was 1:1.5 At St Hilda's, for example, six of the ten girls we interviewed (and nine of the first fifteen assisted-place entrants to that school) were from single-parent families. Although that proportion was unusually high, the evidence from pupil interviews and other information supplied by the schools in which we worked suggested an average figure of about a third — which is what ISIS and other national surveys have consistently reported.

That marked 'over-representation' has been widely used to indicate the Scheme's success in matching opportunity with need. Yet single-parent families are a diverse category in status and circumstances. Almost all those in our sample were headed by women. They were single parents through divorce or separation, the husband's death, or through having children without marrying — different causes with potentially very different material consequences. The Scheme considers income, not wealth, in determining financial eligibility. It also takes account only of parental income. Some mothers we interviewed were supported by cohabitees, or by ex-husbands, without a custodial relationship to the child; in neither circumstance was the other income included in calculating fee remission. Mrs Menton for example (Cathedral College) was surprised that she was eligible for assistance when her ex-husband was earning around £70,000 a year and ought to have paid the full fees immediately a High Court decision made him responsible for them; her son's participation in the Scheme had given Mr Menton what she regarded as a thoroughly undeserved year's grace. We cite other cases later in the chapter where a high level of fee remission co-existed with the high income of a new partner.

Of more general relevance to our own study is the extent to which the single-parent category illustrates the difficulty of using 'low income' as the sole or main indicator of social and cultural disadvantage. Single-parent households are rather more common than is often assumed (Phoenix, 1987) and their incidence is rising. Most of them are headed by women, as was overwhelmingly the case in our own sample. There is a strong tendency in official policy to relate social and educational, as well as economic, disadvantage causally to household form. However, the issue is far more complicated than this in view of the structural position of women in the workforce as predominantly low-paid, often part-time workers with restricted career changes. Difficulties also arise from being dependent on discretionary social security payments and maintenance payments from ex-partners; and from both the direct costs and the limitations on earning power (Pahl, 1983; Jordan and Waine, 1986; Milne *et al.*, 1986). These wider causes suggest that the negative effects attributed to single-parent households are largely direct consequences of low income, which is 'virtually a structural feature' of such families and may in itself 'mediate a large part of the effect on [educational] achievement of the absence of the father' (Milne *et al.*, p. 137). However, more significant in the present context, is the fact that low income may be partly compensated for by the cultural capital available to the child. In the Assisted Places Scheme, it is notable that while children from single-parent families constitute the largest category of beneficiaries identified in relation to social 'need', as successive ISIS surveys have emphasized, children from other kinds of family also thought to be widely disadvantaged are either much less prominent (like the unemployed) or conspicuously under-represented (parents in semi-skilled and unskilled manual work, black and Asian families). The 'structural feature' of low income obviously creates a high level of financial eligibility for assisted places among single parents, but it often co-exists with the kind of educational background which not only gives their children general educational advantages but also makes them particularly alert to new opportunities for 'grammar school education'. Of the thirty-six single parents in our assisted-place sample, twenty-five had been educated at an academically selective or independent secondary school. It is to this aspect of 'social background' that we now turn.

### Educational 'Inheritance'

In examining the 'educational inheritance' of assisted-place pupils, in comparison with their contemporaries, we use that phrase literally to refer to the correspondence between parents' choice of secondary school and their own secondary schooling. To what extent did pupils in each of our categories attend the same kind of school as their parents? What evidence was there of educational mobility between generations? And has the Assisted Places Scheme brought into the private sector, which now contains a high proportion of the remaining grammar schools, parents with little experience of private (or even academically-selective) secondary education who have now been enabled to opt for schools which are both?

A main finding reported by the Oxford Mobility Study was that since 1944, 'sons tend to follow the secondary school examples of their parents' (Halsey *et al.*, 1980, p. 75). The evidence suggested that boys attending private schools were likely to have had one or more parents who were educated in that sector. The likelihood that boys attending non-selective state schools had parents who had also received a non-selective education was even stronger. Our own data on patterns of intergenerational schooling are not strictly comparable, and are certainly too limited in scale to be subjected to similarly sophisticated techniques for mapping social mobility. Our general question, however, was the same. To what extent were the pupils we interviewed following equivalent educational routes to those which their parents had taken? More specifically, did the Assisted Places Scheme seem to be creating new clients for the independent schools, and was it providing for many of its beneficiaries opportunities well beyond those available to their parents?

### Table 8.5 Parents' primary schooling by last school attended

| Parents of | State | | Private | | Missing Data | |
|---|---|---|---|---|---|---|
| | Mothers | Fathers | Mothers | Fathers | Mothers | Fathers |
| Full fee-payers | 59.7 | 56.1 | 39.0 | 39.0 | 1.7 | 4.9 |
| Assisted-place holders | 83.3 | 75.6 | 13.3 | 12.2 | 3.3 | 12.2 |
| Grammar school pupils | 92.0 | 92.0 | 8.0 | 8.0 | 0.0 | 0.0 |
| Able comprehensive pupils | 93.5 | 85.6 | 6.6 | 10.7 | 0.0 | 3.7 |

*Note*: Figures are shown as percentages (N = 319 households).

**Table 8.6 Parents' secondary schooling by last secondary school attended**

| Parents of | | Elem. | Sec. Mod | Tech. | Gram. | Comp. | D.G. | Ind. | Missing Data |
|---|---|---|---|---|---|---|---|---|---|
| Full fee-payers | Mothers | 6.1 | 17.1 | 0.0 | 36.6 | 2.4 | 7.3 | 26.8 | 3.7 |
| | Fathers | 0.0 | 9.8 | 6.1 | 36.6 | 1.2 | 9.8 | 34.1 | 2.4 |
| Assisted-place pupils | Mothers | 7.8 | 20.0 | 6.7 | 41.1 | 3.3 | 8.9 | 11.1 | 1.1 |
| | Fathers | 6.7 | 31.1 | 3.3 | 28.9 | 4.4 | 7.8 | 11.1 | 6.6 |
| Grammar school pupils | Mothers | 4.0 | 16.0 | 0.0 | 60.0 | 0.0 | 8.0 | 12.0 | 0.0 |
| | Fathers | 4.0 | 20.0 | 4.0 | 36.0 | 0.0 | 20.0 | 16.0 | 0.0 |
| Able comprehensive pupils | Mothers | 10.6 | 33.6 | 7.4 | 36.1 | 2.5 | 4.1 | 5.7 | 0.0 |
| | Fathers | 5.7 | 32.0 | 6.6 | 35.2 | 3.3 | 4.9 | 8.2 | 4.1 |

*Note*: Figures are shown as percentages (N = 319 households).

That a majority even of fee-paying parents had not been privately educated at the primary stage, as recorded in table 8.5, is a finding in line with other studies (Fox, 1985, p. 52; Johnson, 1987, p. 86). It reflects a relative lack of perceived advantages at that stage, especially when set against the accumulated costs of paying for thirteen years of schooling.

The pattern of sectoral recruitment changes only slightly when we review the parents' secondary schooling in table 8.6. Again, about 40 per cent of fee-paying parents had been privately educated themselves; that is, a substantial minority were continuing within an 'independent school frame of reference'. The proportion of assisted-place parents who had attended independent or direct-grant schools, noted in table 8.7, was again higher than among parents with children in comprehensive schools.

**Table 8.7 Parents' secondary schooling by sector**

| Parents of | State | | Direct Grant | | Private | | Missing Data | |
|---|---|---|---|---|---|---|---|---|
| | Mothers | Fathers | Mothers | Fathers | Mothers | Fathers | Mothers | Fathers |
| Full fee-payers | 61.8 | 53.7 | 7.3 | 9.8 | 26.8 | 34.1 | 4.1 | 2.4 |
| Assisted-place pupils | 78.9 | 74.4 | 8.9 | 7.8 | 11.1 | 11.1 | 6.7 | |
| Grammar school pupils | 80.0 | 64.0 | 8.0 | 20.0 | 12.0 | 16.0 | 0.0 | 0.0 |
| Able comprehensive pupils | 90.2 | 82.8 | 4.1 | 4.9 | 5.7 | 8.2 | 0.0 | 4.1 |

*Note*: Figures are shown as percentages (N = 319 households).

The range of schools attended by the parents in our study reflects their predominant generational experience of a system of state secondary education which was largely tripartite (or more accurately bipartite) until comprehensive reorganization accelerated in the late 1960s and early 1970s. Most of those 'unsuccessful' in the 11-plus sifting had attended secondary modern schools; a few had remained in the 'upper classes' of elementary schools. It was not surprising that a majority even of the fee-paying parents had gone to state secondary schools. Even Fox's (1985) study of traditionally much more exclusive public schools found only a small minority of parents with no experience at all of state schooling, and our own sample was heavily weighted towards former direct-grant schools which had been 'half-in' the public sector. Nevertheless, in comparison with parents of assisted-place pupils in the same schools, three times as many fee-paying parents had been privately educated at that stage. This might be taken as evidence of the Scheme's success in creating new clients for independent schools. In fact, as we show in detail in the following chapter, it was much more a 'grammar school education' than an independent school education which most of these parents had been seeking.

Our evidence indicates that 68 per cent of the mothers of assisted-place pupils, and 51 per cent of fathers, had received an education that was either private or selective.

These figures are sufficiently high to recall the study by Jackson and Marsden (1962) of working-class pupils in grammar schools — a study in which many of those pupils were thought to be more accurately described as from the 'sunken middle class', and in which the locus of educational ambition in the families was more often the mother than the father. Twenty years later, Halsey was to argue that 'a child's chances of selective education are substantially improved by having a parent who went to a selective school, but it makes very little difference whether it was the mother or the father' (Halsey *et al.*, 1980, p. 86). Our own study also suggests that parents who attended selective schools or independent schools enhance the educational opportunities of their children. In the case of the assisted places pupils, the notable difference between the educational background of mothers and fathers appears to support Jackson and Marsden's findings that mothers are the 'important and pressing parent'. In this category, however, a high proportion of pupils (over a third) also come from single parent families, almost all headed by women, so support for Jackson and Marsden's argument is at best ambiguous.

Of course, reporting the kinds of school attended by the parents in our study does little justice to the notion of 'educational inheritance'. We also need to know about educational outcomes. How did the parents fare at school? With what formal qualifications did they leave, and what proportions continued on into higher and further education?

## Table 8.8 Parents' qualifications

| | 5 + O-levels or equivalent | | A-levels or equivalent | |
|---|---|---|---|---|
| Parents of | Mothers | Fathers | Mothers | Fathers |
| Full fee-payers | 61.0 | 63.4 | 35.4 | 61.0 |
| Assisted-place pupils | 42.2 | 35.6 | 21.1 | 30.0 |
| Grammar school pupils | 72.0 | 68.0 | 52.0 | 64.0 |
| Able comprehensive pupils | 41.0 | 41.8 | 18.0 | 32.0 |

*Note*: Figures are shown as percentages (N = 319 households).

The most obvious (and expected) feature of table 8.8 is the relative 'dropping-out' rate of academically successful males compared with females after the end of compulsory schooling. The gender difference in 18-plus qualifications is considerable. While five or more O-levels were a valuable occupational passport in themselves, they were also the conventional threshold for those judged capable of proceeding through the sixth form to higher education and the occupations to which that gave access. It was in this context that many of the mothers we interviewed stressed the importance of providing their daughters with an education equal to their potential, and we take up this point in the chapter which follows. Table 8.9 shows high proportions of fathers of fee-paying and grammar school pupils (43.9 per cent and 52 per cent respectively) who have attended university. Of the fee paying fathers, nearly half of those who went to university went to Oxford or Cambridge. It is therefore not surprising that their children are in schools with a tradition of preparing a considerable number of pupils for Oxbridge entrance examinations. Of the assisted-place parents, however, a surprisingly high proportion — just over 50 per cent of fathers and over 60 per cent of mothers — had some formal post-school education (excluding apprenticeships).

We now want to draw some conclusions from the evidence we have reported. The preceding 'class' analysis of parental backgrounds showed a continuing domination of the independent schools by professional and middle-class parents. Our examination of their 'educational inheritance', however, presents a rather more complex situation. The key indicators here are the figures relating to intergenerational educational mobility. The level of self-recruitment within our sample of independent school families is quite low; only 30 per cent of the pupils in that sector had one or more parents who had themselves attended fee-paying schools. This reflects the general 'inflow' of new recruits from families previously associated with the state sector, which reverses the trend reported by Halsey *et al.* (1980), and which has been well publicized by ISIS since the early 1980's. There is little doubt that the Assisted Places Scheme has contributed to that process, and made an independent-school education seem feasible to many who had not considered it before. But to echo the point made in chapter 7, and one which is developed in chapter 9, most of the first-time users of independent schools whom we interviewed were not parents whose children would have been trapped in evidently 'inadequate' comprehensive schools, but parents who would otherwise have made 'strategic' choices of maintained schools with a reputation for coping successfully with able children.

In our sample, more than half the assisted places parents (and more than two thirds of the mothers) had themselves attended either a selective or independent secondary school, more than a third had at least five O-levels (compared with a national sample of adults, in which 16 per cent achieved an O-level qualification) and slightly less than a third achieved at least one A level (compared with the national figure of 8 per cent) (General Household Survey, 1987). Even though these parents were not manifestly more educationally advantaged than those of academically able children in comprehensive schools, and were less so than other independent and grammar school pupils, the Scheme does seem to have benefited children of 'educationally-advantaged' parents on a scale far beyond what its advocates predicted when it was being constructed. And while 'educational inheritance' cannot be treated as equivalent to cultural capital, successful passage through the upper reaches of selective secondary education is certainly eased by parental familiarity with its demands and often made more likely by strong and explicit parental ambition. In the final section of this chapter, we illustrate with particular examples, both the 'educated' background from which many assisted-place pupils came and the frequent lack of correlation between low income and cultural disadvantage.

**Table 8.9 Parents' higher and further education**

| Parents of | | University | Polytechnic | College of Education/Higher Education | Further Education/Technical | Nursing | Apprenticeship | No Further Education/Missing Data |
|---|---|---|---|---|---|---|---|---|
| Full fee-payers | Mothers | 24.2 (2.2) | 4.9 | 19.5 | 17.1 | 11.0 | 1.2 | 21.9 |
| | Fathers | 43.9 (20.7) | 3.7 | 8.5 | 17.1 | 0.0 | 13.2 | 13.6 |
| Assisted-place pupils | Mothers | 13.3 (2.2) | 7.8 | 16.7 | 23.3 | 7.8 | 2.2 | 28.9 |
| | Fathers | 24.4 (3.3) | 6.7 | 5.6 | 13.3 | 0.0 | 16.3 | 33.7 |
| Grammar school pupils | Mothers | 40.0 (8.0) | 12.0 | 16.0 | 20.0 | 4.0 | 4.0 | 4.0 |
| | Fathers | 52.0 (16.0) | 4.0 | 10.0 | 8.0 | 0.0 | 16.0 | 10.0 |
| Able comprehensive pupils | Mothers | 9.0 (0.3) | 4.1 | 12.3 | 18.0 | 4.9 | 4.1 | 47.6 |
| | Fathers | 22.0 (0.8) | 6.6 | 4.9 | 13.9 | 0.8 | 28.7 | 23.1 |

*Note:* Figures are shown as percentages. The percentages of parents who attended Oxbridge are shown in brackets (N = 319 households).

**Income, class and cultural capital: examples and conclusions**

The Assisted Places Scheme has certainly benefited large numbers of low-income families. It has also provided a high proportion of places to children of the 'impoverished middle-class', as has been highlighted in other studies (Douse, 1985; Tapper and Salter, 1986). We have noted that the high proportion of single-parent families helps to explain this apparent discrepancy, and how it also illustrates the difficulty of using parental income as a strong indicator of cultural disadvantage.

We begin our illustrations with several families which might have figured in the photo-calls which used to precede the Minister's report to Parliament on the success of assisted places. Mrs Stanning lived in a late Victorian end-of-terrace house, badly in need of repair despite (or perhaps because of) her husband's job as a joiner and painter. Both she and her husband had left school at 15, and had no qualifications apart from his six-year apprenticeship in joinery. Several cousins on the 'clever' side of her family had gone to the Moortown grammar schools in their direct-grant days, but she had needed a great deal of persuading that their son stood a chance of a place in a school which 'is only for the very, very bright'. As with other pupils in our study, the critical influence had been the head of his primary school, who had encouraged, cajoled and provided two years' special preparatory homework. John now had a free place, though they had not sought help with the incidental expenses. An older daughter had gone to a local comprehensive school, where she had been 'denied the chance of O-levels'. Mrs Stanning was still bitter about that 'denial', and was convinced that such schools could not really 'train the brain'.

Mr Kolowski's education had ended at 13, when he was taken from his home in Poland to a forced-labour camp in Germany. Now working as chauffeur to the directors of a local manufacturing company, he was very conscious that the Scheme enabled his son to attend the same school (Weston) as his employers' children but on a free place. Such schools had to be better because they were 'in the market'; state schools were indelibly associated with Left-wing teachers, peace studies and other 'propaganda'.

Mrs Allan had come to this country from West Africa thirty years ago. Divorced and working as a nurse (she had just finished her night shift in time for the interview), she used her single-parent allowance to make up the £120 a year needed to top-up her daughter's assisted place at Nortown High (the fees then being just under £1500). There was no doubt about her relative poverty. But, as so often in our sample, her awareness of the opportunities that place represented was grounded in considerable educational experience. She had gone to secondary school in her country of origin, at a time when most children ended their education at the primary stage; her brother is a geology lecturer in that country; and her elder daughter had recently completed an HND in Business Studies.

Mrs Hardman is another example of low income in association with well-informed educational ambition. She was another single parent, working as a barmaid and living in a house badly in need of repair in a drab locality. Her own small business had collapsed, while her husband's bankruptcy had led him to leave the country and work abroad. He was behind in his maintenance payments, and life was clearly a financial struggle. An ex-grammar school girl, she had left school early to take up a secretarial job, and had then attended a local commercial college for evening classes in typing, shorthand and commercial subjects. She had a high regard for qualifications. Her son Duncan, 'much cleverer' than her other three sons, had become bored at a primary school which had not 'stretched' him at all. She had therefore moved him to a local denominational school which had a better academic reputation, and a history of preparing pupils for independent schools' entrance exams. Her orientation towards independent schooling seemed to be a continuation of that wish for an academically demanding environment. Duncan himself had walked into Nortown Grammar on an open day and — 'that was it, he just loved the atmosphere and feel of the place'. Mrs Hardman paid nothing towards the fees of £1600 per annum; she was getting additional help from the Scheme towards uniforms, bus fares and school dinners, and from the school to meet the costs of school trips and so on.

The Isaacs lived in a modest semi-detached house. Mr Isaacs was formerly a company secretary, but had been unemployed for more than two years at the time of our interview. Mrs Isaacs had not worked for over three years. There were three children in the family and not much money. The two eldest children held assisted places — Adam at Nortown, and Julia at Milltown Girls'. Mr Isaacs talked and practised the importance of education. He had left grammar school with six O-levels, but had taken two A-levels part-time, had passed City and Guilds and HNC commercial examinations, and was currently taking an Open University course. Mrs Isaacs had left her secondary modern at 15 without any qualifications, but had qualified later in commercial and secretarial subjects through the local further education college. Her husband had a fervent regard for Nortown, which he described as 'a very special school', and the family were delighted when David won a Governors' scholarship to go there. He had then been offered an assisted place as soon as the Scheme was introduced, which allowed the family to benefit from a uniform grant and travel allowance in addition to the full fees. His sister took up an assisted place in the same year.

For Mrs Golding, another single parent, the Scheme had been a 'life-saver'. Her son was already in the preparatory department of Cathedral College when he won his place, and she had only been able to pay those fees with borrowed money. Living now in a council flat, and working part-time as an NHS psychotherapist, she could not have gone on borrowing. But she came from a wealthy American family, had been 'well-off' before her marriage ended, and although claiming to have been unaware of the prestige of Cathedral College was strongly oriented towards independent schools.

Mrs Cann, whose fervent objections to the available comprehensives in her area in Milltown we quote in the next chapter, estimated the joint income of herself and her husband as not much more than £6000. Both were working class in origin, Mrs Cann herself being the eldest of nine children and the first to go to grammar school. She had left it at 15 because she had been 'dead keen on hairdressing', and had always regretted it. She was now poised to take O-levels so as to train as a play-group assistant at the polytechnic. Her husband had been the only son of ambitious parents, although his seven years at a grammar school had brought him no occupational success; his 'real block' about pushing his own children too hard seemed to be more than made up for by his wife's ambition for the son who had a free place at Milltown Grammar.

We have mentioned here some of the poorest families in our sample, emphasizing the educational support which some of them clearly provided. Most of the assisted-place families we met, however, lived in more comfortable domestic circumstances. For some, the Scheme had clearly eased rather than created their choice of school. Mrs Sadler had been widowed for four years. She had worked as a speech therapist and was now a theatre administrator; her husband had been a press officer. Her son was already attending an independent secondary school as a fee-payer when her daughter's school had to be chosen, and she had felt that Emily should have the same opportunity. It was also essential that the school should be single-sex, and that it had to be able to 'cope' with academically able children such as Emily. Family investigations of the possibilities had been thorough, and Emily had sat and passed four independent school entrance exams before obtaining an assisted place at St Hilda's which covered all but £90 of the £2400 annual fees. Mrs Servis too was quite clear about the advantages offered by independent schools like St Hilda's — a wide curriculum, many extra-curricular activities, good facilities, generous resources for books and materials, and a demanding environment for able children. But her strong preference for the independent sector preceded her knowledge of the Scheme, and Laura would have attended St Hilda's without its assistance.

Mrs Deeds was yet another single parent, having been divorced for seven years. Both she and her former husband were actors, but both were 'resting' at the time of the interview. Both had gone to maintained grammar schools before entry to a London drama school. Tamsin had attended two local primary schools, the second of which encouraged Mrs Deeds to consider sending her to 'a grammar type school'. The free place offered at Dame Margaret's had been accepted because of its academic selectiveness, Mrs Deeds' mother helping out with some of the incidental expenses. In social and educational background, she (like Mrs Sadler) would have resembled most fee-paying parents at their children's schools.

We found other cases where the financial circumstances would not have been dissimilar either. Mr and Mrs Rowan for example ran a small hotel, and were anxious that details of their family circumstances should not be reported back to the school (Weston) where their son had an assisted place. By any standards, these parents had enjoyed a privileged background. Mr Rowan had attended a leading public school, and had moved on to be on the board of a major public company; his wife had been educated at an exclusive girls' school and been 'finished' on the continent. They were certainly not the kind of beneficiaries the Scheme's architects had had in mind.

The Kendalls qualified for assistance in rather unusual circumstances. The family income was sufficiently low for their daughter Chloe to pay no fees at all at Dame Margaret's, yet the parents were both directors in a family business which manufactured industrial safety equipment and which they admitted was doing 'rather well'. However, the company was also involved in complex litigation in the High Court where they were suing another company. The case had temporarily depressed their income and prevented them from drawing on capital tied up in the company. Once the case had been settled they expected to be paying full fees; meanwhile, they took full advantage of being assisted to send their daughter to a school they would have chosen anyway.

There were other instances of incongruence between the financial eligibility of some beneficiaries and the apparent comfort and expense of their domestic setting. Mrs Wesley (Nortown High) for example was divorced. Her ex-husband was a doctor, since re-married. His maintenance payments covered the children's needs. Mrs Wesley did not work. She lived in a large house, drove a newish mid-priced car, and had a mother sufficiently affluent to pay for the family's overseas holidays. Mrs Garnier (also Nortown High) was in her second marriage, but because she retained sole custody of Julie she was entitled to an assisted place on the basis of her own salary as a secretary. But she lived in a new bungalow, and her second husband was proprietor of an engineering company of which she was also a director.

Although we have highlighted some financially undeserving cases, we emphasize again that most of the parents we interviewed were undoubtedly eligible for the assistance they received towards their children's fees. But their values and aspirations illustrate that aspect of the Scheme's take-up which we discussed earlier — the unreliability of 'relevant income' as a guide to the cultural and educational situations of families. As we report in detail in the following chapter, parents of assisted-place pupils were similar to fee-paying parents in their orientation towards schooling and in their characterization of the private and public sectors. They strongly supported the notion of selective schooling, and a 'grammar school type' of education; in general, they viewed state comprehensives as rough places unable to offer an academically challenging environment to bright children; and they perceived independent schools as offering considerable social as well as educational advantages. They were the most supportive of academic selection, and specifically of grammar schools. This theme is discussed in detail in the next chapter, and we simply illustrate it here with two examples. Mrs Denton (Milltown High) saw what she was buying (with considerable assistance from the Scheme) as a grammar school education which she would have had 'by rights without payment' if they had left the grammar schools alone. She denied any wish to buy social privilege, and agreed with her daughter that most people at Milltown 'were just normal like, not posh like — [she mentioned a prestigious girls' school in nearby

Nortown]'. Mrs Newton (Milltown Grammar) had been recently widowed and was 'finding it quite hard to manage'. Her daughter had gone to Milltown High, and her son had been in the grammar school's junior department when her husband died. The school had responded to her changed circumstances by immediately initiating an application for an assisted place. Both schools had been 'part and parcel of my life', and she was unable to see why 'they had to get rid of grammar schools when some children are suited to that kind of education'.

We began this chapter by asking whether assisted places were reaching the groups for whom they were intended by the Scheme's architects. It was a task made more complex by the changing rhetoric employed by the Scheme's supporters in justifying its introduction and explaining its 'success' in operation. We have reported how its advocates' initial references to disadvantaged inner-city school children as the target group have been superseded by explanations that the Scheme is succeeding because places are being taken up by low-income families. The promulgation of 'income' as the only relevant criterion for judging the Scheme was important to our research for two reasons. First, because the discursive shift from 'class' (or surrogates for that term) to 'income' was an important aspect of the history of the way in which the Scheme was justified. Secondly, the 'official' justification of the Scheme now being employed has effectively introduced a new definition of 'inequality' and 'disadvantage' into educational policy discourse. In our concluding remarks we shall consider the appropriateness of this development through a discussion of early reactions to our own work on the social backgrounds of the beneficiaries of assisted places.

Press coverage of our preliminary report in September 1986 focused mainly on the finding that there were few children of manual workers amongst the holders of assisted places. The conclusions drawn were that 'assisted places are failing to help the working class' and that they were more obviously 'subsidising than widening parental choice'.[6] In responding to the *Guardian*'s editorial comment that our evidence showed the Scheme as failing dismally to achieve even its own aims, the Director of ISIS (David Woodhead) defended it against being judged according to wrong or inappropriate criteria. If 60 per cent of places were going to families with incomes below £8000 a year, as was the case, were such families to be considered 'undeserving of places unless they can prove a certain class background as well as modest parental means?'[7]

When we presented our findings at the Headmasters' Conference later that month to heads of assisted-place schools, we emphasized that we had taken our criteria from how the Scheme itself had been promoted, and recalled the particular concern about the fate of able working-class children which had been expressed within the private sector as the grammar schools disappeared. Commenting on that report in the HMC journal, David Smith (the head of Bradford Grammar School), who had chaired the meeting, noted the 'careful and temperate explanation of what turns out to be a careful and temperate investigation'. But he preferred to regard the findings as 'a challenge rather than a condemnation'. Since the Scheme was 'manifestly reaching lower-income families in large numbers', he was 'tempted to tear up the Hope–Goldthorpe scale of social mobility' which we had used in our analysis, and to demand criteria 'more in keeping with the financial and social realities of Britain today'. Nevertheless, he had to recognize the Scheme's apparently limited success in providing a 'ladder out of the inner-city'. This constituted an 'image-problem', and schools offering places had to try harder to reach those parents who had most to gain from them.[8]

Two years later we have to consider whether the Hope–Goldthorpe scale, which we have again used in our analysis in this chapter, does deserve to be 'torn up'. In the light of the reaction, we need to ask whether our preoccupation with social origins and cultural capital is vulnerable to the charge of importing criteria from outside the Scheme's frame of reference, against our professed intention of judging it as it asks to be judged. Certainly the 'image-problem' has not been seen as a challenge by ministers – or, at least, not explicitly. For Bob Dunn it was enough that the Scheme was not providing a subsidy to the rich. Income was the only appropriate criterion of need and 'we could not inquire about the occupation of the parents'. To do so was not only sociology, which was bad enough; it was 'socialism'.[9] Since Stuart Sexton claimed not to have 'used the word class at all' in promoting the Scheme, it did not bother him if 'all the beneficiaries turned out to be middle-class so long as their parents were otherwise unable to pay the fees'. In the article in which that comment is quoted, Wendy Berliner describes the typical place-holder as 'middle class with plenty of cultural if not financial advantage', and notes that 'the photo calls for the latest batch of dustmen's daughters and cleaners' sons to win places were abandoned long ago', (Berliner, 1987). In fact, though, it was not so long ago. Dunn's own 1984 photo-call with five 'typical' beneficiaries included an electrician, a bus driver and a caretaker among the parental occupations, even though no available evidence would suggest those occupations to be anything but untypical (Hodges, 1984). Similarly, the ISIS annual surveys of the Scheme in operation show a strong tendency to illustrate occupational diversity with a disproportionate number of references to manual occupations – for example, to butcher's assistant, blacksmith, bricklayer, coal miner, bus driver and crane driver (1982); to lorry drivers, miners, butchers and bricklayers (1985); and to cleaners, bus drivers, lorry drivers and postmen (1986). The 1983 survey identified clergymen's children as the largest single occupational category, but the other examples were chosen to emphasize the Scheme's accessibility to all classes. Press coverage has also tended to give prominence to manual working-class backgrounds when giving the Scheme a 'human face'.[10] Altogether, our monitoring of how the Scheme has been publicized shows a considerable (if implicit) unease about its 'failure' to reach in any significant numbers those parents who were seen to have most to gain when it was being promoted and introduced, and a considerable change in the supporting rhetoric. An expedient insistence on low income as the only relevant criterion of open access to assisted places has actually been accompanied by the deliberate selection of working-class examples of the Scheme's success in reaching its target.[11]

In examining the backgrounds from which our sample of assisted-place pupils came, we therefore consider it appropriate to persist in regarding parental occupations as relevant within the Scheme's own terms. Denying that it had been specifically intended to reach out to manual workers, Douse (1985) commented that its architects had not defined the prospective clients in class terms at all 'whether deliberately or because it was not their customary terminology'. To Bob Dunn it was clearly 'socialist' terminology. Yet, as we have noted in exploring the Scheme's institutional and ideological origins, a preoccupation with *working-class* opportunity provided much of its driving force. And we know of no educational research which considers issues of inequality and opportunity solely in terms of the income levels of parents. The use of 'social class' categories in our own study takes it into the mainstream of such research, which has traditionally given prominence to children's 'educational inheritance' or 'cultural capital'. It also focuses attention on the particular 'rescue mission' which the Assisted Places Scheme has been claimed to represent.

On the 'relevant income' criterion, all the families we described at the beginning of this section were similar insofar as they were all eligible for some degree of assistance through the Scheme. But families like the Kendalls, Rowans and the Wesleys, for example, though financially eligible, were also suburban, middle class, possessed property and were well endowed with cultural capital. In this regard they were very unlike the original target families, believed to be disadvantaged by their social and cultural environments and thought to be served by inadequate local secondary schools and in need of some form of special educational provision to put them on the ladder of social mobility. As our study shows, 'income' as a measure of disadvantage fails to provide an adequate basis for distributing assistance in such a way as to compensate for the sorts of disadvantages that were identified as providing the initial justification for the existence of the Scheme. Furthermore low income can disguise other social and cultural (and, on occasions, economic) characteristics of families which can be transformed into educational advantages without the need for assisted places. As a consequence the Scheme has been supporting a relatively high proportion of families, at least in this study, whose general social, cultural and financial situation suggests that they have no obvious need which can only be met through an assisted place. Our findings throughout this chapter indicate the weakness of low income as measured by 'relevant income' as an indicator of cultural impoverishment and educational disadvantage.

The importance of social and cultural factors other than income which have had an important bearing on the distribution of places is evident, paradoxically, when we refer to the few families in this study who do bear a close resemblance to the original target group. In several respects, even the Hardmans and the Isaacs are similar to the majority of other assisted-place families, sharing school experiences of selective education, a belief in the importance of education for their children's future, and identifying the independent schools as the best means of obtaining the equivalent of a grammar school education. This 'educational inheritance', as we have called it, is an important factor explaining the predominant presence of professional and middle-class families in the Scheme. Because families like those cited above share it, they have been able to meet the entry requirements to participating schools, whereas many others who might have been an appropriate target for the Scheme lack those cultural and educational attributes. This in turn suggests that parental occupation, like income, is itself too crude an analytic tool for analyzing the success of the Scheme. A form of class analysis which takes into account the cultural and political resources available to families, as well as their economic market position, is essential to a full assessment of how far the Scheme is achieving its aims and to an understanding of the complex social dynamics which militate against it doing so.

Although even the mode of analysis we have employed here is itself in need of refinement, it has certainly helped us to identify important aspects of the operation of the Scheme that remain completely hidden in the income data collected by the schools and aggregated in the official statistics reported in chapter 5. In the chapter that follows, we look even further beneath the surface of those statistics at the social processes that have produced them. In doing so, we have chosen to give a particular 'voice' to those individual parents and pupils whose choices and perceptions of schooling might themselves easily have remained obscured by our own aggregate statistics as presented in this chapter.

### Notes

1 'Fee-paying' refers to pupils paying the 'full' fees charged by their schools. Of course, most assisted-place pupils also pay some fees. Many of our own sample paid little or nothing, the scale of fee remission illustrating the *Daily Express*'s approval of assisted places as offering 'better bargains than any fashion store'. Where else, the paper asked, could parents find 'up to £3000 of services for virtually nothing?' (6 February 1984).

2 In most schools efficient pupil grapevines soon ensured that our questions contained few surprises.

3 Summaries of the pupil interviews were sent to the schools.

4 We were sometimes made aware that parents had rung the school office to check on us after receiving the letter asking for their agreement to the interviews. Similar experiences of schools' capacity to legitimate researchers is reported in Connell *et al.* (1983), p. 31.

5 Throughout this chapter, and the next, all the parents mentioned have been renamed to conceal their identities.

6 That was how our findings, as reported to the annual conference of the British Educational Research Association in Bristol in September 1986 (Whitty, Fitz and Edwards, 1988), were highlighted in the *Guardian*, 4 September 1986. The Scheme's 'failure' to reach the target groups for whom it was mainly intended was also highlighted in the *Daily Telegraph*, 4 September; the *Times Educational Supplement*, 5 September; *Education*, 5 September; and in the *Teacher*, 8 September.

7 *Guardian*, 16 September 1986.

8 *Conference*, June 1987, p. 39.

9 Standing Committee on Statutory Instruments, 25 April 1984.

10 For example, the son of a West Indian single parent employed as a shop assistant, who won a place at Malvern in 1981 *(Sunday Times*, 20 September 1981); the son of a semi-skilled shipyard worker who gained a place at St Bees (BBC-TV programme, *Educating Michael*, 1 March 1984); and the daughters

of a bus driver and a railway signalman with places at Birkenhead High School (*Liverpool Echo,* 25 January 1983).

11 In the light of our own findings, it is interesting to note that it has recently been reported that the Government is 'poised to launch a national advertising campaign to promote the Scheme. The publicity drive is likely to concentrate on deprived areas with no tradition of independent education' (Hadfield, 1989). This report reflected official concern about places not being taken up in 1988 and the findings of an opinion poll that six out of ten parents had never heard of assisted places.

Chapter 9

# Choice of School and Perceptions of Schooling

In the previous chapter we concentrated mainly on assisted-place pupils and their parents. We now broaden our approach, drawing on evidence of how pupils and parents across the whole sample explained their choice of a secondary school. While our initial focus is on the influences shaping particular decisions and on how individuals explained their preferences, we also locate those responses in the wider context of choice between state and private schooling and between selective and non-selective education. As in other mainstream studies in the sociology of education, we were interested to discover any patterned relationships between choice of school and family background.

It was evident, as many parents talked through their choice of secondary school, that the process of choosing had been worrying. There was widespread awareness that very different kinds of educational experience were available, the choice of which might well critically affect the life chances of their children. A further difficulty was that they were making that choice in an educational landscape that had changed markedly since their own schooldays. While the continuing coexistence of the private and state sectors might be familiar, prominent tripartite (or bipartite) landmarks had disappeared and few of the parents had themselves attended comprehensive schools. We therefore encountered many families who were not only ambivalent about the principles of comprehensive secondary education, but also very unsure about how to evaluate its practice. It is important to emphasize this point because parents so often referred back to a system in which (as Mrs Denton in Milltown put it) 'the decision whether you passed or failed was so clear, and you were graded to where you should be'. How secondary schools used to be, and the relative status of schools of different kinds, was a powerful influence on how many parents judged the current alternatives. For some, independent schools remained privileged places and 'not for the likes of us'. Indeed, many assumed the superiority of the private sector, or approved in principle of the choice it offered, without having ever considered it to be financially or socially within their own reach. There were many others, however, for whom the kind of independent school they wanted represented the only surviving source of 'real' academic education — an 'oasis' of excellence in an otherwise mediocre educational world, which is the image the private sector itself has most zealously propagated.

### Choosing an Independent School

Before reporting how families accounted for their choice of sector, or for never having considered a maintained school at all, we must emphasize how much overlapping there was between the two sectors. As Johnson's (1987) study illustrates, it is incorrect to see independent school pupils as coming exclusively from 'a distinct social stratum' or their parents as thoroughly and consistently committed to private education. Our own evidence however does suggest that the intakes of both full fee-payers and assisted pupils into the assisted-place schools show a marked bias towards children from professional and middle-class backgrounds. Nevertheless there is now considerable 'cross-sectoral movement, many pupils switching several times during their school careers according to their parents' fine judgments of benefits in relation to the costs.[1] In our own interviews with parents we recorded many examples of last-minute decisions to change sectors; of decisions to do so or not to do so which were clearly still regarded with doubt or regret or guilt; of families currently using both maintained and independent secondary schools; and of parents whose attachment to their child's comprehensive school was conditional on academic success, and who clearly saw private education as a safety net if things did not work out.

We begin with parents whose initial choice of secondary school had been made possible, or at least fostered, by the Assisted Places Scheme. Although the Scheme was partly intended to create new clients for the private sector, its primary justification was to provide a 'ladder' of opportunity for able pupils who 'needed' the stimulus of 'academically excellent' selective schools of a kind which comprehensive reorganization had largely removed from the public sector. Almost all the assisted-place pupils and parents we interviewed saw the Scheme in that way, their lack of confidence in any comprehensive alternatives being expressed very much as Irene Fox reported from her study of public schools (Fox, 1984; 1985). In contrast, Johnson (1987) questions the explanation that it is the lack of grammar schools which drives many parents out of the state system. But her sample of only twenty-five families was deliberately drawn from a broad range of independent schools, some of which lacked any academic reputation. Our own sample, reflecting the predominantly meritocratic objectives of the Scheme, came mainly from academically 'strong' schools — most of them from the old direct-grant list. As Johnson remarks, those schools were widely seen as representing the best that had been available in the public sector and so were used by many parents theoretically committed to state education. Her conclusion was that — 'Parents will not choose between public and private education with a consciousness of choosing between two totally separate forms of education until the heyday of the direct-grant school has passed out of living memory' (1987, p. 90).

Our evidence supports that conclusion. Fee-paying and assisted-place parents alike often shared a view of comprehensive schools as 'going at too slow a pace' and so 'holding back the ablest', or as being 'academically appalling'. The alternative for some was a socially prestigious as well as 'academic' independent school like St Hilda's, but few assisted-place parents with children at Nortown High or the other former direct-grant schools seemed especially conscious of those schools' independence. They were very aware of their academic selectiveness. Mrs Waters, with a son at Highgrove County Grammar, saw Nortown High simply as a superior grammar school, and deplored the kind of private school she had attended herself where 'the entrance examination was a farce, and all that counted was money'. She had wanted for her 'very bright' daughter 'an ethos in which academic achievement is given priority', in whichever sector it could be found. Mrs Clough, whose son had an assisted place at Milltown Grammar, is another example of this common theme. A qualified supporter of independent schools ('they have their place, filling in what's missing from the state system . . . '), her first preference would have been for a maintained grammar school. The local state schools however were all comprehensive and, according to her, offered 'very poor standards'. Not believing that there was a 'good' comprehensive school available, as well as being uncertain whether any comprehensive school could cater for her son, she went firmly for a grammar school education. This same sense of having been 'driven' to private education by the 'awfulness' of the entirely non-selective alternatives was conveyed by many of those we interviewed. Mrs Henry's choice, for example, had been against all her political commitments. A long-term Labour voter, she believed that independent schools should be abolished. But while they existed, she would 'do the best' for her son. Adamant in her preference for a kind of (grammar school) education which was only available locally in the private sector, she did not see Milltown Grammar as an 'elite' school, nor did she value its independence except as a necessary condition for its being academically selective. For her and many other parents, comprehensive reorganization had taken out of the state sector the only secondary schools with which they felt comfortable, and it was with a sense of having been 'dispossessed' that they had made their exodus. Mrs Cann's determination to get her eldest son to grammar school had been primarily a reaction against the local comprehensive. Her husband had initially dismissed her application for an assisted place as 'snobbish', and their rows about it had been (she said) almost the last blow to an already rocky marriage. At the height of one row, she had shouted — 'I'll dance on your grave, I'll knife you in the night and use the insurance money to pay the fees. He'll have a gaol-bird for a mother and a dead father, but at least he'll go to grammar school!' Few parents were as vividly expressive in denouncing comprehensives, but it was a common view that there could be no academic virtue in them.

As we note later in the chapter, there were many parents in all categories who recognized that the advantages of the old 11-plus had to be balanced against the distress and diminished opportunities of the 'losers'. Indeed, some of the parents most committed to 'grammar school education' and most prepared to make financial sacrifices to achieve it still seemed hurt or embarrassed by their own failure to obtain it. But hostility in principle to selection between schools was expressed by only 48 per cent of comprehensive school parents, and by 13 per cent and 11 per cent respectively of the parents of fee-payers and holders of assisted places.

Although assisted-place parents were slightly ahead of those paying full fees in their support for academic selection in general (77 per cent and 74 per cent respectively), and for grammar schools in particular (74 per cent and 62 per cent), a strongly academic orientation pervaded our whole independent school sample. Not surprisingly, it was again most evident among fee-paying parents in the former direct-grant schools. For Mr and Mrs West (Milltown High), 'grammar schools did us well enough, and that's what we wanted for our children'. Public schools were 'Eton, Harrow, that sort of thing', and were part of a different world. Mr Barnes, an old boy of Nortown Grammar, saw Nortown High as 'the town grammar school which the town has unwisely deserted'. And although he had sent his younger and less able daughter to Redland Comprehensive, a school to which 'some liberal-minded parents are willing to entrust even their bright children', he had sent his own 'bright' child to Nortown High because 'academic excellence is more securely located in a grammar school'.

This close association between independent schools and 'real' academic education was central to the assumption (common to many parents in all our four categories) that such schools offered their pupils a distinct 'competitive edge' compared with anything available in the public sector. It was a view strongly held by the pupils, with no perceptible differences in this respect between fee-payers and those with assisted places. A 'good education' was one which carried you forward to 'good results' and a 'good career'. Even when we moved out from the explicitly academic tradition of former direct-grant schools, we were again struck by what might be termed a 'pre-vocational' academic emphasis. As indicated in chapter 2, the public schools underwent an 'academic revolution' in the 1960s and early 1970s, and began to place much greater emphasis than before on A-level success and entry to higher education. In our own interviews, especially at Bankside and Cathedral College, there was considerable evidence to support John Rae's (1981) argument that even such prestigious schools no longer rely for their main appeal on a distinctive educational and 'character building' ethos. Weston has a much less distinguished academic reputation. Indeed, it had been chosen by a few of the parents we interviewed for *not* being too high-pressured; as Mrs Carr said of it, in an almost classically Victorian public school compliment — 'At Weston, they really do play games for the game's sake, not to win'. But here too, the better prospects opened up by examination success were mentioned by almost everyone we interviewed. As one assisted-place pupil put it, in typical fashion — 'It's meant to be better teaching at public schools, you get better results and more sport, and getting good results means hopefully a good job'.

Dominant though that orientation was among parents and pupils, we do not want to exaggerate it. Alongside their confident expectations of tangible educational and career advantages, we found many examples among independent school parents of a preference for a 'gentler', safer and more 'civilized' environment than comprehensives were believed to provide — especially for girls. This view was much more common than support, even implicit support, for social segregation for its own sake. Indeed, we encountered no parents who admitted to the motive commonly ascribed to middle-class clients of the Victorian public schools — that of seeking social advancement for their children by associating them with their social betters. What was quite often apparent, however, was a view of the independent school as a social oasis in rough areas. Mr and Mrs Arkwright, for example, living in a private cul-de-sac within a large council estate saw themselves as resisting on their children's behalf the 'less desirable sorts of element' from that estate, and their choice of Milltown High was an essential part of that resistance. Mr and Mrs Cave saw the same school as having an ethos closely aligned with their own cultural and moral standards, and as capable of insulating their only child from the worst excesses of modern youth — from what Mrs Cave referred to as 'discos, hanging around on street corners', and other symptoms of 'adolescent giddiness'. For that protection, they were willing to remain in a rather run-down neighbourhood in order to afford the fees, knowing that their daughter was daily being carried out of it.

Given the high prestige of some of the independent schools in which we worked, it was not surprising that we also encountered parents whose initial application for entry, especially for an assisted place, had needed some social courage. A few still seemed rather overawed by the world in which their children now moved. The Waniewskis, for example, rarely went to Cathedral College functions on their own, and described one visit to the main school as having been 'terrifying'. Mrs Fenton, whose son had a fully-assisted place at Bankside, was relieved that his skill in rugby had both eased his settling in and enabled him to retain some links with his friends on their council estate. Other parents mentioned the difficulties of mixing with markedly more affluent peers, although they were usually reported as having been greater in anticipation than in practice. In this respect, the former direct-grant schools were seen as less socially distant and more accessible. The ethnic dimension in Mr Shawar's perspective was unusual, but his views were otherwise characteristic of many parents. He regarded public schools as schools for the affluent, and as increasingly populated by 'rich Arabs'. In contrast, Milltown Grammar and Milltown High, which his own children attended (two of them with assisted places), represented the ablest and most respectable sections of the local population, and so offered them the best chance of assimilation into mainstream British culture. Although a devout Moslem, his own middle-class origins and westernized education set him apart from his many Asian neighbours whom he regarded as being 'villagers by origin and villagers still in outlook'. Mr and Mrs Harris were convinced that Nortown Grammar (considered by some other parents we interviewed as too far 'above' them) had a wider social mix than the other independent school they had considered, and chose it partly for that reason. Mrs Denton, as we saw in Chapter 8, agreed with her daughter that most pupils at Milltown 'were just normal like,' unlike those in some independent schools. Mr and Mrs Wilson had visited the independent school which had initially been their first choice but had found other parents there to be 'off-putting and snobbish'. In comparison, Milltown Grammar was academically demanding but socially reassuring. Both of them local in background, positive about their working-class roots and 'unable to think of any middle-class friends', they actively encouraged their two sons to maintain neighbourhood friendships by playing in local football and cricket teams, and regarded the Scheme as doing no more than enabling the boys to attend the 'only kind of school that can really foster talent'. That such a school now seemed available only in the private sector was to them, as to many parents we interviewed, a matter for considerable regret.

Throughout this section of the chapter, we have emphasized the similarities in attitude between fee-paying and assisted-place parents in their dislike or distrust of comprehensive secondary education. But did the fee-payers place more value on independence for its own sake rather than as a necessary condition for being academically selective? And was there a much higher proportion among them, as would be expected, who felt committed in principle to private education and who had never seriously considered an alternative? In fact, unqualified approval of private education was expressed by only just over a third (36 per cent) of all the independent school parents we interviewed, with no significant difference between full fee-payers and others. Of those opposed to it in principle, it was interestingly the grammar school parents who were most prominent — 44 per cent expressing that view, compared with 30 per cent of comprehensive school parents and 5 per cent and 13 per cent respectively of the parents of fee-paying and assisted-place pupils. That difference may be yet another reflection of the priority given to academic selectiveness; where independence was not a necessary condition for being or remaining a grammar school, then its significance was diminished. Belief in other distinctive merits of independent schools were more often expressed by fee-paying parents. They were more likely to refer to the benefits of having to compete for custom, of being directly accountable to parents, and of being (as Mr Barnes, with a daughter at Nortown High, put it) 'free of the interfering officialdom of the town hall, trying to impose educational theory and experiment'.

It was entirely predictable that more fee-paying parents reported that they had never seriously considered any maintained secondary school. Dr and Mrs Moorhouse (Milltown Grammar) exemplify the entrenched users of independent schools within our sample, being resolved to have nothing to do with the public sector at all. Paying four sets of fees, including the fees of a pre-preparatory school for their 3-year old son, was an acceptable price for that freedom. Mr and Mrs Hoyle (Bankside), both privately educated themselves, claimed that they would 'like to see the independent schools disappear', but 'wanting to do the best for our children' had kept all of them within the private sector and perpetuated the family tradition. In some cases, a decision to pay for the secondary schooling of an older child based on a judgment of his or her particular needs had clearly produced a sense of obligation to provide the same opportunity for other children; the parents had consequently been carried firmly into the independent school frame of reference. We also found some assisted-place families where the child had already been sent along the private route before the Scheme's introduction made the cost of doing so easier to bear. Vinay Quatar had gained his assisted place at Nortown Grammar from a preparatory school, and his younger sister was intended to do the same. Paul Cooper-Ryan had attended a preparatory school because his parents had wanted him to have some experience of private education, and had ruled out the secondary stage as being beyond their means. The 'Money Mail' newspaper column had alerted them to the possibility of an assisted place, which now enabled them to extend their ambition for their son by providing two-thirds of the annual £3000 tuition fees at Bankside. Theirs had been a late decision. For many families it was a decision which had been made long before the secondary stage. Nearly half (45 per cent) of the fee-paying pupils we interviewed, and 28 per cent of assisted-place holders, had attended the preparatory or junior department of their present school, thereby producing an 'obvious' progression from one stage to another within the same sector. Just over a third of the younger brothers and sisters of the fee-paying pupils were attending independent primary schools at the time of our interview, compared with only 8 per cent of siblings of pupils with assisted places; overall, however, 67 per cent of the brothers and sisters of the fee-paying pupils in our sample were attending an independent school of some kind, compared with the much lower but still substantial figure of 25 per cent among the siblings of assisted-place holders. That paying for primary education was less common is unsurprising. It reflects fewer objections to maintained primary schools, some feeling that the primary stage is more 'dispensable' in terms of a future career, and a high level of satisfaction in some families with maintained primary schools which grouped pupils by ability and prepared them overtly to compete for entry to the private sector.

In addition to asking parents about their reasons for choosing a particular school, we also asked them about 'significant others' in the process of reaching a decision. Predictably, it was the other parent or current partner who was mentioned most often. We discuss later in this chapter the apparently greater weight given to their child's own preferences by parents in the public sector, and end this present section with examples of the sponsoring influence of some primary schools, to which we referred in chapter 7. As we noted then, LEAs had often given their primary schools explicit instructions not to advertise the existence of the Assisted Places Scheme, not to prepare pupils for the entrance examinations, and not to volunteer information about pupils to the independent schools to which they were applying. Despite these various prohibitions, we encountered many cases of active sponsorship by heads and by class teachers. They seemed to be residues of the traditional meritocratic, 'capacity-catching' function of the schools. Mr Kolowski (Weston) and Mrs Fenton (Bankside), for example, had both been alerted to the possibilities offered by the Scheme by primary heads who had argued that their 'bright' children 'needed' a selective secondary school. Neither Mr Lewis nor Mr and Mrs Stanning had realized how 'open' Milltown Grammar was to pupils from many kinds of social background until 'talent-spotting' heads had assured them that their sons could cope perfectly well with its academic curriculum, and then provided both encouragement and special homework. Mrs Bride had already accepted a place for her daughter at a Church of England comprehensive when the deputy head of her daughter's primary school (who had taught both parents years before) intervened to tell them about assisted places and to suggest an application to Milltown High. In this case the head of the school had been overtly hostile to the private sector, while the girl's class teacher had warned them that she would 'fail the exam, you mark my words' — a pessimism which Mrs Bride felt had been politically motivated. It was more usual, however, to find evidence of headteachers who had written to or telephoned the parents of 'promising' pupils, provided information about the Scheme, encouraged application, and provided 'extra' lessons (often 'after hours' to avoid defying the LEA too overtly). As Mrs Galton (Milltown High) said of one such head — 'The girls would not be there without him, and we'll always be grateful'.

### Choosing a maintained secondary school

Given the nature of the Assisted Places Scheme as a scholarship 'ladder', and its genesis as an antidote to a supposed decline in standards in the public sector, our analysis of how and why parents chose a maintained school was bound to focus particularly on how they perceived its academic scope and quality. Was there much evidence of that 'crisis' of parental confidence in comprehensive schools which Irene Fox (1984) has described, and if so how did parents cope with it? Did they share (however reluctantly) the assumption of most private sector parents that independent schools offer substantial relative advantages, or did they assert a broad equality of opportunity?

As a background against which to answer these questions, we report how different categories of parents identified the 'very important' factors which had influenced their choice of secondary school. The responses indicate the widespread importance given to the academic aspects of school choice — to examination results and the ladder of opportunity to higher education and 'good' jobs. That orientation was relatively weaker among comprehensive school parents, who were correspon-

**Table 9.1 Factors influencing parents' choice of school**

| Parents | Total | Private sector | | Public sector | |
|---|---|---|---|---|---|
| | | Fee-payers | Assisted-place | Able Comprehensive | Grammar |
| Examination results | 51.4 | 58.5 | 54.4 | 40.2 | 72.0 |
| Higher education | 49.2 | 58.5 | 56.7 | 32.0 | 76.0 |
| Career prospects | 40.4 | 50.0 | 51.0 | 25.4 | 44.0 |
| School facilities | 41.1 | 43.9 | 46.7 | 36.9 | 32.0 |
| School ethos | 54.2 | 58.5 | 62.2 | 42.6 | 68.0 |
| Family tradition | 8.5 | 7.3 | 7.8 | 9.0 | 12.0 |
| School location | 28.2 | 36.2 | 20.0 | 21.3 | 24.9 |
| Extra-curricular activities | 24.1 | 32.9 | 20.0 | 21.3 | 24.0 |
| Child's friends | 19.4 | 8.5 | 11.1 | 32.8 | 20.0 |

*Note:* Figures are shown as percentages (N = 319 households).

dingly more inclined to mention social aspects like 'learning to mix with children from different backgrounds', and especially prominent among parents of children in maintained grammar schools. The vague concept of 'ethos' has to be included in this 'academic' category because while it certainly included the 'civilizing' characteristics which had been important to some independent school parents, its essential component was a school's perceived capacity to provide a demanding and competitive setting which would 'push' or 'stretch' able pupils. Even among those parents who were paying full fees, family tradition was given little overt weight. Indeed, it was mentioned no more often than was a traditional family link with a particular state school, or a traditional family commitment to state education. Perhaps the most striking difference, commented on later, was the greater weight given by comprehensive school parents to where their child's friends were going.

We now explore, in similar detail to the previous section, the reasons which parents gave for their choice of a maintained school. At the beginning of that section, we emphasized how much movement there is between the public and private sectors and the error of imagining that private education is for a 'distinct social stratum'. There is now another important general point to be made about the pervasive influence which the presence of independent schools can have even on parents who have never seriously thought of using them.

Among its several objectives, the Assisted Places Scheme was intended to provide maintained schools with the challenge of competition. In our concluding chapter, we argue that it is difficult to see how the supposed benefits of this form of competition are being achieved, certainly when set against the damage being done to intakes and to confidence in the public sector. At this stage, we emphasize that the availability of independent schools in the four areas we studied not only presented some parents with a choice between sectors; it also actively shaped many more parents' perceptions of the quality of education in the public sector, and caused them continuing anxiety about whether they had made the right choice.

Mr and Mrs Elwell, for example, were a middle-class couple whose children went to Vicarage Road and who were happy with most aspects of the education it provided. It was, they thought, about as good a comprehensive as there was anywhere around them. Throughout the interview, however, they speculated about whether or not they 'had done right by the children'. Without specifying what additional benefits a private education would have offered, they admitted feeling guilty about their choice and wondered whether they should have made the sacrifice to send their children to fee-paying schools. They were not alone in their uncertainty, nor in recognizing that they had not done what friends and relatives expected. Mrs Arlen, recently returned with her husband from a two-year posting in the United States, approved of the predominance there of the neighbourhood high school. Since their return, however, they had been made acutely aware of local pressures to 'go private', and she described her family as 'one of the very few in our network to use state schools'. Dr and Mrs Dennis had a daughter at Highgrove County Grammar School. He managed a local chemical plant and she worked part-time as a pharmacist. They lived in a conspicuously prosperous suburb on the edge of Nortown, and their daughter's initial preference for a prestigious ex-direct-grant school had been influenced (they thought) by the values and ethos of a primary school which fostered such ambitions because the resulting places were treated by so many parents as evidence of its own 'quality'. Dr Dennis preferred the 'wider social mix' which he saw in the local grammar school, and was satisfied with its academic record. Nevertheless, he spoke of the social pressures in their neighbourhood which had oriented them for a time towards the independent sector; 'the whole environment', he said, 'makes you question your own framework of reference, it makes you think that much harder and you lose that much more sleep'. A similar sense of social pressure was conveyed by Mr Collier when he distinguished carefully between independent schools which were nationally important and those of marked but local significance. He had chosen Rowton himself despite anxieties about whether there were enough 'really able children there to give Steve the necessary stimulus and companionship'. But in his immediate neighbourhood (and we noted earlier how socially diverse Rowton's intake was) the take-up of private education was extensive and he deplored it. Whereas schools like Eton and Winchester were 'an irrelevance', part of the 'traditional pageantry of English life', the independent grammar schools in his own city had to be regarded as damagingly divisive because of the city's tight, overlapping occupational and social networks.

In their very different material and personal circumstances, these families illustrate some of the effects of co-existing sectors with unequal prestige. The hegemonic effect of the private sector caused all of them, for different reasons, to express doubts about the validity of their choice and fears about the relative advantages which they might be denying their children. Indeed, some of the public sector parents we interviewed seemed to be only conditionally attached to their child's present secondary school, and to be fully prepared to escape into private education if it fell below their academic expectations. For such families, an independent school was still there as a safety-net. Mr and Mrs Wilmott, for example, academic economist and social worker respectively, had accepted their son's wish to go to Rowton 'with all his friends', against what they saw as local expectations that they would choose an independent school because he was 'very bright'. Yet they referred explicitly to their willingness to pay for secondary education if 'things at Rowton don't work out'. We encountered that notion of a possible private escape route quite often.

Most of the comprehensive school parents we interviewed had never included an independent school among the realistic alternatives — whether because they regarded such schools as way beyond their means, or as 'not for the likes of us', or as no better (or not sufficiently better) than the maintained schools available, or as objectionable in principle. We return in the final section of the chapter to the many parents whose assumptions about why independent schools are 'better', assumptions which closely resembled the distinctive merits to which fee-paying and assisted-place parents regularly referred, were unaccompanied by any sense that such schools had ever been within their own reach. More interesting at this point in our argument are the families who had at least 'flirted' with the possibility of private education before making a positive choice of a maintained school. Not always untroubled by their eventual choice, they were sometimes robust in defending it. Mrs Mitchell was one example. As a divorced single parent, and unemployed (as a secretary) for some time, she could have benefited from a Scheme she certainly knew about. Indeed, she had visited several independent schools to see what they offered. Her daughter had disliked them all as being 'airy-fairy and girlish', and had wanted in any case to 'stay with her friends'. Unimpressed herself by the independent schools and their facilities, Mrs Mitchell had been entirely won over by Rowton's open evening for prospective parents and by the head's description of the opportunities offered for woodwork, computing and electronics. 'Right' she thought, 'that'll do for Jessica'. Mr and Mrs Scott were professionally employed and comfortably-off. Their son's entry to Rowton had been planned some years ahead, when they moved into Rowton's catchment area to escape their then local comprehensive school's bad reputation. Like Mrs Mitchell, they had considered several of the city's independent schools, obtaining their prospectuses without visiting them. Their eventual decision not to go private reflected their dislike of pupils being 'channelled too early along academic paths', and being set apart from the 'real world' too early. Their experience of running Cub and Scout groups had also left them feeling that some products of independent schools were — 'weird, narrow in views and arrogant'. Rowton, they felt, combined 'a wide social mix with good academic opportunities — the attributes any good comprehensive should have'. They accepted the independent sector on the grounds of parental choice and 'the right to pay', but objected to it being supported by money from public funds and to its creaming off talent from the maintained sector. Mrs Cram's son had been offered a place at a large independent grammar school, and she had got as far as the open evening for new parents only to be put off by 'the stiffness and all that talk about moulding the boys'. Increasingly reassured by all that she heard about Shirebrook High School and its (then new) head, she and her husband had willingly accepted their son's wish to go there with this friends.

We emphasize these instances, which are typical of many in our sample, because our previous highlighting of assumptions about the academic superiority of independent schools may exaggerate the strength and extent of parental scepticism about the capacity of maintained schools to cope with able pupils. Of course, it is against the 'denial of opportunity' in comprehensive schools that the Scheme is mainly directed. And as might be expected from our earlier discussion of the many parents who saw themselves as buying or being assisted to buy a 'real' academic education in the only sector they now believed could provide it, it was among parents of pupils in the two maintained grammar schools that a view of the private sector as unnecessary was most apparent. Mrs Hanson, for example, declared herself to be 'bigoted, not biased but really bigoted' about comprehensive schools. Educated herself first at a girls' independent school which she described as 'little more than a finishing school' and then at an academically tougher maintained grammar school, she was strongly in favour of selection. For her, keeping children under the right kind of academic pressure depended on keeping out too many working-class pupils (at the end of the interview, commented that she'd been 'horrified by some of the things I've said — I didn't realize I was so conservative, or such an educational and social snob!'). If Highgrove had gone comprehensive, she would have 'scrubbed floors' to get her only daughter into Nortown High. As it was, the County Grammar School was good enough because it offered a sufficiently academic education (with the additional advantage of a single-sex setting) without the burden of fees. Mrs Larch, a laboratory technician married to a dentist, reflected a common view among parents at Archbishop Ambrose's Grammar School. 'We wanted the best education available', she said, 'which wasn't going to cost us a fortune'. As another parent (Mrs Dressel) explained — 'The comprehensive schools don't give everyone a chance. I was put in the middle of the pile and was lost . . . Ambrose produces results, they have dedicated teachers, and they keep the kids in line'. Her reasons closely resembled those given by fee-paying and assisted-place parents, and even when her son had been offered a place at an independent school she had chosen what she regarded as a free equivalent.

Archbishop Ambrose is much more selective, academically and socially, than Highgrove County. Both schools, however, were regarded by many of the parents we interviewed as offering a happy compromise — academically more acceptable than a comprehensive but not as pressured or potentially as uprooting as the independent schools nearby. But these parents should not be seen one-dimensionally as middle-class opportunists still able to take advantage of free grammar schools. Some were clearly uneasy about the consequences of selection for those who 'failed'. The Revd Andrews had been upset by parishioners' questions when his own son failed to get into Highgrove County Boys, and while he might have paid for his abler daughter if she had not been able to go to the Girls' Grammar he was insistent that an academically-oriented comprehensive was perfectly feasible in a residential area like his. Mrs Menton, a fairly affluent resident of the same district, had considered private education for a daughter whom she described as — 'a typical grammar school child, she epitomizes the type'. She and her husband, an industrial chemist, had chosen Highgrove because the fees would have curtailed other activities and would also have made it impossible to 'bail out' either of their younger sons 'if things went wrong and they failed the 11-plus'. Yet that examination had caused her daughter a great deal of worrying and crying at night, and she was herself well aware of the vagaries of a once-and-for all test which could do lasting damage to some who 'failed' it. She defined as her ideal 'a really flexible comprehensive school in a good catchment area'. And despite her own consideration of private education, she disapproved in principle of independent schools because their disappearance would bring 'less agonizing by middle-class parents' about which sector to use, and more pressure from them to improve the state system.

Shirebrook High School resembled Mrs Menton's ideal. By the measures we used, the 'able' children we interviewed there came from backgrounds as socially and culturally advantaged as any we encountered. A 'successful' school academically, with a large sixth form and a high rate of entry to higher education, it also offered a range of extra-curricular activities which matched those at the independent schools. Asked why they had chosen the school, many pupils and their parents responded — 'Why go elsewhere?' Certainly parents who could clearly have afforded private education saw no need to do so. In other comprehensive schools too we found considerable confidence in the quality of education being offered. Rowton was widely regarded as the 'best state school around', and some of its pupils and parents were explicitly dismissive of nearby independent schools as being 'not worth the money'. Parkside was seen as still shaped by the traditions and values of the girls' grammar school it had previously been, and some parents approved strongly of that continuity. Moorside lacked that inherited character, and seemed largely to have lost to independent schools in Milltown and elsewhere that substantial professional stratum which was most apparent in Shirebrook but also evident in Parkside, Vicarage Road and Cherry Tree. But its rural and commuter catchment area was still sufficiently reassuring to ambitious parents that it would have its 'share' of able pupils. Mr Gould, a self-employed bricklayer, for example, had wanted 'an academically sound, well-disciplined school', and Moorside provided it. Although his son had sat the entrance examination (unsuccessfully) for Milltown Grammar, he claimed it had been only 'a test to see what his level was' and he had rejected the same tactic for his younger daughter because he was satisfied with his son's progress. Mrs Westgate, working as a dinner lady to eke out her husband's earnings as a mechanic, had discounted Milltown High for her daughter because of the fees, because 'I don't want my child feeling ashamed of me', but principally because she could see no reason why her educational ambitions for the girl could not be catered for at a school which did well by its abler pupils.

Many parents in this part of our sample gave us the impression of having carefully chosen the only comprehensive they considered sufficiently 'academic' to cater for an able child, or of having needed some reassurance that there was a sufficient 'leaven' of other able, ambitious children in the neighbourhood school to provide stimulus and challenge. Almost all of them were strongly in favour of streaming or some broader form of ability grouping, seeing this as a necessary barrier against carrying non-selectivity too far. Indeed, academic selection *within* schools was approved by almost all parents in all four categories.

It was interesting to find much less support 'in principle' for comprehensive schools among parents who used them than there was for the particular schools that their children attended. We return later in the chapter to the stereotyped 'descriptions' of comprehensives which were offered by so many of the pupils and parents we interviewed, because such responses reflect a formidable barrier to their acceptance as the normal form of secondary schooling. And in highlighting parental preoccupations with academic opportunity, we are both following our own evidence and illustrating a main theme in the long debate about comprehensive schools — briefly, whether they can be both 'meritocratic' and 'egalitarian'(Marsden, 1969; Shaw, 1984; Weeks, 1986; Green and Ball, 1988). Their possible contribution to social cohesion also emerged quite strongly, both directly and indirectly. Its most conspicuous manifestation was the explanation given most often by pupils for their choice of school — 'It's the school all my friends were going to, and it's the closest'. Many parents too mentioned the appeal of a local school to which 'everybody went', often indicating their own sympathy with a child's wish to 'be with her mates'. Both these aspects of 'choice' were, for obvious reasons, much more evident in the public sector than in the often widely-dispersed intakes to independent schools. And both of them raise questions about parents as 'consumers', a notion which we want briefly to explore.

### Parents as Consumers

One justification of the Scheme, offered at its inception and insisted on with some force as it developed, is that it enhances parental choice. Its supporters have encouraged parents to see themselves as 'consumers'. In this sense the Scheme offers parents dissatisfied with the state of education the opportunity to look elsewhere without disadvantaging those amongst them who are unable to afford fees. Before examining the force of this particular claim, we take a broader view and look comparatively at various aspects of 'consumer choice' we encountered in our research.

We want to begin by emphasizing again the careful 'strategic planning' of their children's secondary schooling which was apparent in many of our interviews and which is illustrated in many of the families mentioned in the previous two sections. Such parental 'strategists' were encountered in both sectors, and included of course those families which had deliberately moved into the area of a favoured comprehensive school (sometimes years before their child's entry into it) or which had included independent schools among the possible alternatives before being reassured that comparable academic opportunities existed outside private education. The most conspicuous cases, of course, were found among those able (though sometimes with difficulty) to consider a wide range of alternatives. Mr and Mrs Cross and Mr Grayson exemplify them. Mr Cross already had Nortown Grammar in view for his son when they moved to Nortown years before. The boy had been sent to a preparatory school to enhance his chances of an eventual free place, and the unanticipated ending of the direct-grant arrangements had greatly increased the potential cost of his schooling. While Mr Cross had no doubt that the reputation of Nortown was worth a considerable financial sacrifice, he had compared results in other independent schools and decided that their superiority to several surviving maintained grammar schools was not enough to justify the expense. In his order of preference, the secondary modern school which was literally opposite their front gate had been rejected as entirely unacceptable; a small private grammar school would have been a last resort; Highgrove and other grammar schools in the same LEA would have been second- or third-best. Now that his son was coping successfully with the intense academic pressure at Nortown, he was certain that he was buying tangible advantages for him in an increasingly competitive labour market. Mr Grayson had been satisfied with his son's state primary school (which he had once attended himself), but was eloquently dismissive of all the comprehensive schools in and around Milltown. While any of them would have been a 'last resort', he had still identified the 'least bad'. His main efforts, however, had gone into a systematic comparison of facilities and examination results at four independent schools. Milltown Grammar had moved up from fourth to first choice because it had taken trouble with its public relations, and because he had been particularly impressed by its blend of discipline and openness. After a place there had been accepted, and one offered elsewhere had been turned down, the rejected school had written to inform the family 'in strict confidence' that the boy had been fourth in their entrance examination and to offer a school scholarship of £500 per annum. The school then pretended that the letter should not have been sent. But since it had, wouldn't they like to consider the offer? It was rejected, even though the payment of Milltown's full fees was a difficulty only partly overcome by Mrs Grayson's part-time work as a barmaid and by a loan at a preferential rate of interest from the bank for which Mr Grayson worked. Both parents expressed complete support for the school, and complete confidence in the opportunities it offered.

We have noted similarly confident expectations among comprehensive school parents, especially those convinced that they too had made a real choice. But in particular parts of two of our study areas, we recorded some forceful expressions of belief that children had simply been allocated to a school. These were from families living in LEAs which still operated in practice a strict neighbourhood catchment policy, making exceptions for more distant schools only if siblings already attended them. Few of the parents we interviewed here had used, or even considered, the statutory appeals procedure. Not surprisingly, then, a rather fatalistic view of the transition from primary to secondary school was common among parents and children in these areas. It was not uncommon for pupils to respond 'Everyone comes here' or 'We just got sent' to the question, 'Why did you choose this school?' Some Frampton parents in particular, affected by the catchment area policy, were adamant that no choice of state schools existed for them. As Mrs Pugh explained — 'It was all cut and dried because there were no places at Waverley [a nearby, much favoured, comprehensive]. So there was no choice really'. Like some other parents in this working-class area, she claimed that if she had 'had the money all my children would have gone to private schools', but that alternative was rarely seen as a serious possibility. However, Mrs Voss's daughter had sat and passed the entrance exam for one of the city's leading independent schools. She applied for, but did not obtain, an assisted place and had also attempted to obtain one at another school. The first choice in the state sector was Waverley. Knowing the difficulties of obtaining a place there, she put the family house on the market with every intention of purchasing another in Waverley's catchment area. The LEA refused her request for a place at Waverely. She invoked the appeals procedure and wrote to the Secretary of State. Both appeals failed. While this case indicates how constraining the catchment area policy could be, we were struck by its symbolic importance because it was cited by other parents as evidence of the difficulty of securing any choice at all. Yet few had even considered the alternative of an assisted place which had been pursued by Mrs Voss.

Even an informal neighbourhood catchment policy has serious implications, not only for the families who see themselves as bureaucratically locked into less desirable schools, but for the schools themselves. Just over 20 per cent of parents with children at comprehensive schools reported that the school their children attended had not been their first choice — a figure which is significantly higher than that usually quoted even by ministers when they argue the case for open enrolment. It was Frampton parents especially who seemed to tolerate rather than support their school, and in some cases to be generally doubtful about state secondary education. This might be taken as evidence for the Connell thesis about working-class parents feeling no sense of control over their children's schooling (Connell *et al.*, 1983). But we would not want to exaggerate the point, and they were very much the exception. Even at Rowton, in a different LEA but not far away and with a similarly 'zoned' intake, a high degree of satisfaction with the school was expressed by parents and pupils alike. If there were many families there (as there were in Cherry Tree) who seemed not to have considered any alternative, it was because they were confident that it was 'simply the best school around'. The Assisted Places Scheme did not apparently even enter their frame of reference.

We have referred to the process of 'pupil-drift' — the inertia of simply progressing to the school that 'everyone' went to. We have also referred to the more positive aspect of this — the strong desire of many maintained school pupils to 'go where my friends were going', a preference which many parents had respected even when it went against their own wishes. Clearly, we have insufficient evidence to argue that families in the public sector were more democratic in how they chose a secondary school, or more willing to give children a positive voice. Nevertheless, the clearest instances where parental preferences had overridden the child's wishes were in the private sector. This may have been a reflection of the generally stronger instrumental orientation among independent school parents, with a much greater emphasis on examination results as a 'very important factor' determining their choice of school (see

Finally, we return to another aspect of choice referred to earlier — the stronger stereotyping of different kinds of school which appeared in many of our interviews with pupils and parents. In general, independent schools were seen as being stricter, fussier about uniform and related matters, and more demanding about pupils' behaviour in and out of school. Work there was thought to be 'harder' and 'more academically advanced' because 'they have brighter pupils'. They were also widely regarded as being socially selective, 'a bit snobbish', but as offering 'better chances'. Indeed, many parents seemed to have no doubt at all that they were 'better' schools, with abler pupils and 'better qualified teachers' and a proven capacity to give their pupils advantages of style and substance in competition for places in higher education and for jobs. Those beliefs were commonly expressed by many parents whose own children were in maintained schools, and often seemed to arise not from any knowledge of what such schools were actually like but from a simple assumption that education which is paid for 'had to be better'. Private sector parents and pupils seemed even readier to judge from ignorance, and to pronounce confidently on the failings of particular comprehensive schools and of comprehensives in general. The schools were seen generally as being larger, rougher, rowdier, and full of diversions from work. The comments of three girls at Dame Margaret's exemplify views which surfaced repeatedly in our school and home interviews. Comprehensive schools 'don't teach you so hard and let you waste time'; 'the whole atmosphere there is not to work'; and 'those at the top are dragged down by those behind'.

## Perceptions of school and of education opportunity

Having explored how parents accounted for their choice of secondary school, and how far the presence of independent schools was seen as extending or improving the alternatives, we now turn to parents' and pupils' perceptions of the outcomes of their choice. In first reporting the views of pupils, we emphasize that the diversity of schools in which we worked brought considerable differences in the age of pupils at the time we interviewed them. We therefore have to take care not to make misleading comparisons — for example, between first-year pupils in 13-18 public schools or comprehensive high schools still enthusiastic about a new and challenging environment, and contemporaries in independent (or maintained) schools who were already relatively hardened veterans in those schools and perhaps more disposed to criticize. Of course the interview situation itself was not conducive to strong criticisms of the established order, however firmly we assured pupils of confidentiality. Opportunities for complaint were certainly there, and were occasionally taken with enthusiasm. But in general, the level of expressed dissatisfaction was low. Any differences which we identify between pupils in maintained and independent schools have to be set against the background of a high level of pro-school feeling. Except where we explicitly indicate otherwise, comments from independent schools are from assisted-place holders or their parents. While this reflects our specific focus on the Scheme, we also found no notable differences in attitude between them and their fee-paying contemporaries.

The predominant contrast between independent school and comprehensive school pupils lay in the more evidently and confidently ambitious responses of the former. We illustrate this from two contrasting pairs of schools. In Rowton, a large city comprehensive with a very socially-mixed intake, positive comments outnumbered the criticisms by four to one. There was appreciation of 'good' and 'helpful' teachers, the wide range of facilities, the variety of extra-curricular activities (even though our interviews were within the period of the teachers' industrial action), and the friendly atmosphere. Occasional disapproval centred on boring subjects or lessons, boring assemblies, and teachers 'who can't keep order' or who 'don't consider people'. In Nortown Grammar School, a large city boys' independent school, the level of appreciation was similarly strong, and a similar proportion (about a third) could think of nothing that they actively disliked. Friends and friendliness were mentioned often, as were the array of extra-curricular activities — 'If you're interested in anything, there's a good chance you can find a club'. There was however a much clearer view of the benefits to be expected from being at a school which (to quote two fee-paying pupils) is 'known instantly and nationally as good' and where a place was clearly 'an investment in the future'. Most boys seemed to approve of the high pace of academic work which the school set and maintained; as two of them said, 'they seem to push you to get a lot out of you', and 'you get used to being graded'. It was similarly recognized by pupils at Milltown Grammar that they were probably getting a better start in life than at any of the comprehensive schools available. But it was more often accompanied by a somewhat negative or ritualistic response to that school's demands. The label 'instrumentally compliant' seemed to apply to a high proportion of those we spoke to, especially in the third year, and there were more comments of a kind we rarely recorded elsewhere in the private sector, that 'school is school'. In Frampton, a mixed urban comprehensive with an almost entirely working-class intake, two-thirds of the references to specific features of the school were favourable, while thirteen of the thirty-three pupils we interviewed identified nothing they really disliked. There were almost as many favourable comments about good teachers or the attractions of particular subjects as about 'being with friends' or 'having some laughs'. Criticisms were mainly about the drabness of uniform (when it was worn!), and the few teachers who could not control classes or who were boring. But, with some lively exceptions, most pupils seemed to regard school more as a necessary fact of life than as something about which to have strong feelings. It was certainly not seen with any confidence as a source of opportunities to 'get on'.

It was this difference which came through most clearly in our general comparisons of responses from independent and maintained schools. To the question 'What is important to you about being at this school?', references to 'being with my friends' were more numerous in Frampton (as they were in other comprehensives) than were references to 'getting good results' or 'doing well enough to get a good job'. At least at the age when we interviewed boys and girls alike, friendship appeared as the most powerful influence on how enjoyable school life was found to be. Of course a balance had to be found. As one boy in Cherry Tree put it, 'I want to do pretty well, work hard, and enjoy myself'; or, in the words of two pupils at Rowton, it was most important to 'do well in exams and have as many friends as possible', and to 'get good qualifications, good friends, and have a good time'. But getting good results seemed to be a generalized objective, less firmly attached to particular ambitions (or to 'levels' of occupational ambition) than in independent schools, and much less a matter of success being confidently assumed. As might be expected from our earlier evidence of a high level of instrumentalism, independent school pupils were far more likely to refer explicitly to the sequence of a good education, good results and a good start in life. Many of them also spoke appreciatively of the academic orientation of their schools, schools in which 'there's no shame in being serious and hard-working' (Milltown High). 'It's nice not to be made fun of because you work hard', said an assisted-place pupil at Nortown High; 'in my old school, there was no pride in coming top because you were called a swot' (Nortown High). The pressure to 'get on with your work' was accepted more easily because of the assurance of future benefits, even where other disadvantages were also apparent — as at Milltown Grammar, where there were sharp criticisms of poor buildings, inadequate facilities in comparison with neighbouring comprehensive schools, limited subject choice (especially for the most academically able), and a lack of provision for technical and practical subjects.

Any impression of remorseless dedication to academic results, however, would be misleading. 'Friendliness' was a recurring theme in our independent school interviews too. However elusive 'ethos' may be as a concept in organizational analysis, references to a 'nice' or 'pleasant' atmosphere were numerous. Both at Milltown High and Nortown High, for example, awareness of limited facilities and a marked dislike of irksome rules about uniform were more than offset by enjoyment of what was seen as the homeliness of a small school — 'We all know each other, everybody is pleasant, and makes you feel welcome'; 'It's small, homely and easy to cope with', and 'manageable and comfortable'. That impression of friendliness was no more conspicuous, however, in the smaller schools. It was a frequently noted quality at one of the largest independent schools in the country, while at Shirebrook (a state school with about 1000 pupils) there were repeated references to 'being trusted', 'being treated like adults', and to 'a homely atmosphere that makes you feel confident'. 'There's just something about it', as one girl said; 'it just doesn't feel like a school'. Again, our overall impression from interviews at Vicarage Road, an 11-16 school of nearly a thousand, was of a similarly relaxed confidence and even enjoyment. In each case, these impressions were confirmed by the parental interviews.

We have emphasized these impressions because comprehensive schools are so often associated with large sites, large numbers and impersonality. Such associations or stereotypes came through strongly in many interviews with parents of assisted-place and fee-paying pupils as being among the reasons for having chosen an independent school. Yet most of our sample schools are large, as we noted in chapter 7, and many of them are on extensive and sprawling sites. For most pupils, their primary school had been 'midget compared with this place', with 'life a bit simpler then than now' (Vicarage Road). When we asked them how difficult they had found it to settle in to their present schools, there were predictable reports of having felt initially frightened and lost. 'I was nervous at first — I was small, and everyone towered above me'. In addition there were intense anxieties, of the kind which Measor and Woods (1984) describe, about not finding the right classrooms in time. Some pupils, more especially girls, expressed a certain nostalgia for the smaller, familiar, more intimate environment of a primary school where you are 'closer to all the teachers', 'get more attention', and 'knew all the faces'. Indeed, comments on the 'family atmosphere' of the previous school sometimes highlighted features which some independent school parents seemed to have been looking for at the secondary stage, especially for their daughters. As one Shirebrook pupil remarked of her middle school, without apparent irony — 'It's a nice little school, with nice teachers and nice children'. But this was certainly not the predominant view among pupils. Some recalled their previous school with disdain. It was 'like a play-school' (Moorside boy), or 'just like a day nursery where you dropped the kids off before doing some shopping' (Cathedral College). More typically, pupils claimed strongly to prefer the greater diversity of their secondary schools — the new facilities, the wider choice of friends, and especially the escape from 'having the same teacher all the time, which is so boring'. Most of them either denied that the size of their new school had ever been a problem, or (more commonly) presented it as a problem which they had very quickly overcome. The most frequent response was a variation on the comment of a Shirebrook girl — 'I was terrified at first, but I stopped being nervous in two to three days'.

As with the pupils, we found no conspicuous general differences between fee-paying, assisted-place and maintained school parents in their appreciation of the schools their children attended. Of course there were strongly expressed individual criticisms — for example, of the replacement of a disciplinarian head by 'the wet nelly we have now' or of the deterioration of a comprehensive school said to have 'gone back' academically under the influence of 'idiot subjects' like cookery and typing which supposedly got in the way of 'proper work'. But the general level of expressed satisfaction was high. Certainly nostalgia was rare, except for that pervasive regret at the passing of the grammar schools, a point to which we will return. It was a frequent theme among all categories of parents that their children's secondary education was a marked improvement on their own, schools being now more humane and open, and relationships between teachers and pupils significantly better. In no instance, however, did this represent an endorsement of anything which could be called 'progressivism'. Like the Australian parents interviewed by Connell and his colleagues (1983, p. 60), independent school and maintained school parents alike 'clearly supported firm discipline, teacher-centred pedagogy, and job-oriented curricula'. And, as we noted earlier, there was almost unanimous support for academic selection *within* schools.

Some contrasts might have been expected in a sense of control over their children's schools, the main sectoral (and class) difference emphasized by Connell. It was most apparent among the minority of parents described in the previous section who had felt 'bureaucratically' constrained to accept the local comprehensive school even where 'better' alternatives were technically available, and who had also felt excluded from even considering an independent school by lack of money or a sense that such schools were not for them. As we commented then, this feeling was especially marked in Frampton, the most working-class and also the most intensely local of our areas. Knowledge that a more socially-favoured school with better results was swamped with applications had deterred some parents from even applying, but had not removed their resentment at having been allocated second-best. Generally, the view that fee-charging schools are necessarily more accountable to parents seemed to be more strongly held among working-class parents who admired such schools from a distance than among the fee-payers themselves. We should note however that our private sector samples, even of 'full' fee-payers, included far fewer than those interviewed by Connell (or by Irene Fox) who could be described as 'ruling class', and this may explain why we were made much less aware of teachers being regarded as 'paid agents', and of the schools as being 'owned' (Connell *et al.*, 1983, pp. 128–35).

At various points in the chapter, we have noted the strongly instrumental attitudes to secondary schooling among many independent school pupils and parents, the widely-held belief in the competitive edge provided by a private education, and the anxiety among many state school parents that their children would not be left behind.

We now examine in more detail some sectoral differences in perceived opportunity.

There were, for example, obvious residues of a difference noted by the Crowther Committee thirty years ago. For most independent school pupils, staying on into the sixth form was something which they assumed would happen. It was the obvious course to take in that kind of school. Comprehensive pupils of comparable ability seemed to be less certain, more aware of contingencies and alternatives, and less precise about their intentions afterwards. In general, they were much less aware of the necessary routes into and from higher education to the kinds of careers they said they would like. Since our interviews were conducted some years before the relevant decisions had actually to be made, comparisons cannot be taken too seriously. Nevertheless, some differences were apparent apart from the much greater level of certainty among independent school pupils about their educational and occupational futures. While the proportion of 'able' comprehensive pupils considering higher education was quite high, that stage was defined much less exclusively in terms of going to university, and particular universities were referred to very much less often. For example, some expectation of higher education was mentioned by twenty-four of the forty pupils at Cherry Tree and twenty-seven of the forty at Shirebrook. But only thirteen pupils in the two schools together named a university or polytechnic. At Frampton, none of the eighteen aspirants to higher education cited a particular institution (although one did say 'the nearest'!). In contrast, the near unanimity at Nortown Grammar about staying on was accompanied by almost as much unanimity about the desirability of higher education; more than half had some idea of what they might study, and more than half also named a university, 40 per cent of those references being to Oxford or Cambridge. At Milltown Girls', most pupils seemed to see higher education as a necessary step to the kind of occupation they wanted, and references to Oxbridge and to the local civic university were numerous. At Cathedral College, all the assisted-place pupils named Oxbridge as the obvious next step for them to take. At the two grammar schools, relatively specific ambitions were also common, and the popularity of Oxbridge in the boys' school was as high as in most independent schools.

Our questions about possible careers were not intended to do more than touch whether even vague ambitions currently existed. At the age most pupils were when we interviewed them, few were likely to reveal more than a broad level of aspiration, together perhaps with a basic optimism or pessimism about their 'life chances'. We recorded some engaging examples of playing the field — for example, the Frampton girl who wanted to be 'a pop singer if all goes well, or an export marketing manager'! Where fairly precise careers were mentioned, it was mainly by pupils in independent schools — strikingly illustrated by the Nortown boy who saw a clear progression for himself from barrister to Queen's Counsel to High Court judge. But in the context of continuing debates about the 'decline of the industrial spirit' in the UK (Mathieson and Bernbaum, 1988), and about the low status and weak influence of technological culture in elite education, we should note that the professional/managerial ambitions of independent school pupils were overwhelmingly concentrated in the 'higher professions' (especially law and medicine), and that references to jobs in industry were strikingly low. 'Something in science' was a much more common response than anything in engineering, and something in the arts (journalism, writing, acting, fashion design) was much more common than either.

Among parents, there were no significant overall differences between fee-paying, assisted-place and maintained school parents in their views of the occupational opportunities open to their children. There was a predominant optimism, qualified by concern that unemployment was becoming a significant risk even for the well-qualified, and more general alarm at the 'collapse' of the job market. Yet neither national statistics nor personal experience had apparently undermined the traditional conviction that educational success was 'very important' in determining children's futures. The proportions of parents whose answers fell broadly into that category were 82 per cent of fee-payers, 74 per cent of assisted-place holders, and 75 per cent in maintained schools. Christopher Jencks' (1979) assertion that success is largely dependent on luck was a view which rarely appeared even by implication, and the openness of British society to the meritorious still seemed to be largely accepted. We recorded occasional objections to the barriers 'which stop people like us going too far', and more frequent comments on the benefits of wearing the 'right school tie' which we elaborate in the section which follows. But, generally, opportunities were still seen as being substantial for the able, the ambitious, and those prepared to work.

We have commented repeatedly on parents in all our categories whose own experience of academically selective secondary schooling had made them dubious about all alternatives. More interesting in many ways were those parents in both sectors who, although occupationally successful themselves without formal qualifications, nevertheless regarded such qualifications as being essential for their children. Indeed, a view of schooling which was both meritocratic and instrumental pervaded many of the home interviews. Mr Marshall (Rowton) illustrates this perspective. He had moved house some years before, partly to escape the tensions of being 'in private housing in a sea of council estates', but mainly to escape the catchment area of a 'bad' comprehensive offering no prospects. Having left school at 15 himself, he had only got a job as a glass-blower in the local university because his mother already worked there as a laboratory assistant, and had acquired his technical qualifications by the arduous night-school route. Turning to his daughter, he said firmly — 'Without qualifications you're not even on the bottom rung of the ladder, and if you're not on the bottom rung Andrea you can't climb the ladder'. His main theme, repeated often during the interview, was that 'if you're prepared to work you should go up and if you don't you should go down'. The saving grace of Rowton Comprehensive was that it allowed able children like Andrea to work, and so to equip herself to 'go up'. It was the doubt and uncertainty about the capacity of most comprehensives to provide that opportunity which seemed to us to be a main theme in many parents' response to secondary schooling.

Much of the corresponding attraction of independent schools, and of any remaining maintained grammar schools, lies in the large 'critical mass' of able pupils, the assumptions about future educational and occupational careers which are therefore believed to pervade the schools, and the consequent pressure on pupils. We have mentioned several times the fast academic pace which parents and pupils saw as a significant advantage. It was one aspect of social segregation of which they were often prepared to approve. Independent schools are often criticized for creating or at least intensifying social divisions. Those most firmly within the independent school frame of reference are seen as being carried along a segregated fee-paying route from the outset of their schooling, and we encountered some pupils of whom that was certainly true. The much larger numbers for whom the assumed benefits of a private education are not bought until the secondary stage are then likely to be separated from those with whom they were friendly at primary school and launched into different social networks. A similar if milder sorting process is associated with grammar schools, and reactions against it shaped the social integration claims made for the 'common' secondary school. In turn, as we noted in chapter 4, advocates both of the private sector and of grammar schools argued that such social engineering does not work; that even if it did, the academic costs would be too high; and that neighbourhood comprehensive schools were often less socially diverse than the grammar schools they replaced. It was in this context that we were interested not only in the influence on pupils' preference for a particular secondary school of where friends were going, but in which schools their 'best friends' at that stage now attended and whether these older friendships had survived the change of schools.

We certainly found expectedly large differences in how socially disruptive the transition to secondary school had been, and how far it had carried the children into an initially unfamiliar social world. At one extreme were pupils in those neighbourhood comprehensives which had been the 'obvious' next step to pupils and parents alike. For example, fifty-five of sixty-three 'best friends' mentioned by Frampton pupils had moved on with them, and the fact that 'all my friends were coming' was the school's most frequently mentioned attraction. At Rowton, more than half the pupils we interviewed reported that all their best friends from primary school had moved with them. In other comprehensives, like Shirebrook, where intakes were drawn almost entirely from a few local feeder schools, most best friends from the previous stage were still around and about several years later. At none of the independent schools, however, was that figure higher than 10 per cent for assisted-place pupils or (except at Bankside) higher than 25 per cent for those paying full fees. At the other extreme from Frampton was Weston, where no two of our sample had come from the same school; Cathedral College, where the fee-paying pupils we interviewed had joined at six different ages from 8–13; and at Highgrove County where the twenty-three girls we spoke to had come from fourteen different schools. There were some independent schools where either their own junior departments or especially strong links with a few local preparatory and primary schools had produced clusters of pupils who had known each other well before their arrival. And, as we saw in chapter 7, there were some former direct-grant grammar schools which remained very much 'town grammar schools' with predominantly local intakes. In contrast, however, schools like Nortown Grammar have traditionally served a region rather than a locality, and continue to recruit geographically-dispersed intakes which must present new pupils at first with a bewildering array of strangers and few familiar faces.

Although friendship is the saving grace of school life for many pupils, the school itself is an absorbing source of conversational topics. It provides a common frame of reference, and a common store of anecdotes to be regularly recalled and embellished. It was not surprising, then, to find that most of the previous 'best friends' who had gone to other secondary schools, whether maintained or independent, were no longer or only rarely seen. Of course, old friendships had often been superseded even for children whose wish to 'be with my friends' had been a decisive factor in their own choice of school. There was now a new and much larger population in which to find friends, while new teaching and tutorial groups had often brought an end to what had previously been daily, intensive classroom contacts. As a Shirebrook girl commented — 'If they're in different bands, it's like being in a different school, and that's a pity'. But it is still not the same as being in a different and 'superior' school. Mrs Schooner, who thought her son was 'happy enough' at Frampton but would have bought a private education for him if 'we hadn't been just ordinary people', had gone to a local grammar school herself thirty years before. It had separated her from her former friends, who had shouted 'swot' at her on the bus and mocked her uniform. Those still living nearby 'talk to me now, but they didn't talk to me then'.

The divisiveness otherwise fostered by selection for different schools was attenuated for some independent school pupils by having 'school friends' and 'home friends'. Wide catchment areas often meant that best friends from school were out of reach at weekends and holidays anyway, while membership of the same youth clubs or sports clubs helped some to overcome what would otherwise have been considerable social isolation. As we noted earlier, some parents actively encouraged such social mixing, and none referred openly to a wish to preserve their children from possible 'contamination' by less able or ambitious contemporaries. But assisted-place pupils in our sample, who were particularly likely to have been 'uprooted' educationally from their local area, were predictably more likely to report and to regret the loss of contact with former friends. They were also more likely to report having been ostracized in their home areas for being 'swots' or 'poshies', and for attending 'snob schools'. At Milltown High, for example, almost all of them referred to some experience of this kind, a still strictly enforced school uniform making them uncomfortably conspicuous.

Even where such hostility had not been a problem, heavy homework demands often left little time for fraternization during the school week. Public schools have long been noted for their efforts to take over the whole of their pupils' lives during term-time. Highly selective day schools have also traditionally sought to extend their influence, not only by setting substantial amounts of homework but also by containing much of their pupils' 'spare' time under the schools's influence. In fact, several of the comprehensive schools we visited matched any in the private sector in the range of extra-curricular activities they offered. But there remained a large generalizable difference in responses to our questions to pupils about their leisure time, which was that independent school pupils had much less of it.

Our general conclusion from the pupil interviews is that while the transition to secondary school had unscrambled many old friendships even for those moving forward together, the move to an independent school detached many pupils (especially those holding assisted places) from their local social networks and placed them in a more 'cosmopolitan' world. Where contacts continued across the public sector-private sector 'border', they tended to reinforce and even intensify perceived differences between types of school in curriculum, work demands and destinations. It is to these perceived differences that we now turn.

### Comparative Judgments of Secondary Schooling

In explaining and justifying their choice of secondary school, both pupils and their parents often expressed strong beliefs about the distinctive qualities and weaknesses of types of school. In doing so, they looked both to alternative (or rival) schools of the same kind and to schools thought to be different in kind. The knowledge on which their beliefs were grounded was often very insubstantial. As we have emphasized already, many comprehensive pupils had moved almost *en bloc* from their previous schools and had few contacts of any kind with pupils elsewhere. They may have believed that they were in 'the best comprehensive around', but some forceful claims to that effect were unsupported by any information about alternatives. Very few indeed had any personal knowledge, however indirect, of independent schools. Many were therefore understandably unwilling to make any comparisons. At Frampton, for example, almost half those we interviewed claimed to know nothing about any other secondary school. None had friends or relatives in the private sector, except for one girl whose cousin at an independent school in another part of the country 'doesn't pay 'cos she's the brainiest there, and they're all swotty at that kind of school'. In this area there was none of that network of example and advice which had tempted some pupils elsewhere to at least consider trying for an assisted place.

Whatever the knowledge on which they were based, some comparisons emerged, explicitly or implicitly, in many of our interviews. They were sometimes accompanied by firm assertions of parity. In Cherry Tree, for example, the local independent schools (of which there were several) were often described by pupils as being quite different in overall character. 'People who go there get pushed more, so they get higher grades'. They do some different subjects, wear uniforms, have prefects, and 'would be a different class of people, not the ones you were with at primary school'. Such schools 'can get people to work faster, because they'll all have passed the test'. But accompanying these sometimes reluctant admissions of superiority was a considerable scepticism about the claims commonly made, especially about a neighbouring independent grammar school formerly on the direct-grant list. 'All the brainy people don't go there'; it was 'not a better school — I've been comparing exam results and they seem about the same'; 'I know a lot of kids from there, they say it's brainier but not much brainier'. As one pupil summed it up, 'It's no big deal going there, you get the same sort of chances here'. At Rowton, those who had no doubt that it was as good as the nearby independent schools outnumbered those who conceded some inferiority. 'If you do well from here', said one girl in a slightly ambivalent testimonial, 'you can do well from anywhere, but if you do well from [naming the city's largest girls' independent school] it's only what's expected. There's more of a mixture here, I prefer that'. Admitting that Rowton might be 'a little worse', another girl identified the difference as 'so slight that it's not worth paying'. At Moorside, the reputation of the two local independent schools for being strict, getting good results and being 'snobby' was referred to by several pupils who were still not prepared to accept at face value those schools' claims to be academically better, or who asserted the superiority of a 'good' comprehensive like theirs because it had to 'cope with a wider range of intelligence'. We quote the following comments to illustrate both the main dimensions on which comparisons were made, and the ways in which equality was typically asserted.

> It's a lot stricter there [at King Henry's Grammar School], and you get loads of homework, but chances are just as good here. (Shirebrook)

> In private schools, everyone's richer. Here you get the average, well-off and not-so-well-off and I prefer that. In a private school, you'd be driven to keep up with them. (Rowton)

> Private schools are no better, it's just that children who go there are led to believe it's a better education. (Shirebrook)

> Private schools are too posh. Comprehensives have more common people. I don't mix much with the upper class, and I couldn't go to one of those schools. (Shirebrook)

> I prefer this to a private school because the sexes are equal and you mix with all sorts here. Friends from private school describe some of their friends as pretty thick. (Moorside)

We noted earlier in the chapter the relatively greater readiness of independent school pupils (and sometimes their parents) to identify confidently the weaknesses of state schools of which they had no direct knowledge. They seemed to measure the differences on the two main dimensions of academic ethos and discipline. There was a general feeling of being well ahead of their contemporaries in such schools, and for that advantage they were prepared to pay the price of stricter rules and heavier homework. At Milltown High, for example, the local comprehensives were widely seen as places where 'kids muck about', 'kids swear at teachers', 'teachers can't handle the children so that they're not learning much', and where 'it's very rough, with truancy, bad behaviour, more lax'. These were all comments from assisted-place pupils who had been at state schools until the age of 11. Boys at Nortown Grammar described the comprehensives available to them as being 'rough', 'full of yobs for a start', 'unsympathetic to anyone who worked', and unable to offer 'as good an education or a job'. A few were more cautious, prepared to concede that 'the standard of teaching may not be higher, but that's the way it seems'. A much more frequent response, however, was that where 'everyone is clever, that means more competition and everyone works hard', and that the academic pressure was impossible to escape. These beliefs were pervasive. They were sometimes accompanied by a perceived contrast not only in standards, but also between a traditional and a more modern curriculum — for example, a belief that 'they do crafts, we do double maths, they have a free choice at O-level and we have to do two Englishes' (Milltown Girls). But by far the most usual comparisons were in terms of better behaviour and better results.

Parents' general attitudes to different types of secondary school rarely fell into neat, dogmatic categories. Indeed, the views expressed most frequently can best be described as ambivalent — reservations about the divisive effects of private education accompanying pragmatic recognition of its benefits; admiration for the 'old grammar schools' qualified by criticisms that selection for them had been carried out too early and too rigidly; support for the 'idea' of comprehensive education combined with the judgment that comprehensive schools themselves were unable to cope with 'really able' children.

Favourable views of independent schools seemed to be based most commonly on the related assumptions that schools which had to win customers in the market-place 'had to be' good, and that they were in fact better disciplined, more academic, more insistent on hard work, and more likely to promote ability and ambition. Mr Walewski's perceptions were very much those highlighted in ISIS publicity. We mentioned him in the previous chapter as insistently proud that an assisted place had enabled his son to attend the same school as the sons of his employers. He had no doubt that state schools were inherently prone to propaganda and that independent schools were an essential defence against it. But the latter were superior anyway, having to attract their pupils with smaller classes and better teachers and so giving them far better opportunities. Such unhesitating acceptance of the distinctive quality of independent schools was predictably apparent in the comments of parents who had never at any stage considered state schooling for their children. More notable was the frequency with which state school parents took the same virtues for granted. Over our whole sample, the proportions agreeing that independent schools offered 'particular advantages' were strikingly similar — 78 per cent of fee payers, 82 per cent with assisted place, 79 per cent in the public sector. Opinions about the source of those advantages were more divided. Mr and Mrs Southcott, for example, had deferred to their daughter's wish to go with her friends to Cherry Tree, despite their own conviction that an independent school would have provided more individual attention, better discipline, and more encouragement for academic achievement. Mrs Gates had sent her son to preparatory school before her divorce made the fees impossible, regretted bitterly that he had failed to gain an assisted place, and was not deflected by his evident enjoyment of Shirebrook from believing that it could never match in teaching or academic 'challenge' the independent school he might have attended. This was, however, very much a minority view amongst Shirebrook parents.

Prominent in some parental responses were references to the special 'poise' and 'polish' which independent schools were thought to develop. As Mr Keane (Rowton) put it — 'There's a self-confidence that goes with elitism'. This view was especially marked in our Frampton interviews, despite the absence of even vicarious experience of what independent schools are actually like. Mr Wilson, a postman and ex-seaman still active in the RNVR, knew nothing about the Assisted Places Scheme and felt that the presence of much richer pupils would have been too much for Sharon anyway. Yet if he had had the money, 'and it's all a question of money isn't it', he would have bought a secondary place to make much more likely his ambition that she should go to university. Mr Morrow, a just-retired police constable, could never regard a comprehensive school as anything more than an unavoidable second-best when independent schools 'can do so much more for you'. Mrs Sullivan believed that even mere attendance at an independent school was an advantage — 'They even sound different — it's the accent and the label and the old-school-tie brigade — they prefer their own'. Mr and Mrs Gable had both left secondary modern schools at 15, and worked hard since for their occupational and financial success. Although all three children seemed to be doing well at Frampton, they would have sent all of them to an independent school if they could have afforded three sets of fees, and resented the fact that such schools recruited 'so many with money but thick'. On the matter of academic selection, they reflected the ambivalence of so many parents we interviewed. Their own experiences as 'secondary modern cast-offs' had turned them against early selection because 'if you missed the boat early you really missed it'. Yet they also wanted their own children to be 'pushed hard', doubted if Frampton would do that, and had no doubt that independent schools gave able children a far better chance through their better facilities, possibly better teachers, greater parental involvement ('because they're paying and would kick up a fuss if they weren't getting what they wanted'), tighter organization, and greater capacity to exclude 'undesirable' influences.

These were the benefits identified most often by those independent school parents who also recognized the damage which the existence of private alternatives might be doing to the public sector. If they offered unequal opportunities, then parents 'wanting to do the best for our children' would find them impossible to resist, even while supporting in theory (as Mr and Mrs Hoyle did) their eventual abolition. Dr Allen, a parent and a teacher at the same school (Bankside), could see no case for a private sector if state schools were adequately funded. Mr Crosbie had a prestigious local independent school clearly in view from the time he moved house years before, and his son had been enrolled in a preparatory school at the age of 3 to enhance his chances of gaining a place there. Yet he was 'against independent schools in principle', denied that the state system needed private alternatives, and saw the buying of educational and subsequent occupational advantages as unfair. But as long as the independent schools were there, ambitious parents like himself would use them to secure better credentials for their children in what was becoming an increasingly competitive labour market. This was a commonly-expressed view. In other families, we recorded the rather different ambivalence of parents who seemed anxious to explain their choice of an independent school as a response to the special needs of an individual child — a child too clever, too easily bored, too eccentric or too introverted to be happy in the relative rough-and-tumble of the local comprehensive — rather than as an expression of any general preference for private education.

Outright opponents of private education sometimes derived their opposition quite explicitly from their Labour politics, seeing it as a logical consequence. They argued that the state should provide the education, and the health care, of all its citizens. Mrs Clements (Cherry Tree) saw the existence of independent schools as entirely incompatible with equality of opportunity because they 'structured career chances unfairly' in higher-status occupations, and was critical of her own sister for 'betraying her class' by buying a secondary school place. Mrs Grace (Moorside) deplored the divisive effects of private education, which creamed off talented pupils and teachers and so made comprehensive schools uncomprehensive. Mr Martin, a teacher at another comprehensive and with a son at Moorside, had found his own opposition to independent schools strengthened by the teachers' industrial action because the dispute had emphasized that as long as Tories and their supporters could buy their way out of an under-resourced state sector they could 'leave it to flounder'. Mr Davies was happy with Shirebrook High School, would not have sent any of his children to independent schools, but approved of their existence because of his commitment to 'freedom of choice'. His wife was thoroughly against them because they drew away from comprehensive schools many able children and many articulate parents. 'Their freedom of choice', she said, 'diminishes my children's opportunities'.

### The Limitations of 'Choice'

This chapter and the last have focused on many of the families we encountered in our research and on their choice and perceptions of secondary schools. We conclude this chapter by relating our findings to the more general political ideology of 'choice' which has been both a sustaining justification of the Assisted Places Scheme and which, as embodied in more recent initiatives, is discussed in our final chapter.

As we noted earlier, in recent Conservative Party thinking, parents have figured largely as consumers — in the tradition of neoclassical economics, as independent actors making decisions based on calculations of self-interest (Hula, 1984, p. 194). From this perspective, the Assisted Places Scheme can be seen as enabling a greater number of parents to select a secondary school from either sector according to what they judge to be the relative advantages and disadvantages. Our own analysis of parents' accounts, however, indicates some serious inadequacies in that consumer model.

On the supply side, the image of a range of schools of varying quality and qualities competing for parental attention is a rosy-hued version of the 'market' as perceived by many families managing the transition from primary to secondary school. As the present Government recognizes, choice is still contrained in the public sector. Although the 1980 Act gave parents greater *de jure* rights in their choice of school, it also placed a statutory duty on LEAs to make efficient use of their resources. Where the two conflict, the managerial priorities of the authority sometimes take precedence. But there are also limitations on choice in the private sector. Available schools are not equally accessible — because of the fees they charge, their entrance examinations, their reputation for being socially exclusive, their location, or a popularity which enables them to reject 'unsuitable' applicants. As we have seen, by no means all these constraints on the availability of independent school places are removed by the existence of the Assisted Places Scheme. And, in some senses, the 'market' is distorted rather than enhanced by its existence, particularly in its present form.

Furthermore, the 'consumerist' model of parents has a number of shortcomings which are all too evident when applied to real families making decisions about their children's schooling in the contemporary setting. Parents in our study, for example, had individual biographies which shaped or determined their perspectives on different kinds of schools. They gave rise to preference and prejudices, loyalties and resentments which were powerful referents when choices were made. Additionally there were divergent views in households where contrasting school experiences sometimes led to considerable disagreements about parents' priorities and values.[2] As our study also makes clear, the young have a voice, powers of persuasion and often their own agendas, and it was their wishes which were often the determining factor. We observed, however, that parents determined to send their children to private schools were rather more inclined to press their choice on unwilling children than were parents with children in the state sector. A simple rational choice model is certainly inconvenienced by all these factors, and it looks rather weaker than an interpretation of educational decision-making at this level as a continuously negotiated process taking place between pupils and their parents.

In this study, for example, the parents were of an age where they had experienced or were familiar with selective schooling of one kind or another. For many of them, as we noted earlier, the grammar schools still best represented the model of 'a good education', even for the parents who were themselves 11-plus 'failures' (and who often felt that they had suffered the consequences ever since). The grammar schools had provided many of them with an educational route to social mobility and, as we suggested previously, many regretted that opportunity was no longer available for their children. Without that history of association with selective education the comprehensive school pupils had a very different perspective. In the absence of a divisive 11-plus examination other criteria applied. They preferred to attend the same school as their friends, or followed a route trailed by their brothers and sisters. However, the differences in generational perceptions of the nature and purpose of schooling should not hide the decisive similarity between parental schooling and that of their children.

The broad sweep of intergenerational stability has its disturbing aspects. Most notable in our sample is the under-representation of working-class children in the maintained grammar schools and in the Assisted Places Scheme and, perhaps even more disconcertingly, in the upper ability bands of comprehensive schools, especially those locally regarded as strong competitors with the independent schools. Critics of the Assisted Places Scheme have to come to terms with the fact that those comprehensive schools themselves seem to have had little success in redressing the considerable educational advantages that accrue from tacitly transmitted and acquired cultural capital. Even so, despite the obvious good intentions of some of its sponsors, the Scheme has not so far proved a particularly effective way of sponsoring working-class talent that would not be developed within the maintained system. We end this chapter by summarizing some of those factors affecting choices made by working-class families which seem to account most strongly for the findings of our study.

Firstly, by their own account, many working-class families cannot buy their way out of state schooling in specific instances where it was poorly regarded. But secondly, neither do they have the educational and cultural capital necessary to unlock the gate to an assisted passage through the fee-paying independent schools. And the same principle evidently operates in respect of the 11-plus exam for places at the maintained grammar schools. Thirdly, very few of the working-class families committed themselves as far as entering children for entrance examinations. This point is significant because it was at this stage that many of the assisted-place beneficiaries were first alerted to the financial support offered by the Scheme. Fourthly, not only were many of the highly regarded comprehensive schools in our research physically distanced from working-class communities, additionally some working-class families we encountered felt administratively 'locked out' of them through the operation of neighbourhood catchment policies. But, while this might seem to justify the availability of assisted places as a route of 'escape' from poor schools, our own evidence is that those with the cultural and political resources (including primary school sponsorship) to gain assisted places were also those already well placed to effect their escape within the state system. The failure of some clearly disgruntled working-class parents, like those at Frampton, to pursue assisted places suggests that the converse is also the case. In that sense, the Scheme has not in practice yet opened up real opportunities for that very group which, according to the Scheme's original rhetoric of legitimation, would otherwise be trapped in poor neighbourhood comprehensives in the inner city.

These difficulties indicate the limitations of formally extending 'choice' as a means of enabling 'socially disadvantaged' families to make the most of educational opportunities thought to have been denied them prior to the inception of the Scheme. The class-related social, educational and cultural factors which we have identified in this chapter and the previous one not only inform 'choice' but, more importantly, they enable some groups to recognize its possibilities and execute it more advantageously than others.[3] We return to this issue in our concluding chapter when we discuss more recent educational initiatives which, like the Assisted Places Scheme, are justified on the grounds that they will enhance parental choice and improve all schools through the enhanced competition they engender.

### Notes

1  See Moncur (1984), Tapper and Salter (1986b), ISIS (1988).
2  As we indicated in the previous chapter, many of our home interviews were with both parents. There were occasions when our questions elicited arguments between parents about their views of independent schools, in some cases revealing differences of which they had apparently not been aware before. We left a few interviews with a feeling that these arguments would continue into the night!
3  As with Stillman's study of parental choice (1986, pp. 11–12), our broad findings on the relationship between parental education and employment and the exercise of choice must not be allowed to obscure the variety of choices actually made by parents within all social classes. Some of the case-studies selected for inclusion in chapters 8 and 9 are designed to emphasize this very point.

Chapter 10

---

## *The Assisted Places Scheme and Beyond*

---

When the Thatcher Government came to power in 1979, there was little to suggest that it would seek significantly to alter the structure of the education system. Its education policy responded to that range of concerns and interests that has traditionally influenced the Conservative Party in Britain, even if the balance between the different strands had shifted somewhat since the days of the Heath Government (Dale, 1983; Edwards *et al.*, 1984). A broad commitment to raising standards by making schools more accountable to parents was accompanied by specific pledges to end compulsory comprehensive reorganization and to restore the 'direct-grant principle'. Although the Assisted Places Scheme was certainly one of the more contentious items in the Government's early policy-making, because it used public funds to sponsor the removal of pupils from the public sector at a time when cuts were being announced and made in public expenditure, it was not in itself a radical departure. Indeed, the central thrust of the Scheme was the restoration of a traditional 'ladder of opportunity' for poor but able pupils which was seen as having been cut down by the disappearance of maintained and direct-grant grammar schools.

The limited scope of the Scheme also reflected the peculiar nature of English private schooling. Where private schools in other industrial countries are commonly defended as expressions of religious, ethnic and cultural diversity, their predominant function here has been to provide appropriate training for high-status occupations within the cultural mainstream (Mason, 1983; 1985; Edwards *et al.*, 1985; Whitty *et al.*, 1989). More particularly, they have been increasingly seen as complementing the public sector by offering a form of academic education no longer available within it. Although the Scheme also enhanced parental choice, as did other elements of the 1980 Education Act, it did so only for those parents whose children were eligible to be sponsored on academic 'merit'. And, as in the case of earlier scholarship ladders, the extension of access to highly academic schools through the Scheme was presented as making a contribution to educational and social mobility through a system that itself remained largely unchanged.

The evidence reported in this book suggests that the advocates of the Assisted

Scheme have had some degree of success in mobilizing a constituency of parents behind the Scheme as originally conceived. These parents share the belief of the architects of the Scheme in the distinctive academic education offered by good grammar schools, and their doubts about the capacity of some comprehensive schools (or even of any comprehensive school) to extend very able children. We have shown how such parents have come, sometimes reluctantly, to regard independent schools as synonomous with selective schools and thus with high levels of academic achievement. Not surprisingly, this view is less prominent in areas that have retained maintained grammar schools. Despite the fact that the presumed association between academically-selective schools and academic achievement has not been demonstrated by research,[1] our own evidence suggests that the supporters of comprehensive education have yet to convince many parents, including some traditional Labour voters, of its potential as a source of educational achievement and social advancement. There clearly remains a market for selective education amongst some parents whose children would, in the past, have attended maintained or direct-grant grammar schools, though other parents with similar circumstances appear happy with the academic (as well as other) opportunities offered in comprehensive schools.

As we noted in chapter 4, advocates of the Scheme have tended to stress its benefits for individuals while critics concentrate on the damage that it causes to the educational system as a whole. While we shall have to await longitudinal evidence before pronouncing confidently on the issue, there is evidence that some of the individual benefits claimed by supporters of the Scheme have indeed been forthcoming, insofar as assisted-place pupils have already been conspicuously successful in public examinations and in gaining entry to higher education.[2] But there is no evidence so far that the main beneficiaries have been from the target groups originally envisaged. Insofar as the 'right' academic advantages have not gone to the 'right' people, the Scheme seems to have been yet another example of an educational reform targeted towards the working class but mainly benefiting children from middle-class backgrounds.[3] In this sense, it might be argued that most of the beneficiaries are amongst those with least need for the Scheme, since they are drawn from groups whose educational performance tends to be relatively high in any context. Although there is no way of knowing how the particular assisted-place holders in our study would have performed within the maintained sector, many of them come from the very groups shown in a recent analysis to gain least advantage from attending independent schools in terms of their chances of entering higher education (OPCS, 1987).

Critics of the Scheme have certainly challenged the assumption that comprehensive schools cannot cater for the full range of ability, and thus themselves provide the academic benefits ascribed too exclusively to independent and grammar schools. They often point out, however, that the chances of comprehensive schools doing so are significantly diminished (especially at the sixth-form stage) by the 'pirating' of scholastic talent which the Assisted Places Scheme is said to have encouraged. At this systemic level, there is wide disagreement about the Scheme's effects. Some of its advocates suggest that even this limited extension of parental choice will eventually have systemic as well as individual benefits by exerting an additional competitive pressure on state schools to improve their own standards and thereby contributing to their success. Our own findings, as reported in chapters 7–9, make us highly sceptical about this claim. We found rather more evidence that the capacity of maintained schools to attract the most able pupils is inhibited by the existence of the independent sector, and that this problem has been made marginally worse by the introduction of the Scheme. How state schools are to be prompted to do a better job by the competitive existence of assisted places remains unclear. About a third of the assisted places available each year are allocated to pupils already in independent schools, and many others would not have considered a state school anyway at the secondary stage. And by increasing the academic selectiveness of some independent schools, and thus enhancing their 'results' and consequently their market appeal beyond what would have been attainable through the operation of 'pure' market forces, the Scheme has provided an 'artificial boost' to their prospects in competing with the public sector (Walford, 1987).

In fact, the editorial anxiety which we noted earlier was expressed in the HMC journal *Conference* before the Scheme got under way has been justified by events; our own findings suggest that the Scheme has indeed attracted pupils from 'good' comprehensives in suburban or mixed catchment areas rather than those from 'poor' inner-city neighbourhood schools. The academically successful comprehensives seem to have lost at least some of those pupils whose future examination performance would have contributed to continuing parental perceptions of those schools as 'good'. This, in turn, is likely to have negative long-term consequences for the capacity even of such 'good' schools to compete with their independent school rivals. In these circumstances, any suggestion that those schools which are currently perceived as 'poor' will be spurred into improvement by the operation of this Scheme seems rather naive, especially as we found little evidence that such schools saw themselves as competing with that part of the private sector involved in the Scheme.

Furthermore, the symbolic consequences of the Assisted Places Scheme probably far outweigh its direct creaming effects on the maintained sector or the 'opportunity costs' of not spending the money devoted to the Scheme on the maintained sector, had it indeed been available for that purpose.[5] Even though the Scheme is currently available to only 1 per cent of pupils entering secondary schools for the first time, its very existence reinforces a belief in the inability of state schools to match the quality of private provision, and of comprehensive schools in particular to maintain high academic standards amid all their other tasks. Furthermore, it inhibits the development of credible alternatives to the type of education which the Scheme has so powerfully sponsored. Thus, those comprehensive schools that do currently manage to compete successfully for academically able pupils may sometimes have to do so at some cost to their provision of an appropriate education for the other market segments that they, unlike the schools participating in the Scheme, are expected to serve. Though the success of some of the schools in our study should caution us against the conclusion that comprehensive schooling is an 'impossible dream' (Shaw, 1984), the existence of the Assisted Places Scheme is likely to make the dream that much more difficult to realize.

In this connection, it is important to note that systemic consequences of this sort also have individual effects. As a leading Conservative critic of this and other more recent government initiatives has put it:

> They do nothing to improve the quality of education in schools that the vast majority of young people are educated in. These schemes all help most those children with parents best able to play the system to escape from poor schools. They do nothing for the quality of education of the majority who remain behind. (Argyropulo, 1986a)

Thus, while acknowledging that the Scheme might bring tangible benefits to the individuals holding assisted places, Argyropulo recognizes (like some of the parents in our study) that its systemic consequences are translated into potential costs for those individuals not themselves participating in it (see also Argyropulo, 1987).

Despite these arguments and counter-arguments, it is hard to see how the Scheme in itself has fundamentally changed the traditional pattern of education in England and Wales. Neither, in terms of the objectives that were originally defined for it or our own findings to date, does there seem to be much scope or justification for extending it substantially in its present form. The limited reallocation of places since 1981, and especially the 260 additional places available from September 1989, have slightly reduced the unequal provision for girls and the very unequal provision for different parts of the country, to which we pointed in chapter 5. But while the fifty-two schools allocated places for the first time in 1989 include some whose academic excellence is much less apparent than was the case with those which survived the original sifting, it remains a Scheme framed in ways which limit it to pupils who can demonstrate a considerable degree of conventional academic merit, and which therefore seems also to require schools with some credible claim to 'academic excellence'. In these circumstances, even the improved targeting of publicity now proposed (Hadfield, 1989) seems unlikely to bring major changes to the patterns of take-up described in chapters 8 and 9 in the absence of broader changes in the culture of educational choice.

It is in this context that we now have to ask whether the Assisted Places Scheme has in any way been reconceptualized since it has been in operation, and whether it is now in any sense part of a 'grand design' to restructure the education system. We also need to consider whether, whatever the Government's own intentions, it might have unintended consequences of that kind.

## The Scheme as a Precursor of Privatization?

The Scheme is now seen by some commentators as part of a wider Government strategy to transform the education system and is even identified as a precursor of its widespread privatization (for example, Pring, 1987). There have certainly been persistent attempts from the Right to persuade the Government that its apparent success, at least as measured by the take-up of places by those on low incomes, justifies more extensive measures to offer parents alternatives to mainstream state education. Indeed, we saw earlier that Boyson placed the Scheme in a broader context from an early stage of its existence and soon urged on his ministerial colleagues the much more radical ventures in extending parental choice which he had been advocating since the mid-1970s. In the fourth set of *Black Papers*, for example, the usual 'Letter to MPs' is also a 'Letter to Parents'. It refers to a lack of 'real parental choice', urges parents to 'hold schools accountable for standards', and asserts the efficacy of vouchers as a mechanism for empowering them to do so. Boyson's own contribution to that collection outlines the 'developing case for the educational voucher', which would reinforce the constraints of national attainment tests at 7, 11 and 14 (which he also advocated) with the sanctions that parents-as-consumers could bring to bear on 'inefficient' schools by taking or threatening to take their business elsewhere (Cox and Boyson, 1975, pp. 3–6 and 27–8). From that perspective, he welcomed the Assisted Places Scheme because able working-class children 'needed' a grammar school environment, but saw it as illogical to limit the evident 'good things' of choice and variety to able children (Albert, 1982). Also from that perspective, it is possible to detect some preparing of the ground for a re-definition of the Scheme as the precursor of a radical new policy of privatization rather than merely a 'natural' extension of the traditional scholarship ladder. We have found no evidence, however, of any significant support for that kind of re-definition from within that part of the private sector involved with the Assisted Places Scheme;[6] such support has instead been rooted in the broad commitment of neo-liberal elements within the New Right to giving a free rein to market forces.

Carlisle's replacement by Keith Joseph as part of the distinctly New Right reshaping of the Cabinet in September 1981 had certainly brought very different convictions about education into the DES. Joseph settled to the task of 'reconstructing the principles of the British educational system with a relish he never displayed in any earlier Cabinet post' (Cosgrove 1985, p. 137). Yet educational policy was only intermittently near the top of the first Thatcher Government's priorities. Ideologically-driven innovations are not readily identified in that period, and there are few references to education at all in most contemporary accounts of 'Thatcherism' in action (Behrens, 1980; Bruce-Gardyne, 1984; Cosgrove, 1985; Holmes, 1985; Lindsay and Harrington, 1979; Riddell, 1985; Stephenson, 1980). Even under Joseph, the Assisted Places Scheme was neither significantly expanded as some hoped it would be (West, 1982), nor followed by any more radical mechanisms for increasing the capacity of private enterprise to compete with public provision and perhaps eventually to replace it altogether.

Yet both developments were anticipated by some of its advocates, especially in the run-up to the election of 1983 and as the ideas of bodies such as the Institute of Economic Affairs began to take hold in other spheres of Government policy. The IEA had included vouchers as the favoured New Right mechanism for extending parental choice quite prominently in its self-appointed task of investigating how 'market principles and pricing can be introduced into the disposition of goods and services organized by the Government'. Particularly notable was E. G. West's celebrated attack on the state's 'virtual monopoly of educational resources', a monopoly which insulated LEAs from the necessity of improving unpopular schools and 'abolished practical choice for poorer families'; vouchers were presented as the only way of treating parents as 'competent choosers' able to make their own decisions about competing suppliers (West, 1965; 1976; 1982; see also Peacock and Wiseman, 1964; Maynard, 1975; Harris and Seldon, 1979, pp. 85–97; M. Seldon, 1982; Dennison, 1984). Yet even with a ruling party which had committed itself as early as 1976 to trying out how vouchers might work, a Government generally committed to giving a freer rein to market forces, and a Secretary of State especially identified with that orientation, the Friends of the Education Voucher Experiment (an organization founded in 1974) could get no further in 1981 than to have its arguments referred to DES officials for comment. When the DES response turned out to be a list of legislative and practical objections, FEVER's refuting of the refutations elicited no further official response (Seldon, 1986, pp. 20–38). Keith Joseph remained consistent in being attracted to the idea, but unpersuaded of its practicality. A fully-developed system of educational vouchers remained an idea whose time had still not come.

There was then some evidence of diffidence, even confusion, in Government circles about how far it was appropriate to move towards a more market-centred and privatized approach to educational provision. During the 1983 general election campaign this was one of the few issues on which the Government was wrong-footed, when the press picked up a suggestion in briefing notes for candidates that the coded reference in the Conservative Party's manifesto to extending parental choice might actually mean the introduction of vouchers.[7] Yet even in his major speech to the 1984 North of England Conference, in which he emphasized the Government's determination to 'reduce the share of national resources taken by the public sector', Joseph made no reference to vouchers, or to 'open' enrolment, or to any of the other measures for radically extending parental choice or privatizing education which some on the Right had been urging so strenuously (Joseph, 1984). In the following year he again declared a voucher system to be practically unworkable, only to hear the Prime Minister the very next day voice her own continuing wish to see something of the sort develop.[8] However uncertain and even contradictory, such speculation about new initiatives had a powerful backwash effect on morale in the state sector and increased expectations that more radical measures were on the way. For the more extreme marketeers in and around the Conservative Party, of course, vouchers were only a large step towards the ultimate goal of a largely privatized education service with the state providing only a 'safety-net' for those unable or unwilling to compete in the market.[9]

How far, then, can the Assisted Places Scheme, despite its rather different origins, be seen in retrospect as making a contribution towards the implementation of the current education policies of the New Right? The links between the influential *Black Papers* and neo-conservative elements of New Right thinking are undeniable but the Scheme's role in neo-liberal thinking, despite Stuart Sexton's recent emergence as Head of the Education Unit of the Institute of Economic Affairs, is much less clear. Certainly as a contribution to the neo-liberals' long-term goal of privatization, the Scheme is decidedly ambiguous.[10] It can hardly be seen as a measure of privatization in a narrow budgetary sense, since (if we are to believe Carlisle's claim that the finance for it did not come out of the mainstream education budget) it actually involved an increase in public expenditure. But a cross-sector voucher scheme would also have that effect, at least in the short to medium term, and at a level of expenditure much higher than that incurred by the Assisted Places Scheme.[11] Nevertheless, like a voucher system, the Scheme can be seen as a privatization measure in that it involves the use of public money to buy services that otherwise might have been provided directly by the state — though only, it is claimed in this case, where such services are no longer available in the maintained sector. The Scheme might also be seen as a privatization measure in the ideological sense of providing an extension of choice to families who might otherwise be denied the right to make private decisions in the market-place.

It is a basic New Right premise that parents have to be empowered as 'competent choosers' if all schools are to face the disciplining consequences of having to operate in a market. Representation on governing bodies, even a freer initial choice of school, are not enough. Parents need not merely a 'voice', but an effective right of 'exit' from schools they regard as unsatisfactory. State schools will only become fully responsive to their clients' wishes when those clients can take their business elsewhere. 'Consumer sovereignty', as the director of the Institute of Economic Affairs defined it as early as the second *Black Papers*, 'rests securely on the power to choose between competing suppliers' (Harris, 1969, p. 71). It was on the basis of that premise that Rhodes Boyson, while emphasizing the distinctive virtues of grammar schools and of pulling more able working-class children on to the 'lifeboat of 11-plus selection', identified as a fundamental obligation on any 'truly radical' government to extend to all families that freedom of choice currently restricted to the very small minority able and willing to pay fees. Only then would 'popularity with parents' rightly become the 'real test of a school's efficiency', those not good enough to fill their places being 'reduced in size, or closed, or taken over' (Boyson, 1975a, pp. 148–50; 1975b, pp. 127–8; 1973, pp. 27–8). Similar arguments represent a continuing and major theme in New Right policy proposals. If 'the only true parent power ... [is] parent purchasing power' (Sexton, 1987, p. 4), then its exercise requires a thorough-going system of customer preference created through vouchers, 'education credits' or 'pupil entitlements' (Marsland, 1986; Flew, 1987; 1988; Sexton, 1987; Hillgate Group, 1986; 1987; Ashworth *et al.*, 1988). Among the short-term outcomes would be a substantial increase in private education and in 'state independent' schools, the eventual goal being the wholesale privatization of the state education system (Sexton, 1987, p. 10). Demaine (1988) argues that the neo-liberal tendency within the New Right wants to go much further 'in its plans to dismantle the system' than what he calls 'the "old Right" Black Papers'. He suggests that 'in New Right plans, most schools would be privatised eventually' and he quotes Marsland of the Social Affairs Unit as arguing that 'in the longer run a substantial expansion of independent education, with schools having to regard their pupils' parents as customers or clients, will be necessary if the balance is to be tipped back in favour of family instead of professional bureaucratic control' (pp. 250–1).

From that perspective, as we argued earlier, the enhancement of parental choice achieved through the Assisted Places Scheme is so constrained as to make it largely irrelevant to the ideological aspirations of the New Right. It is true that the Scheme was contained in an Education Act which also reinforced parental rights to choose between state schools, and which required the schools to publish the kind of market information about their organization, curriculum and examination results on which parents could make a more knowledgeable 'consumer choice'. But, as we described in chapter 3, the schools offering assisted places were drawn from the upper academic reaches of a private sector which contained only 7 per cent of pupils overall. Being both socially and academically selective, they are schools which choose parents at least as much as they are themselves chosen, and the reward of 'success' is to become more selective rather than larger. So while the academic excellence of independent schools is certainly cited as evidence of the beneficial effects of being directly accountable to parents, it is hard to generalize those benefits to the other 93 per cent of children. We have certainly found no evidence that the Scheme has even begun to produce the kind of 'open' or 'free' market in educational services that advocates of a market-oriented approach to education suggest will lead to the improvement of poor schools in the maintained sector — or indeed in the private sector itself. On the other hand, we have suggested that the Scheme may be having a progressively debilitating effect on the capacity of good schools in the state sector to compete, thus potentially making the private sector even more attractive to the parents of academically able children in the long term. If this turned out to be the case, then it would indeed be possible to see the Scheme as a privatization measure in the strong sense of encouraging a growth in private education at the expense of the public sector.

Examined as a single initiative, though, it would be difficult to argue that the Assisted Places Scheme has effectively shaken off its origins and taken on a new guise as a flagship of New Right education policy. Thus while Sexton suggests retaining the

Scheme's 'scholarship character' for the time being while doubling the number of places — a suggestion consistent with his advocacy of 12,000–15,000 places a year during the negotiations which preceded the Scheme's introduction (see chapters 2 and 3) — his real recommendation is that it should be replaced by a universal system of education credits (Sexton, 1987, p. 14). A clearer case can be made, however, for viewing the Scheme alongside other Government attempts to go far beyond the provisions of the 1980 Education, and even the 1986 (no. 2) Act, in creating a quasi-market in educational provision within the public sector and blurring its boundaries with the private sector. Such policies have sometimes been described as 'creeping privatization' (Inman, 1987; see also Pring, 1986; 1987) in that they gradually introduce elements of the New Right approach to the provision of services. Such policies involve both greater involvement of private interests in the provision and/or financing of education and attempts to make the public sector behave more like the private sector. It is to such policies, and their relationship to the Assisted Places Scheme, that we now turn.

### City Technology Colleges: The Start of a New Agenda?

In announcing the city technology colleges, the Government stated that it was seeking to work with 'interested individuals and organisations to establish with financial assistance from the Department of Education and Science a network of City Technology Colleges (CTCs) in urban areas'. It went on to say:

> Their purpose will be to provide broadly-based secondary education with a strong technological element thereby offering a wider choice of secondary school to parents in certain cities and a surer preparation for adult and working life to their children. It is in our cities that the education system is at present under most pressure. (DES 1986)

These city technology colleges might be seen as a logical response to the failure of the Assisted Places Scheme to do something positive about the education of those groups of inner-city pupils whose absence from the Scheme has been one of the most striking features of our own findings. As the announcement of the initiative at the Conservative Party conference in 1986 by the new Secretary of State, Kenneth Baker, came within weeks of the Cabinet Office requesting a copy of our interim report on the Assisted Places Scheme, we might have been tempted in more vainglorious moments to see the new initiative as a response to our evidence about the failures of the earlier one! In fact Government belief in the success of assisted places was immovable, as we indicated in chapter 8. And the new initiative, though heralded as the brainchild of an ambitious Secretary of State determined to make his mark early, had its origins in proposals that had already been floated within the Department of Science under his predecessor Sir Keith Joseph.[12]

There are though some strong parallels between the Assisted Places Scheme and the city technology college initiative which make it feasible to regard them in some respects as indicating a consistent policy thrust. For example, the city technology colleges were originally intended to be located in or adjacent to inner-city areas and to provide a further alternative to 'failed' neighbourhood comprehensive schools (especially in areas dominated by left-wing Labour authorities). Both the Assisted Places Scheme and the city technology colleges claim to 'complement' LEA provision, but also serve to reduce the influence of LEAs over education in their own areas. Opponents of the Scheme have objected to the 'creaming off' of academically able pupils from the maintained sector. They have also seen the Scheme as introducing academic selection by the back door. The city technology college proposals have raised similar fears that academic selection is again 'on the agenda', with particular concern being expressed at the early age at which specific 'aptitudes' will have to be identified, and at the serious consequences for intakes to comprehensive schools already suffering from falling rolls.[13] Furthermore, while the city technology colleges are also presented as extending parental choice, improving standards in the maintained sector by example, and repairing some of the damage caused by the inadequacy attributed to many comprehensives, they resemble Assisted Places in falling well short of the full-blown policy of privatization advocated by some of the Government's own policy advisers.

If these are some of the similarities, there are also important differences. The way in which this new initiative emerged contrasts sharply with the origins of the Assisted Places Scheme as we described them in chapters 2 and 3. That Scheme was initiated within the private sector in the early 1970s, subsequently attracted political support, and was preceded and prepared for by extensive negotiations to establish whether there were sufficient independent schools of appropriate academic quality which were willing to participate in it. By contrast, the city technology colleges were a political initiative apparently preceded by little advance planning. Despite the earlier floating of ideas about both privately-sponsored schools and directly-funded Crown schools in inner-city areas, the specific announcement came as a surprise. The lack of careful preparation produced embarrassing rebuffs from some of those from whom the Government had expected support, considerable high-level pressure on potential sponsors so that the initiative could take off, and some significant redefinition of the concept, particularly concerning how the colleges were to be funded.[14]

The Assisted Places Scheme was introduced to give able children from low-income families opportunities to attend 'academically-excellent schools' as defined by entirely traditional academic standards. Indeed, while its introduction coincided with the Technical and Vocational Education Initiative, it included no encouragement whatsoever for the kind of technologically-relevant curriculum which TVEI was intended to foster in those LEAs which bid successfully for the substantial extra funding involved. As we noted in chapter 3, independent schools were selected for 'assisted-place status' on the basis of their success in traditional 'grammar school' subjects. While also seeking to foster high standards in education, the city technology colleges are to offer a broad curriculum, but with a 'strong technical and practical element which is essential preparation for the changing demands of adult and working life in an advanced industrial society' (DES, 1986). In this initiative, the support of the 'business community' is openly enlisted for a form of secondary schooling which is seen as being directly relevant to its needs, whereas this was not a central issue in the thinking behind the Assisted Places Scheme. Although the point is complicated by the approving references to TVEI in the launch document, the city technology colleges are presented primarily as offering a different kind of education to that available in most maintained schools rather than (as with the Assisted Places Scheme) a superior version of the same. And rather than leaving the curriculum to market forces, as remains the case with independent schools, a condition of funding for city technology colleges is that they have to adhere broadly to a particular curriculum model.[15]

The mechanisms for government funding of the two schemes are also quite different. In the Assisted Places Scheme, money is channelled to parents through means-tested remission of fees and some supplementary grants, with no (direct) financial benefits to the 'fully independent' schools their children attend and so no consequences for those schools' independent status. In contrast, the city technology colleges were originally to be newly created with initial capital costs being met by their private promoters and central government meeting their recurrent expenditure, although a dearth of enthusiastic sponsors has forced the Government to agree to meet up to 80 per cent of capital costs as well.[16] The city technology colleges will be registered as independent schools, but will charge no fees and receive their income direct from the government. They thus represent a 'semi-independent' form of secondary schooling, with the colleges substantially subsidized as institutions. In the discussions which led to the establishment of the Assisted Places Scheme, as we reported in chapter 3, such an intermediate status was explicitly rejected — as was the idea of subsidizing schools rather than individuals.

## The Scheme in the Context of the 1988 Education Reform Act

By the time of the 1987 general election, the Thatcher Government appeared to have abandoned the idea of a voucher system (or its equivalent) and of widespread privatization as a strategy for reforming the education system. In addition to confirming its intention to create City Technology Colleges, it committed itself to legislate for a radical extension of market forces within the system through open enrolment to LEA maintained schools and, perhaps most significantly, through allowing schools to opt out of LEA control. These proposals have subsequently been enshrined in law through the Education Reform Act of 1988. On a majority vote of parents, schools will be able to opt out of their LEAs but remain part of the state system and receive their funds direct from central government. The Government claims that these grant maintained schools will 'add a new and powerful dimension to the ability of parents to exercise choice within the publicly provided sector of education', and that 'parents and local communities [will] have new opportunities to secure the development of their schools in ways appropriate to the needs of their children and in accordance with their wishes, within the legal framework of the national curriculum'.[17] In this latter respect, however, they will remain more constrained than both independent schools, which (even when receiving public funds through the Assisted Places Scheme) are not required to conform to the national curriculum, and city technology colleges, which are required to adhere only to its 'broad substance'.[18]

Although grant maintained schools will not normally be permitted to change their character or admissions policies within five years of opting out, their governors may then apply to change by publishing statutory proposals for public comment. This has been seen by critics as another 'back-door' means of re-introducing selection, albeit after a decent delay. Certainly Kenneth Baker indicated that he would be willing to receive such proposals after five years.[19] It is also the case that LEA maintained grammar schools threatened with comprehensivization can immediately apply for grant maintained status and receive a decision before any reorganization proposals are acted upon. They can then retain their existing character, and a number of the early school applying for grant maintained status have come into this category.[20] In the longer term, grant maintained status could lead to an increasing number of academically selective schools within the maintained sector.

There was some initial confusion between senior ministers at the time of the 1987 election about whether such a plan signalled a preference for new forms of state education or a policy of 'creeping' privatization, with the Prime Minister and her Secretary of State publicly contradicting each other about the nature and scope of these proposed schools and whether they would eventually charge fees.[21] Nevertheless, rather than directly encouraging the growth of the fee-paying sector, the Government's preferred strategy for encouraging market forces within education now seems quite clearly to be the creation of a range of what Kenneth Baker has described as 'half-way houses' between the LEA maintained and private sectors.[22] Unlike city technology colleges, grant maintained schools will remain in the state (though not the LEA) sector. Significantly, and despite their different origins, the Government has now chosen to group the administration of both these initiatives and the Assisted Places Scheme in a newly-created section of the Department of Education and Science, School Branch IV.[23] All these initiatives are thus seen by the Government as increasing parental choice and promoting the sort of competition between schools that will improve overall standards. As Kenneth Baker put it, in defending the concept of grant maintained schools to the North of England Conference in January 1988:

> Our policies seek to encourage all parents to take their responsibilities seriously and create opportunities for the conscientious majority to set an example to the rest . . . If the product is not all it should be, parents should not be put in the position of having to like it or lump it. Grant Maintained Schools will be a threat to the complacent and to the second best . . . I want to give people a chance to press for excellence; I want to give them the means to demand excellence; and I want to create a spur which will oblige all LEAs to deliver excellence.[24]

Such developments, together with other policies enshrined in the Act that permit open enrolment to LEA schools and local control of their budgets, are likely to alter radically the shape and function of the state education system in the coming years because the central tendency of the changes is to allow the market to discipline poor schools by putting them out of business. Unlike the planned admissions limit of the 1980 Act, which recognized a need to temper market forces with a modicum of planning, these proposals effectively give parental choice its head. Critics suggest, however, that administrative chaos is likely in the short term and that the longer-term outlook is one in which many of the positive benefits of the old partnership between government, local government and the teaching profession are likely to be lost along with its shortcomings, especially if Mrs Thatcher is right about the number of schools that will opt out of their LEAs.[25] Many commentators argue that in this situation a resegmentation of the system and a widespread return to academic selection will become real possibilities. Though they differ as to whether this is a result of conscious policy or merely the outcome of a series of apparently unrelated decisions, such critics of current policies predict the emergence of a clear hierarchy of schools (Campbell *et al.*, 1987; Cordingley and Wilby, 1987). This might run from independent schools at the pinnacle through city technology colleges, grant maintained schools and voluntary-aided schools to LEA maintained schools at the base. The likelihood of this happening will be greatly increased if grant maintained schools eventually exercise their right to apply to the Secretary of State to change their status and then become overtly selective.

The financial calculations involved in devolving budgets to individual schools, whether of grant maintained or LEA maintained status, have also been seen by some observers as a back-door method of determining the value of vouchers or educational credits to be introduced by a future New Right administration. Demaine (1988, p. 251–2) sees differential top-up payments eventually being charged by different schools, and this could potentially reinforce the sort of hierarchy described above. In that situation, LEA maintained or 'council' schools might again become the paupers of the system and the preserve of those unable or unwilling to compete in the market. As such, they might well become straightforward institutions of social control for the inner cities. Yet the legitimacy of the system and the notion of an open society could still be maintained by devices such as the Assisted Places Scheme, which ostensibly offer opportunities to worthy disadvantaged children to 'escape' from their backgrounds, while actually attracting middle-class pupils and helping to increase the market appeal of the private sector. Our own study of the Assisted Places Scheme reported in this book certainly indicates that such a development is possible.

Seen in this broader context, then, a Scheme that has so far had only marginal effects on the education system as a whole could take on a new significance. Yet while it remains in itself an ambiguous example of privatization within education (Fitz *et al.*, 1989), even in combination with the initiatives enshrined in the 1988 Education Reform Act, it hardly fulfills the criteria of the more extreme privatizers of the New Right. Indeed, it is possible that these latest initiatives, which at one level constitute a further development of the idea of a market, will be even more ambiguous in their effects. Whereas the Assisted Places Scheme has probably enhanced the capacity of the private sector to compete with the state system, the spectre of extensive funding by central government of free education outside LEA control is viewed with trepidation by some of the independent schools. It is seen as a distortion of the educational market that could eventually threaten their own position within it (Ainley, 1988). At the 1988 Headmasters' Conference, the Director of ISIS warned members that they were not safe under a Conservative Government either, and so should improve their marketing.[26] And, as if to reinforce his warning, the Education Minister, Angela Rumbold, was reported in the same week as looking forward to the demise of private education because the Education Act would now enable the state sector to 'provide parents with standards and choice that are currently provided in the independent sector'.[27] As this situation developed, the Assisted Places Scheme would presumably become progressively harder to justify politically as it became less 'necessary' as a rescue operation.

It seems just as likely though that parts of the Reform Act will further threaten the capacity of local authority schools to compete for academically able pupils, especially those parts which will effectively increase the distance (in status, resources and 'quality' of intake) between an 'independent' sector enlarged by city technology colleges and grant maintained or (state independent) schools, and the increasingly under-resourced schools (especially in the inner cities) which are supposed to be either improved or eradicated by the 'bracing' operation of market forces. Mrs Thatcher's suggestion during the election that grant maintained schools would be permitted to charge fees might eventually turn out to have been a statement of aspiration rather than an uncharacteristic error. And, whatever the intention, prolonged uncertainty about the future shape of the education system could still lead to just that process of sponsored withdrawal from the state sector which we noted in chapter 4 as having been predicted by the then Chief Officer of the ILEA as the Assisted Places Scheme was getting under way. He then predicted that in the longer term the Scheme could create a fee-paying grammar school system and a secondary modern maintained sector.[28] In this situation, there would clearly be a need for a ladder of opportunity along the lines of the Assisted Places Scheme in order to maintain the legitimacy of the system by holding out at least a possibility of sponsorship for the 'poor but able'.

However, it must be recognized that though such speculation gains some credence from our own observations of the limited effects of the Assisted Places Scheme, we can be far from certain how a system allowing much greater parental choice would actually operate. As soon as we try to interpret our data for this purpose, we are forced like Coleman *et al.* (1982) to make informed guesses about the effects of possible future policies on the basis of evidence collected from a system in which those policies have hardly taken root. It remains to be seen whether the combined effects of various measures of 'creeping privatization' will eventually produce a system embodying the ideology of the New Right, or whether it will merely produce confusion. Insofar as the proliferation of such initiatives will make it far more difficult to plan a coherent system of state education at local or national level, they may well produce the sort of self-fulfilling prophecy that will justify the Right's critique of the state system. By itself, the Assisted Places Scheme has been an irritant rather than a threat to that system. In the new context, its role is potentially more significant.

## Notes

1  For an account of the conflicting evidence (and interpretation of evidence) about the relative effectiveness of selective and non-selective secondary schools see the references in Chapter 6, note 2.

2  As might be expected from the competitive nature of the Scheme, assisted-place pupils have done relatively well in examinations. In 1985, for example, 55 per cent of sixth-form leavers with assisted places went on to university and 74 per cent to higher education, compared with equivalent figures for all sixth-form leavers of 44 per cent and 61 per cent in HMC schools and 26 per cent and 44 per cent in GSA/GBA schools (see Chapter 6).

3  For other evidence of this tendency, see Halsey *et al.* (1980). Our own evidence is reported in detail in chapter 8 and (as we noted there) compares closely with that of Douse (1985).

4  *Conference*, February 1981.

5  Carlisle always claimed that the money for the Scheme was additional to that which would have available for support of the maintained system. See, for example, the *Times Educational Supplement*, 15 February 1980. Critics, of course, maintained that he could have argued for further money for state schools as an alternative and that these schools incurred 'opportunity costs' as a result of the existence of the Scheme.

6  However, as we noted in chapter 3, there has been persistent if unsuccessful pressure from within the private sector to extend the criteria of eligibility to include boarding 'need', and some pressure to dilute the academic orientation of the Scheme.

7  Speakers' Notes, Conservative Central Office, 1983.

8  Responding to a listener's question on BBC Radio 4 programme *Tuesday Call*, 16 July 1985, Sir Keith Joseph commented that a radical transformation of the education system through a voucher scheme was 'off the agenda'. On the following day, Mrs Thatcher remarked on a TV Channel 4 programme (*Diverse Reports*) that she might 'have another go at it'.

9  In a statement typical of a thoroughgoing commitment to market forces, Arthur Seldon argued that state provision should be reduced to — 'a reasonable minimum above which individuals are left free to rise, rather than an imposed maximum which stifles initiative'. (Seldon, 1981, p.18)

10  For a fuller discussion of the Assisted Places Scheme as an example of privatization, see Fitz *et al.* (1989). For general discussions of the strong consumerist strand in New Right thinking, see Quicke, 1988; Demaine, 1988; McLean, 1988.

11  This, of course, was the Treasury's main objection to vouchers being given to independent school parents, despite their attractions in the longer term if the 'topping up' of vouchers with parental contributions were eventually to become acceptable in both sectors.

12  See the *Times Educational Supplement*, 28 February, 7 March, and 4 April 1986; also the *Financial Times*, 3 March 1986.

13  See, for example, a leaflet produced by the Socialist Educational Association in 1987 entitled *Against City Technology Schools (sic) and For Comprehensive Education.*

14  See the *Times Educational Supplement*, 17 June 1988.

15  The Education Reform Act states that city technology colleges must have a 'broad curriculum with an emphasis on science and technology'. That emphasis is seen as being compatible with conformity to the 'substance' of the National Curriculum.

16  *Education*, 8 July 1988.

17  Consultation paper on Grant Maintained Schools, 1987.

18  See note 15 above.

19  *Financial Times*, 30 November 1987.

20  Amongst the first grammar schools seeking to maintain their selective status by opting out were Skegness (Lincs), Colyton (Devon), Heckmondwicke (Kirklees), Ribston Hall Girls' (Gloucs), and King's School Grantham (Lincs). Other grammar schools considering opting out to avoid amalgamation or closure on their present sites included Sale Boys' (Trafford), Wilmington Girls' (Kent) and Wilsons' (Sutton).

21  See the *Times Educational Supplement*, 18 September 1987.

22  *Times Educational Supplement*, 13 March 1987.

23  Schools Branch IV is responsible for grant maintained schools and the Assisted Places Scheme; it also includes the Registrar for Independent Schools and the City Technology Colleges Unit.

24  *Times Educational Supplement*, 8 January 1988.

25  On occasions she has been quoted as predicting that 'most schools will opt out'. See the *Times Educational Supplement*, 18 September 1987.

26  *Guardian*, 27 September 1988.

27  *Times Educational Supplement*, 30 September 1988.

28  Peter Newsam in *Starting Out*, London Weekend Television, 11 September 1981.

# Gazeteer of Schools mentioned in the text (by Pseudonym)

**Archbishop Ambrose** A maintained grammar school for boys. It has about 850 pupils aged 11–18. Many of its sixth-formers proceed into higher education, including a considerable number going up to Oxbridge. Its head is one of the few state school members of HMC.

**Bankside College** A traditional boys' public school, it has over 600 pupils, mainly boarders. Girls were formerly admitted into the sixth form but recently it opened its doors to girls at 13. Over 80 per cent of its pupils move into the sixth form, with over 50 per cent entering university.

**Brampton School** An independent day school for girls, it has 800 pupils aged 11–18. It shares a site with a boys' school, both of which belong to the same foundation and both are former direct-grant schools. There is a small junior division, admitting girls aged 5–11. Approximately half the A-level leavers proceed to university, with five to ten each year going to Oxbridge.

**Cathedral College** A leading public school which takes day boys and boarders. There are 700 pupils in the school. A small number of girls are admitted into the sixth form. It has a small preparatory school which prepares boys for the Common Entrance examination. Pupils enter the college at 13. The school offers a small number of assisted places and a large number of its own scholarships.

**Cherry Tree** A coeducational comprehensive of over 1500 pupils. Based on two former secondary modern schools, it is well supported by local parents. Some 60 per cent of fifth-year pupils enter its sixth form. 75 per cent of A-level leavers go on to higher or further education.

**Christchurch School** A religious foundation, this private day school for boys has over 600 pupils aged 13–18. In addition to assisted places it offers a small number of foundation bursaries for meritorious entrants. Over 70 per cent of its sixth formers enter university.

**Clifton Grammar School** Formerly serving as a maintained grammar school with voluntary status, this school is now a fully independent day school for over 800 boys. Entrance is at 11, and by Common Entrance exam at 13. It has a strong sixth form, with 60 per cent going on to university.

**Cranmer School** A private school for boys with entry at 13 through the Common Entrance examination. It is a member of HMC, and although most of the 700-plus pupils are day boys more than fifty boarding places are available. As well as offering assisted places, it awards more than thirty of its own scholarships each year. Ninety per cent of the A-level leavers go into higher education.

**Dame Margaret's High School** An independent school for girls with about 550 pupils on roll, aged 11–18. It also has a small preparatory school, taking girls aged 7–11. It awards its own bursaries in the senior school in addition to the assisted places available.

**Fanshawe School** A private school for over 500 girls, pupils enter aged 7 onwards as boarders or day girls. Foundation scholarships are available for new entrants and sixth formers. Over 80 per cent stay on for sixth-form study and about half its leavers go to university.

**Forsyth School** A large private day school for boys, it has over 1000 pupils who enter the school at 11 or 13 years. As an ancient foundation, it is able to offer a considerable number of bursaries to its 11-year-olds in addition to assisted places. Ninety per cent of its pupils stay on to the sixth form.

**Frampton** A mixed comprehensive with 800 pupils aged 11–18, it was formerly a secondary modern school. That history, and the predominantly working-class catchment area it serves, are reflected in its relatively small sixth form.

**Highgrove County School for Girls** This maintained grammar school has nearly 1000 pupils. They are selected by a borough-wide entrance examination conducted by the LEA, supplemented by primary school reports. It has a strong sixth form with a high proportion of its leavers moving into further and higher education.

**King Henry's Grammar School** This large independent school of ancient foundation has about 1000 boys attending it. Its sixth form numbers about 300 and over 80 per cent of its entrants go on to higher education. It is a former direct-grant school and has a large allocation of assisted places.

**Knotley High School** An inner city comprehensive of the kind often referred to unfavourably by the Scheme's supporters. It is a mixed school, with over 1000 pupils of predominantly working-class backgrounds.

**Milltown Grammar** A former direct-grant school, it is now a fully independent day school attended by 650 boys. It shares a site with the girls' division and both are administered by the same foundation. Ninety per cent of its pupils stay on to the sixth form, and over 60 per cent of its A-level leavers go on to university.

**Milltown High** The girls' equivalent of Milltown Grammar, it has 500 pupils aged 11–18 on roll. There is a junior division attached to the school for girls aged 9–11. A strong sixth form shares some facilities with the boys' school. Many of the A-level leavers move into further or higher education.

**Moorside Comprehensive** A mixed comprehensive with 1500 pupils, this school is organized on traditional lines and it has a good reputation locally. It has developed a large sixth form which has helped convince parents that it will cater for academically able pupils.

**Nortown Grammar School** Formerly a direct-grant school, this large day school for boys has a formidable academic reputation. Over three-quarters of its leavers go on to university including a large number to Oxbridge. From its own resources it was able to offer scholarships to many of its meritorious pupils.

**Nortown High School** A girls' independent school, with 500 pupils aged 11–18. A former direct-grant school, it has retained that earlier tradition by its performance in public examinations and by the large proportion of its A-level leavers entering higher education.

**Oaklands High School** An independent day school for girls which has 700 pupils aged 11–18 and its own preparatory school, its catchment area covers several LEAs. It was formerly a direct-grant school.

**Parkside** This girls' comprehensive school has 950 pupils aged 11–16, and it was formerly a maintained grammar school. It has strong support from those parents who believe that a single-sex education has significant academic benefits for girls but who wish their daughters to be educated in a state school.

**Queen's High School** Administered by an educational trust, it was a direct-grant school before 1976 and has 550 pupils aged 11–18. There is a small junior school attached for girls aged 4–11. It has a strong sixth form, achieving A-level pass rates of over 90 per cent.

**Redland Comprehensive School** A mixed school of nearly 1600 pupils aged 11–18. It has a successful sixth form, which has survived attempts by the LEA to remove it. Its A-level leavers include many university entrants, some going up to Oxbridge.

**Riverside College** This tertiary college offers a wide range of courses to students in post-compulsory education, including A-levels. It attracts students from independent schools and from neighbouring LEAs.

**Rowton Comprehensive School** Formed by the amalgamation of two secondary modern schools, this mixed comprehensive has 1600 pupils aged 11–18. There are nearly 150 pupils in the sixth form though. Its socially mixed catchment area includes council estates and more affluent middle-class suburbs.

**St Hilda's Girls'** An independent day school for approximately 600 pupils, its catchment area covers the Riverside area and beyond. Most of its pupils stay on for A-levels and it has an impressive pass rate in those examinations. About 90 per cent of its leavers go on to higher education. Founders' scholarships are available for academically meritorious pupils.

**St Wilfred's High School** This girls' independent day school has over 400 pupils. It is a religious foundation and offers reduced fees to members of the clergy. About three-quarters of the pupils stay on for A-levels.

**Sandgate School** A large 13–18 mixed comprehensive with more than 1000 pupils with a strong sixth form. More than half of its intake achieve good passes at O-level, while its A-level students achieve a 70 per cent pass rate.

**Shirebrook School** This mixed comprehensive school of 1000 pupils aged 13–18 draws pupils from a socially mixed, mainly rural catchment area. However it has attracted numbers of educationally ambitious parents, satisfied that its academic performance at O- and A-levels and its success in providing university entrants meets their needs.

**Sir James's School For Boys** A religious foundation, the school has about 450 boys aged 11–18, with a significant number of assisted places and a strong sixth form. Over 90 per cent of leavers enter higher education.

**Smythe School** Non-denominational independent school for girls. Entry to the main school is at 11, but there is a junior school which admits girls at 7. It is a large school with over 700 pupils and more than fifty staff. Over 80 per cent of A-level leavers go into higher education.

**Stoneyford High School** A former voluntary grammar school, now a fully independent day school for over 650 girls aged 11–18, though the junior division admits girls at 9. Over 90 per cent of the pupils stay on to the sixth form, of whom more than 80 per cent go on to degree courses.

**Thomas Darby High School** A multi-ethnic inner-city comprehensive school with more than 850 pupils aged 11–16, from the kinds of social backgrounds that the Assisted Places Scheme's architects thought would benefit from the opportunity to attend an 'academic' independent school.

**Vicarage Road** A mixed comprehensive school with approximately 950 pupils aged 11–16. It is a former secondary modern school and has had to work hard to throw off that image locally. However, with buildings recently refurbished and a new head teacher, it has been recruiting well in the borough and in the adjacent LEA.

**Weston** A small independent boys' school in a rural location, it is predominantly a boarding school but now admits some day pupils. Girls have recently been admitted to its sixth form. Entry is at 13 and there are about 300 pupils in the main school.

**York Road** This secondary modern school for boys has about 1000 pupils aged 11–18. Modelled on public school lines by its previous head, it has a strong sixth form, a reputation for strict discipline and prefects in gowns.

# Bibliography

AINLEY, P. (1988) 'Private fears', *Teacher*, 6 June 1988, pp. 12–13.

ALBERT, T. (1982) 'The cheapest way to help the brightest and best', *Guardian*, 23 November.

ANDERSON, D. (Ed.) (1980) *The Ignorance of Social Intervention*, London, Croom Helm.

ARGYROPULO, D. (1986a) 'Inner city quality', *Times Educational Supplement*, 1 August 1986, p. 4.

ARGYROPULO, D. (1986b) 'Vouchers can damage your health', *Times Educational Supplement*, 7 March 1986, p. 2.

ARGYROPULO, D. (Ed.) (1987) *Education: One Last Chance*, London, Conservative Education Association.

ASHWORTH, J., PAPP, I. and THOMAS, B. (1988) *Increased Parental Choice*, Warlingham, Institute of Economic Affairs Education Unit.

AYER, J. (1988) 'High fliers . . . and low incomes', *Observer*, 14 February, p. 28.

BAMFORD, T. (1974) *Public School Data*, Aids to Research No. 2, Hull, Hull University Institute of Education.

BANKS, O. (1965) *Parity and Prestige in English Secondary Education*, London, Routledge and Kegan Paul.

BANTOCK, G. H. (1980) *Dilemmas of the Curriculum*, Oxford, Martin Robertson.

BARKER, R. (1972) *Education and Politics 1900–1951: A Study of the Labour Party*, Oxford, Clarendon Press.

BEHRENS, R. (1980) *The Conservative Party from Heath to Thatcher: Policies and Politics 1974–1979*, Farnborough, Saxon House.

BENN, C. (1974) *We Must Choose Which We Want: Co-existence and the Problems of Incomplete Reorganisation*, London, National Union of Teachers/Campaign for Comprehensive Education.

BENN, C. (1980) 'A new 11-plus for the old divided system', *Forum*, 22, pp. 36–42.

BENN, C. and SIMON, B. (1972) *Half Way There: Report on the British Comprehensive School Reform*, 2nd ed., Harmondsworth, Penguin Books.

BERLINER, W. (1987) 'Helped out of state schooling', *Independent*, 10 September.

BLAKE, R. (1976) 'A changed climate', in BLAKE, R. and PATTEN, J. (Eds) *The Conservative Opportunity*, London, Macmillan.

BLAKE, R. (1985) *The Conservative Party from Peel to Thatcher*, 2nd ed., London, Methuen.

BLAKE, R. and PATTEN, J. (Eds) (1976) *The Conservative Opportunity*, London, Macmillan.

BOGDANOR, V. (1976) 'Education', in BLAKE, R. and PATTEN, J. (Eds) *The Conservative Opportunity*, op. cit.

BOSANQUET, N. (1983) *After the New Right*, London, Heinemann.

BOYSON, R. (1974) *Oversubscribed: The Story of Highbury Grove School*, London, Ward Lock.

BOYSON, R. (1975) *The Crisis in Education*, London, Woburn Press.

BRUCE-GARDYNE, J. (1984) *Mrs Thatcher's First Administration: The Prophets Confounded*, London, Macmillan.

BURGESS, R. (1984) *In the Field*, London, Allen and Unwin.

BUTLER, R. A. (1971) *The Art of the Possible*, London, Hamish Hamilton.

CAMPBELL, J., LITTLE, V. and TOMLINSON, J. (1987) 'Multiplying the divisions? Intimations of educational policy post-1987', *Journal of Education Policy*, 2, 4, pp. 369–378.

CENTRE FOR CONTEMPORARY CULTURAL STUDIES (1981) *Unpopular Education: Schooling and social democracy in England since 1944*, London, Hutchinson.

CLARKE, D. (1978) *The Conservative Party*, London, Conservative Central Office.

COBBAN, J. (1969) 'The direct-grant school', in COX, B. and DYSON, A. (Eds) *Fight for Education: A Black Paper*, London, Critical Quarterly Society.

COBBAN, J. (1980) 'The great public school debate: The case for Carlisle', *Sunday Times*, 8 June.

COLEMAN, J., HOFFER, T. and KILGORE, S. (1982) *High School Achievement: Public, Catholic and Other Private Schools Compared*, New York, Basic Books.

CONNELL, R., ASHENDEN, D., KESSLER, S. and DOWSETT, G. (1983) *Making the Difference: Schools, Families and Social Division*, London, Allen and Unwin.

CORDINGLEY, P. and WILBY, P. *Opting Out of Mr. Baker's Proposals*, London, Education Reform Group.

COSGRAVE, P. (1978) *Margaret Thatcher: A Tory and Her Party*, London, Hutchinson.

COSGRAVE, P. (1985) *Thatcher: The First Term*, London, Bodley Head.

COTTRELL, E. (1982) 'The two nations in education', in COX, C. and MARKS, J. (Eds) *The Right to Learn*, London, Centre for Policy Studies.

COWLING, M. (Ed.) (1978) *Conservative Essays*, London, Cassell.

COX, C. B. (1982) 'Progressive collapse: The counter revolution in English education' *Quadrant*, 26, 3, pp. 20–8.

COX, C. B. and BOYSON, R. (Eds) (1975) *The Fight for Education: Black Paper 1975*, London, Dent.

COX, C. B. and BOYSON, R. (Eds) (1977) *Black Paper 1977*, London, Temple.

COX, C. B. and DYSON, A. (Eds) (1969a) *Fight for Education: A Black Paper*, London, Critical Quarterly Society.

COX, C. B. and DYSON, A. (Eds) (1969b) *Black Paper Two: The Crisis in Education*, London, Critical Quarterly Society.

COX, C. B. and DYSON, A. (Eds) (1970) *Goodbye Mr Short*, London, Critical Quarterly Society.

COX, C. B. and DYSON, A. (Eds) (1971) *The Black Papers on Education*, London, Davis-Poynter.

COX, C. and MARKS, J. (Eds) (1982) *The Right to Learn*, London, Centre for Policy Studies.

COX, C. and MARKS, J. (1988) *The Insolence of Office*, London, Claridge Press.

CRAIG, F. (1982) *Conservative and Labour Party Conference Decisions 1945–1981*, London, Parliamentary Research Services.

CROSLAND, C. A. R. (1956) *The Future of Socialism*, London, Cape.

CROSLAND, C. A. R. (1962) *The Conservative Enemy*, London, Cape.

CROSLAND, C. A. R. (1968) 'Comprehensive education', in CROSLAND, C. *Socialism Now and Other Essays*, London, Cape.

CROSLAND, S. (1983) *Tony Crosland*, London, Coronet Books.

DALE, R. (1983) 'Thatcherism and education', in AHIER, J. and FLUDE, M. (Eds) *Contemporary Education Policy*, London, Croom Helm.

DANCY, J. (1963) *The Public Schools and the Future*, London, Faber.

DEAN, D. (1986) 'Planning for a post-war generation: Ellen Wilkinson and George Tomlinson at the Ministry of Education 1945–1951', *History of Education*, 15, 2, pp. 95–117.

DELPHY, C. (1981) 'Women in stratification studies' in ROBERTS, H. (Ed.) *Doing Feminist Research*, London, Routledge and Kegan Paul.

DEMAINE, J. (1988) 'Teachers' work, curriculum and the New Right', *British Journal of Sociology of Education*, 9, 3, pp. 247–264.

DENNISON, S. (1984) *Choice in Education: An Analysis of the Political Economy of State and Private Education*, London, Institute of Economic Affairs.

DEPARTMENT OF EDUCATION AND SCIENCE (1986) *City Technology Colleges: A New Choice of School*, London, DES and Central Office of Information.

DOUSE, M. (1985) 'The background of assisted place scheme students', *Educational Studies* 11, 3, pp. 211–217.

DUKE, V. and EDGELL, S. (1987) 'The operationalization of social class in British sociology: Theoretical and empirical considerations, *British Journal of Sociology*, 38, pp. 446–461.

EDWARDS, A. (1983) 'An elite transformed? continuity and change in 16–19 education policy' in AHEIR, J. and FLUDE, M. (Eds) *Contemporary Education Policy*, London, Croom Helm.

EDWARDS, A., FITZ, J. and WHITTY, G. (1985) 'Private schools and public funding — a comparison of policies and arguments in England and Australia', *Comparative Education*, 21, 1, pp. 29–45.

EDWARDS, A., FULBROOK, M. and WHITTY, G. (1984) 'The state and the independent sector: Policies, ideologies and theories', in BARTON, L. and WALKER, S. (Eds) *Social Crisis and Educational Research*, London, Croom Helm.

FITZ, J., EDWARDS, A. and WHITTY, G. (1986) 'Beneficiaries, benefits and costs: An investigation of the Assisted Places Scheme', *Research Papers in Education*, 1, pp. 169–193.

FITZ, J., EDWARDS, A. and WHITTY, G. (1989) 'The Assisted Places Scheme: An ambiguous case of privatization', *British Journal of Educational Studies*, 37.

FLEMING COMMITTEE (1944) *The Public Schools and the General Educational System* (Report of the Committee on Public Schools appointed by the President of the Board of Education), London HMSO.

FLEW, A. (1987) *Power to the Parents*, London, Sherwood Press.

FLEW, A. (1988) *Education Tax Credits*, Warlingham, Institute of Economic Affairs Education Unit.

FLEW, A., MARKS, J., COX, C., HONEY, J., O'KEEFFE, D., DAWSON, G. and ANDERSON, D. (1981) *The Pied Pipers of Education*, London, Social Affairs Unit.

FOX, I. (1984) 'The demand for a public school education: A crisis of confidence in comprehensive schooling', in WALFORD, G. (Ed.) *British Public Schools: Policy and Practice*, Lewes, Falmer Press.

FOX, I. (1985) *Private Schools and Public Issues: The Parents' View*, London, Macmillan.

GAMBLE, A. (1983) 'Thatcherism and Conservative Politics', in HALL, S. and JACQUES, M. (Eds) *The Politics of Thatcherism*, London, Lawrence and Wishart.

GATHORNE-HARDY, J. (1977) *The Public School Phenomenon*, London, Hodder and Stoughton.

GILMOUR, I. (1977) *Inside Right: A Study of Conservatism*, London, Hutchinson.

GIRLS' SCHOOLS ASSOCIATION (1987) *Girls First*, London, GSA.

GLENNERSTER, H. and WILSON, G, (1970) *Paying for Private Schools*, London, Allen Lane, The Penguin Press.

GOLDTHORPE, J. (1983) 'Women and class analysis; in defence of the conventional view', *Sociology* 17, 4, pp. 465–488.

GOLDTHORPE, J. and HOPE, K. (1974) *The Social Grading of Occupations: A New Approach and Scale*, Oxford, Clarendon Press.

GOLDTHORPE, J., LLEWELLYN, C. and PAYNE, C. (1980) *Social Mobility and Class Structure in Modern Britain*, Oxford, Clarendon Press.

GOSDEN, P. (1976) *Education and the Second World War*, London, Methuen.

GRAY, J., JESSON, D. and JONES, B. (1984) 'Predicting differences in examination results between LEAs: Does school organization matter? *Oxford Review of Education*, 10, pp. 45–68.

GREEN, T. and BALL, S. (Eds) (1988) *Inequality and Progress in Comprehensive Education: A Reconsideration for the 1980s*, London, Routledge and Kegan Paul.

HADFIELD, G. (1989) 'Poorer pupils miss places at top schools' *Sunday Times*, 29 January, p. 5.

HALSEY, A., HEATH, A. and RIDGE, J. (1980) *Origins and Destinations: Family, Class and Education in Modern Britain*, Oxford, Clarendon Press.

HALSEY, A., HEATH, A. and RIDGE, J. (1984) 'The political arithmetic of public schools', in WALFORD, G. (Ed.) *British Public Schools: Policy and Practice*, Lewes, Falmer Press.

HARRIS, R. (1969) 'The larger lessons from Enfield', in COX, C. B. and DYSON, A. (Eds) *Black Paper Two, op. cit.*

HARRIS, R. (1980) *The Challenge of a Radical Reactionary*, London, Centre for Policy Studies.

HARRIS, R. and SELDON, A. (1970) *Choice in Welfare: Third Report on Knowledge and Preference in Education, Health Services and Pensions*, London, Institute of Economic Affairs.

HARRIS, R. and SELDON, A. (1979) *Over-ruled on Welfare*, London, Institute of Economic Affairs.

HATTON, E. (1985) 'Equality, class and power: A case study', *British Journal of Sociology of Education* 6, 3, pp. 255–272.

HEADMASTERS CONFERENCE, DIRECT-GRANT COMMITTEE (1968) *The Direct-Grant School*, London, Headmasters Conference.

HEATH, A. (1980) 'Class and meritocracy in British education', in FINCH, A. and SCRIMSHAW, P. (Eds) *Standards, Schooling and Education*, London, Hodder and Stoughton and the Open University Press.

HEATH, A. and BRITTEN, N. (1984), 'Women's jobs do make a difference', *Sociology*, 18, pp. 475–490.

HEATH, A. and RIDGE, J. (1983) 'Schools, examinations and occupational attainment', in PURVIS, J. and HALES, M. (Eds) *Achievement and Inequality in Education*, London, Routledge and Kegan Paul.

HILDITCH, C. (1970) 'Prove all things: a test for comprehensives', in COX, C. B. and DYSON, A. (Eds) *Goodbye Mr Short*, op. cit.

HILLGATE GROUP (1986) *Whose Schools? A Radical Manifesto*, London, Claridge Press.

HILLGATE GROUP (1987) *The Reform of British Education*, London, Claridge Press.

HODGES, L. (1984) 'Assisted Places Scheme welcomed by parents', *The Times*, 13 January.

HOLMES, M. (1985) *The First Thatcher Government*, Brighton, Harvester Press.

HONEY, J. (1977) *Tom Brown's Universe: The Development of the Victorian Public School*, London, Millington Books.

HOWARTH, T. (1969) *Culture, Anarchy and the Public Schools*, London, Cassell.

HOWELL, D. (1981) *Freedom and Capital*, Oxford, Blackwell.

HULA, R. (1984) 'Market strategies as policy tools', *Journal of Public Policy*, 4, 33, pp. 181–200.

INDEPENDENT SCHOOLS INFORMATION SERVICE (ISIS) (1973) *What is a Direct-Grant School?* London, ISIS.

ISIS (1974) *The Case for Independence*, London, ISIS.

ISIS (1975) *If the Grant Goes: The Threat to the Direct-Grant and Grant-Aided Schools of Britain*, London, ISIS.

ISIS (1976) *Selection: Modern Education's Dirty Word*, London, ISIS.

ISIS (1981) *The Case for Collaboration*, London, ISIS.

ISIS (1988) *Annual Census*, London, ISIS.

INMAN, M. (1986) 'Creeping privatization', *Schoolmaster and Career Teacher*, Winter, p. 5.

JACKSON, B. and MARSDEN, D. (1962) *Education and the Working Class*, London, Routledge and Kegan Paul.

JENCKS, C. (1979) *Who gets Ahead?* New York, Basic Books.

JOHNSON, D. (1987) *Private Schools and State Schools: Two Systems or One?* Milton Keynes, Open University Press.

JORDAN, L. and WAINE, B. (1986/87) 'Women's income in and out of employment', *Critical Social Policy*, 18, pp. 63–78.

JOSEPH, K. (1976) *Stranded on the Middle Ground*, London, Centre for Policy Studies.

JOSEPH, K. (1984) 'Speech to the North of England Education Conference', *Oxford Review of Education*, 10, pp. 137–146.

KALTON, G. (1966) *The Public Schools: A Factual Survey*, London, Longmans.

KAMM, J. (1971) *Indicative Past: One Hundred Years of the Girls Public Day School Trust*, London, Allen and Unwin.

KAVANAGH, D. (1987) *Thatcherism and British Politics: The End of Consensus*, London, Oxford University Press.

KOGAN, M. (1971) *The Politics of Education: Conversations with Edward Boyle and Tony Crosland*, Harmondsworth, Penguin Books.

LABOUR PARTY (1980) *Private Schools: A Discussion Document*, London, Labour Party.

LAMBERT, R. (1966) *The State and Boarding Education*, London, Methuen.

LAMBERT, R. (1968) *The Hothouse Society*, London, Weidenfeld and Nicholson.

LATHER, P. (1986) 'Research as praxis', *Harvard Educational Review*, 56, 3, pp. 257–277.

LEVITAS, R. (Ed.) (1986) *The Ideology of the New Right*, London, Polity Press.

LINDSAY, T. and HARRINGTON, M. (1979) *The Conservative Party 1918–1979*, London, Macmillan.

LORD, R. (1984) *Value for Money in Education*, London, Public Money (Chartered Institute of Public Finance and Accountancy).

LYNN, R. (1969) 'The quest for the unattainable', in COX, C. and DYSON, A. (Eds) *Black Paper Two*, op. cit.

MARSDEN, D. (1969) 'Which comprehensive principle?' *Comprehensive Education*, 13, pp. 2–5

MARSLAND, D. (1986) 'Young people, the family and the state', in ANDERSON, D. and DAWSON, G. (Eds) *Family Portraits*, London, Social Affairs Unit.

MARKS, J., COX, C. and POMIAN-SRZEDNICKI, M. (1983) *Standards in English Schools*, London, National Council for Educational Standards.

MASON, P. (1983) *Private Education in the EEC*, London, ISIS.

MASON, P. (1985) *Private Education in the United States and Canada*, London, ISIS.

MASON, P. (1986) 'Patterns of independent education', *American Educational Research Association Conference*, San Francisco, 16 April.

MATHIESON, M. and BERNBAUM, G. (1988) 'The British disease: A British tradition?' *British Journal of Educational Studies*, 26, 2, 126–174.

MAUDE, A. (1969) *The Common Problem*, London, Constable.

MAYNARD, A. (1975) *Experiment with Choice in Education*, London, Institute of Economic Affairs.

MEASOR, L. and WOODS, P. (1984) *Changing Schools: Pupil Perspectives on Transfer to a Comprehensive*, Milton Keynes, Open University Press.

MILNE, A., MYERS, D., ROSENTHAL, A. and GINSBERG, A. (1986) 'Single parents, working mothers and the educational achievement of school children', *Sociology of Education*, 59, 3, pp. 156–166.

MONCUR, A. (1984) 'How to move among the upper classes', *Guardian*, 8 April.

MURDOCH, I. (1975) 'Socialism and selection', in COX, C. and BOYSON, R. (Eds) *The Fight for Education, op. cit.*

MURGATROYD, L. (1982) 'Gender and occupational stratification', *Sociological Review*, 4, 30, pp. 574–602.

MUSGROVE, F. (1979) *School and the Social Order*, London, Wiley.

MUSGROVE, F. (1987) 'The Black Paper movement', in LOWE, R. (Ed.) *The Changing Primary School*, Lewes, Falmer Press.

NORTON, P. and AUGHEY, A. (1981) *Conservatives and Conservatism*, London, Temple Smith.

OPCS (1987) *Young People's Intentions to Enter Higher Education*, London, HMSO.

PAHL, J. (1983) 'The allocation of money and the structuring of inequality within marriage', *Sociological Review*, 31, 2, pp. 237–262.

PARKINSON, M. (1970) *The Labour Party and the Organisation of Secondary Education 1918–1965*, London, Routledge and Kegan Paul.

PATTEN, C. (1983) *The Tory Case*, London, Longmans.

PEACOCK, A. and WISEMAN, J. (1964) *Education for Democrats*, London, Institute of Economic Affairs.

PEDLEY, R. (1969) 'The comprehensive disaster', in COX, C. and DYSON, A. (Eds) *Fight for Education, op. cit.*

PEDLEY, R. (1970) 'The destructive element — has a trend been reversed?' in COX, C. and DYSON, A. (Eds) *Goodbye Mr Short, op. cit.*

PEELE, G. (1976) 'The Conservative dilemma' in BLAKE, R. and PATTEN, J. (Eds) *The Conservative Opportunity, op. cit.*

PHOENIX, A. (1987) 'Theories of gender and black families', in WEINER, G and ARNOT, M. (Eds) *Gender Under Scrutiny*, London, Hutchinson.

PRING, R. (1986) 'Privatisation of education', in ROGERS, R. (Ed) *Education and Social Class*, Lewes, Falmer Press.

PRING, R. (1987) 'Privatization in education', *Journal of Education Policy*, 2, 4, pp. 289–299.

PUBLIC SCHOOLS COMMISSION (1968) *First Report*, 2 Volumes, London, HMSO.

PUBLIC SCHOOLS COMMISSION (1970) *Second Report*, 2 Volumes, London, HMSO.

QUICKE, J. (1988) 'The New Right and education', *British Journal of Educational Studies*, 26, 1, pp. 5–20.

RAE, J. (1981) *The Public School Revolution: Britain's Independent Schools 1964–79*, London, Faber and Faber.

RAE, J. (1982) 'What future for the private sector?' *Times Educational Supplement*, 17 September, p. 19.

REIMER, E. (1971) *School is Dead*, Harmondsworth, Penguin.

RIDDELL, P. (1985) *The Thatcher Government*, 2nd ed., Oxford, Blackwell.

ROBERTS, H. (Ed.) (1981) *Doing Feminist Research*, London, Routledge and Kegan Paul.

ROBINSON, G. (1971) *Private Schools and Public Policy*, Loughborough, Loughborough University, Department of Social Science and Economics.

RUFFETT, F. and CHRESESON, J. (1984) *Secondary Education: The Next Step*, London, Policy Studies Institute.

SABATIER, P. (1986) 'Top-down and bottom-up approaches to implementation research', *Journal of Public Policy*, 6, 1, pp. 21–48.

SALTER, B and TAPPER, T. (1981) *Education, Politics and the State*, London, Grant McIntyre.

SALTER, B. and TAPPER, T. (1985) *Power and Policy in Education: The Case of Independent Schooling*, Lewes, Falmer Press.

SAMPSON, A. (1983) *The Changing Anatomy of Britain*, London, Coronet Books.

SARAN, R. (1973) *Policy Making in Secondary Education: A Case Study*, Oxford, Clarendon Press.

SCRUTON, R. (1984) *The Meaning of Conservatism*, London, Macmillan.

SELDON, A. (1981a) *Wither the Welfare State*, London, Institute of Economic Affairs.

SELDON, A. (Ed.) (1981b) *The Emerging Consensus?* London, Institute of Economic Affairs.

SELDON, A. (1986) *The Riddle of the Voucher: An Inquiry into the Obstacles to Introducing Choice and Competition in State Schools*, London, Institute of Economic Affairs.

SELDON, M. (1982) 'Education vouchers', in COX, C. and MARKS, J. (Eds) *The Right to Learn*, London, Centre for Policy Studies.

SEXTON, S. (1977) 'Evolution by choice' in COX, C. B. and BOYSON, R. (Eds), *Black Paper 1977*, pp 86–9.

SEXTON, S. (1987) *Our Schools: A Radical Policy*, Warlinghman, Institute of Economic Affairs Education Unit.

SHAW, B. (1983) *Comprehensive Schooling: The Impossible Dream*, Oxford, Blackwell.

SHERMAN, A. (1986) 'A great momentum runs out of steam', *Guardian*, 7 April.

STANWORTH, M. (1984) 'Women and class analysis: A reply to John Goldthorpe', *Sociology*, 18, 2, pp. 159–170.

STEEDMAN, J. (1983) *Examination Results in Selective and Non-selective Schools*, London, National Children's Bureau.

STEPHENSON, H. (1980) *Mrs Thatcher's First Year*, London, Jill Norman.

STILLMAN, A. (1986) 'Preference or choice? Parents, LEAs and the Education Act 1980', *Educational Research*, 28, 1, pp. 3–13.

SZAMUELY, T. (1969) 'Comprehensive inequality', in COX, C. B. and DYSON, A. (Eds) *Black Paper Two*, op. cit.

TAPPER, T. and SALTER, B. (1986a) 'The Assisted Places Scheme: A policy evaluation', *Journal of Education Policy* 1, 4, pp. 315–330.

TAPPER, T. and SALTER, B. (1986b) 'Choice factors', *Guardian*, 8 April.

TUC—LABOUR PARTY LIAISON COMMITTEE (1981) *A Plan for Private Schools*, London, Labour Party.

WALDEGRAVE, W. (1978) *The Binding of Leviathan: Conservatism and the Future*, London, Hamish Hamilton.

WALFORD, G. (1983) 'Girls in boys' public schools: A prelude to further research', *British Journal of Sociology of Education* 4, 1, pp. 39–54.

WALFORD, G. (1986) *Life in Public Schools*, London, Methuen.

WALFORD, G. (1987) 'How dependent is the independent sector?' *Oxford Review of Education*, 13, 3, pp. 175–196.

WALFORD, G. (1988) 'The Scottish Assisted Places Scheme: A comparative study of the origins, nature and practice of the Assisted Places Scheme in Scotland, England and Wales', *Journal of Education Policy*, 3, 2, pp. 137–154.

WALL, D. (1986) 'The Assisted Places Scheme and its operation in GPDST schools', unpublished MA dissertation, London University Institute of Education.

WAPSHOTT, N. and BROCK, G. (1983) *Thatcher*, London, Macdonald.

WEEKS, A. (1986) *Comprehensive Schools: Past, Present and Future*, London, Methuen.

WEST, E. (1965) *Education and the State: A Study in Political Economy*, London, Institute of Economic Affairs.

WEST, E. (1982) 'Education vouchers — evolution or revolution?' *Journal of Economic Affairs*, 3, 1, pp. 14–19.

WHITTY, G. and EDWARDS, A. (1984) 'Evaluating policy change: The Assisted Places Scheme', in WALFORD, G. (Ed.) *British Public Schools: Policy and Practice*, Lewes, Falmer Press.

WHITTY, G., FITZ, J. and EDWARDS, A. (1988), 'Assisting whom?' Benefits and costs of the Assisted Places Scheme, in HARGREAVES, A. and REYNOLDS, D. (1988) *Controversies and Critiques: Issues in educational policy*, Lewes, Falmer Press.

WHITTY, G., FITZ, J. and EDWARDS, A. (1989) 'England and Wales: Private Schools', in WALFORD, G. (Ed.) *Private Schools in Ten Countries*, London, Routledge and Kegan Paul.

WILKINSON, R. (1986) 'The Assisted Places Scheme', *Aspects of Education*, 35, University of Hull, pp. 49–62.

# Index